MANAGING INFORMATION

Understanding the impact of IT on the financial services

Phil Fawcett

institute of financial services

UMIST

CIB Publishing
c/o The Chartered Institute of Bankers
Emmanuel House
4-9 Burgate Lane
Canterbury
Kent
CT1 2XJ
United Kingdom

Telephone: 01227 762600

CIB Publishing publications are published by The Chartered Institute of Bankers, a non-profit making registered educational charity.

The Chartered Institute of Bankers believes that the sources of information upon which the book is based are reliable and has made every effort to ensure the complete accuracy of the text. However, neither CIB, the author nor any contributor can accept any legal responsibility whatsoever for consequences that may arise from errors or omissions or any opinion or advice given.

Trademarks

Many words in this publication in which the author and publisher believe trademarks or other proprietary rights may exist have been designated as such by use of Initial Capital Letters. However, in so designating or failing to designate such words, neither the author nor the publisher intends to express any judgment on the validity or legal status of any proprietary right that may be claimed in the words.

Typeset by Kevin O'Connor

Printed by Redwood Books, Trowbridge, Wiltshire

© Chartered Institute of Bankers 1999

ISBN 0-85297-513-9

Managing Information

This textbook has been written for both students and practitioners of the subject. It has been written to a syllabus drawn up by subject experts, including current senior practitioners, which forms part of the Diploma in Financial Services Management (DFSM). This qualification is administered by the Institute of Financial Services, a wholly owned subsidiary of The Chartered Institute of Bankers and is awarded jointly by The CIB and the University of Manchester Institute of Science and Technology (UMIST). The role of UMIST in this partnership is to benchmark all aspects of the delivery of the DFSM, including this text, to first year undergraduate standard.

Though written to a syllabus specific to the DFSM it is intended that this text will serve a useful purpose for anybody studying for a business or finance-related qualification. Furthermore, this book will serve as an excellent reference tool for practitioners already working in this or related fields. All books in the DFSM series reflect the very latest regulations, legislation and reporting requirements.

Students of the DFSM will also receive a separate Study Guide to be used in conjunction with this text. This Study Guide refers the reader to further reading on the topic and helps to enhance learning through exercises based upon the contents of this book.

CONTENTS

Contents

1

CHARACTERISTICS OF INFORMATION

We are sometimes described as living in the 'information age'. Information is all around us. A weekday edition of the *New York Times* is said to contain more information than the average person was likely to come across in a lifetime in seventeenth-century England. In this book we discuss how we can manage this.

1.1   Data, information and knowledge

If this book had been written 20 years ago it would probably have been given the title *Managing Data*. Within ten years it is likely to be called *Managing Knowledge*. What used to be called data processing is now called information technology, and knowledge management is one of the terms most commonly found in the computer press. What is the difference between data, information and knowledge?

- Data is facts. A statement such as 'the number of this account is 12345678' is a piece of data.

- To transform data into information, we need to put it into some form of context. If I know that account number 12345678 is the account of John Smith of 1 Acacia Avenue, this is information.

  Another way of expressing the difference between data and information is to say that information reduces uncertainty. The fact that an account number is 12345678 does not tell us the identity of the account holder. Having a name and address reduces our uncertainty about who holds the account.

- Knowledge relates this information to something we need to do. If I am monitoring limit excesses, and I know that John Smith has significant financial assets in the form of shareholdings, this is knowledge. I am likely to use this in making a decision as to whether or not to refer a cheque that would take John Smith over limit. Knowledge takes us much further than information. We need an objective and also an awareness of how to apply the information : '... to use information productively, i.e. towards some valued end or purpose, people must know what they are doing and why'.

In this book we shall focus on information, while recognizing the importance of data. We shall briefly touch on knowledge in Chapter 14.

1.2   Using Information

Why do we need information? This will be a recurrent theme throughout this book, but some of the most important uses are:

- *As a basis for decision making.* Information is an essential component of the decision making process. This is discussed in Chapter 12.

- *For planning and control.* We need adequate information to produce plans and to estimate the time and resources needed to implement them. We also need information to monitor and control the progress of these plans. This is discussed in Chapter 12.

- *To manage the customer relationship.* Customer, marketing and product information are essential to develop and maintain customer relationships. This is discussed in Chapter 3.

- *To manage others.* Henry Mintzberg defined three 'informational' roles of management – monitor, disseminator and spokesman. Information is also important for other staff management activities such as selection, training and appraisal. This is discussed in Chapter 2.

- *To manage ourselves.* We need information for self management, and techniques such as time management rely heavily on our having sufficient information to plan and prioritize our work.

- *As an enabler.* Information allows us to take actions that would otherwise be impossible. This is the basis of delegation, and providing first-line staff with the information and authority they need to take decisions is described as *empowerment*. This is discussed in Chapter 2.

1.3   Information technology

Information technology (IT) is a term that encompasses all forms of technology used to create, exchange and use information in its various forms (business data, voice conversations, still images, motion pictures, multimedia presentations and other forms).

It is quite common to hear about a number of 'generations' of information technology. Unfortunately the various writers disagree on what these generations include! The version we shall use ignores the early technological developments and identifies four generations as follows:

Generation	Period	Technology
First	1965–1975	Automation
Second	1975 – 1985	On-line
Third	1985 – 1995	Client/server
Fourth	1995 – ????	Web/Internet

First generation

The first generation was concerned with data processing, and was the dominant model from the mid-1960s until the mid-1970s.

The main business driver was automation. Technology was used to support existing manual processes. These were almost entirely back-office processes, and many financial services organizations developed their clearing and core accounting systems during this period.

Users interacted with the systems through paper. Printed reports were produced that contained the same information as the manually produced reports they replaced.

Transactions were processed in batches. Information was sorted into batches of the same type of form and sent to a data entry section who would type the information onto punch cards for input into the computer.

The advance in technology that made this possible was the availability of reliable, affordable mainframe computers. The mainframe computers were stand-alone – there were no connections between them and the rest of the business. They were located in special-purpose buildings called *data centres*.

Second generation

The second generation provided the bridge from data processing to information technology, and was the dominant model from the mid-1970s until the mid-1980s.

The main business driver was the need to access information on-line or in realtime. At the start of the period on-line enquiry systems were developed to allow financial services organizations' staff to access the information held in their mainframe systems.

The next stage was remote batch, where information could be collected and used to update the mainframe systems later. This replaced the data entry section. Many early ATM networks operated in this way, with transactions being recorded at the ATM and sent to the mainframe at night. This minimized telecommunications costs and fitted with the batch processing approach used in the other mainframe systems.

The third stage was on-line or real-time updating, where information entered would immediately update the mainframe systems.

This generation saw the use of IT being extended into the front office. This occurred mainly in wholesale applications such as foreign exchange dealing rooms where the benefit of up-to-date information was sufficient to outweigh the costs of the system.

Users interacted with the system using a computer terminal. This is a screen and keyboard with no processing or data storage capability of its own. Unlike the first generation, the terminal is both an input and an output device allowing users to interact directly with the computer for the first time.

The processing of transactions using on-line transaction processing (OLTP) increased during this period, although batch processing was still important. Hybrid approaches were also common, for example:

- Using on-line processing to update 'shadow files' so up-to-date balances were available during the day. The transactions were stored on-line and used as remote batch files to update the mainframe systems overnight.

- Using OLTP only for a small amount of processing. One example – an approach that is still used – is to process house cheque encashments online while other cheques are processed in batch or remote batch. House cheque encashments carry more risk as they involve paying out money immediately and the additional cost of online processing could be justified.

The main advance in technology that made this possible was the availability of affordable data communications networks. The network was arranged on a centralized basis with terminals connected to the central mainframe computer, still located in a data centre. Another important technology was the development of the database, which had a critical role in transforming data into information.

Third generation

The third generation completed the transition to information technology, and was the dominant model from the mid-1980s until the mid-1990s.

The main business driver was business process re-engineering (BPR). The processes automated in the first and second generations were developed before IT. The availability of IT allowed the development of new, more efficient processes.

Users interacted with the system using a workstation capable of displaying multiple windows. Windows technology, discussed in Chapter 10, allowed staff to carry out more than one computer operation at the same time. This in turn allowed a single member of staff to carry out more complex work unaided. Rather than passing the form or document through many hands it could be processed by one individual.

Transactions were processed on-line but an approach called *client/server* was used. This is discussed in Chapter 16; it means that processing and data storage are shared between the mainframe computer and another computer – either the workstation or (more usually) a server connected to workstations in a local area network. Local area networks are discussed in Chapter 10.

The advance in technology that made this possible was the availability of workstations capable of storing data and carrying out processing without reference to the central mainframe computer. The network was distributed – data and processing were shared between the workstations, the server and the central mainframe computer. Workstations could also be used independently of the mainframe computer, as a local area network or as stand-alone personal computers.

Fourth generation

The fourth generation is the bridge from information technology to knowledge management, and is emerging as the predicted dominant model from the mid-1990s.

The main business driver is the growth in electronic business or e-business. This is the use of electronic methods (such as the Internet) for ordering and delivering services. Another factor is the continuing fall in telecommunications costs, which has undermined the cost justification for the client/server approach.

This is discussed in detail in the final section of this book (Chapters 14 – 17).

Files and databases

These generations also show a move from structured to less structured data. First-generation systems could process only a small amount of data. This was held in *files* similar to card files, containing *records* corresponding to the record cards in a card file. There was no relationship between files, and data was usually compared by sorting the files into the same order and then matching them.

For example, accounting transactions entered during the day would be stored in a transaction file, which would be sorted into account number order at the end of the day. There would be an account file that was already stored in account number order, and a computer program would read through the files matching the account numbers to update the account balances.

Second-generation systems needed on-line access, perhaps to more than one file at a time. Therefore they needed to be able to link a record in one file to the corresponding record in another file, without the need to sort the files. Second-generation systems used databases (discussed in Chapter 10) to achieve this. This gave context to the data, and started the move from data processing towards information technology.

These early databases were very limited. The relational database was an improved form that was important in third generation systems. This made it much easier to create relationships between rows in different tables (in relational databases, records are called *rows* and files are called *tables*). This allowed much more information to be held, and for the first time, it became feasible to store data other than text and numbers. An early example was the Model 204 database, which was used by the US Navy to store naval charts. Relational databases increasingly became able to hold multimedia data such as pictures and drawings.

The fourth generation was the result of the technology of the Internet and the Web, which was designed to hold multimedia data. In addition to pictures and drawings, other forms of multimedia such as video, animation and sound could be held.

Another difference between the third and fourth generations was the ability of the latter to understand multimedia data. Relational databases typically held this data as *binary large objects* (blobs). The relational database management system could store multimedia data but it would have to be interpreted by a different computer program. Internet browsers can both access and interpret multimedia data.

Moore's Law

A unique feature of information technology is the speed of technological innovation. This is reflected in Moore's Law.

Gordon Moore was one of the founders of computer chip maker Intel. Moore's Law predicts that the processing power of computer chips will double every 18 months. This rule has held true since the early 1960s, and is predicted to continue until 2010.

As well as this increase in processing power, there has also been an increase in the amount of storage available and the amount of information that can be transmitted over data communications networks. This itself has increased the use of information within organizations. Fourth-generation systems and the Internet now provide individuals with access to a quantity of information that is, for all practical purposes, unlimited.

Businesses have exploited this opportunity, and collect an increasing amount of information that is now critical to their operations. Computer Associates' chief executive officer Charles Wang says:

> *Your core business is information. I don't care if your operation makes door knobs or services fire alarms, your core business is information.*

In this view, information is not only the business's most important asset but is also a tradable asset. This has been described as the *information economy*.

1.4   Characteristics of information

We have discussed the idea of information as the reduction of uncertainty. But the wrong type of information can increase uncertainty. We can define some important characteristics that information should possess:

● *It must be relevant to its purpose.* For example, strategic information about market share should not include information about production costs, as this might distract or even confuse the manager using it.

● *It must be sufficiently timely for its purpose.* This means that the manager needs to get the information in time to take some action. There is no point in telling the manager that his or her costs will be over budget after the end of the financial year.

- *It must be sufficiently accurate for its purpose.* The accuracy needed varies depending on how the information is going to be used. Balance sheets are usually shown in thousands of pounds, and this is sufficiently accurate for this purpose. To calculate rates of return on products balances need to be much more accurate, as a small difference in the rate might have a big effect on how the financial services organization markets the product.

- *It must be reliable.* The information user must have confidence in it. The information may be verifiable or may come from a trusted source. Some information varies naturally, and it may be difficult to rely on it if the natural variation is large compared with the information itself. Statistical techniques may be used to identify the variability and to specify a confidence level for the information.

- *It must be robust.* It must not be subject to distortion. Some economic statistics (such as the balance of trade) are the difference between two very large numbers. Therefore a relatively small error in either of these numbers has a much larger effect on the statistic itself. Another cause of distortion is changes over time (another economic statistic – the average earnings series – has been affected by this).

- *It must be presented in the right way and to the right person.* Information for senior management should generally be presented as charts, perhaps showing trends over time or market share. The lower the level of management receiving the information, the more detail should generally be shown.

- Information should not cost more to produce than its value to the business.

In *Managing Information – Avoiding Overload*, Trevor Bentley identifies four laws that apply to information:

- *The law of diminishing returns.* As we obtain more information, the value of each additional item is less than that of the previous item. Therefore as we continue to request more information we shall eventually reach the point where the cost of producing information is greater than its value to the business – contravening the final characteristic of information discussed above.

- *The law of praxis.* We specify our information needs in terms of the way we do things. Therefore the information we ask for is not what is needed to solve the problem – if we are trying to decide whether to refer a cheque do we really need the customer's balance and limit or do we simply need to know if the cheque will put the customer over limit? Another effect of the law of praxis is that once information has been requested it continues to be produced – even if praxis has changed and it is no longer needed.

- *The law of escalating demand.* As we obtain more information we want more information. This is sometimes called data hunger or even data addiction. The additional information can be useful – providing a better basis for decisions or warning of control problems, for example – but it can also be used as an excuse to avoid decisions, and the law of diminishing returns applies.

- *The law of necessity.* Today's luxuries become tomorrow's necessities. Once we know that it is possible to obtain an item of information, we expect it to be produced.

The laws of escalating demand and of necessity in particular tend to increase the amount of information produced.

1.5 Information overload and stress

The amount of information to which we are exposed has led to concern about information overload, as people are overwhelmed by the amount of information with which they are presented.

The term *(information) overload* comes from George Simmel, who described how people shield themselves from 'indiscriminate suggestibility to protect themselves from an overload of sensations, which results in an incapacity ... to react to new situations with the appropriate energy'. What Simmel is describing the paralysis that may affect individuals faced with a huge amount of information to absorb – the feeling of 'where do I start?' that most of us must have encountered at one time or another.

Another effect of information overload is stress. Some writers distinguish between:

- *Eustress,* in which the level of stress is sufficient to push the individual to peak performance. This results in satisfaction in a job well done – euphoria, hence eustress. A more common term for this type of stress is stretch.

- *Distress,* in which the level of stress is excessive and can lead to the medical conditions commonly associated with stress, such as ulcers, high blood pressure and alcoholism. A more common term for this type of stress is strain.

The type of stress associated with information overload is usually distress. Absorbing information is not inherently satisfying (although using this information, for example in making a decision, may be), and does not lead to the rewards associated with eustress.

We can minimize information overload by considering the characteristics of information we discussed earlier. For example, we should ensure that information is relevant, and present it in a way that meets the needs of the recipient.

Most *electronic office* software now allows the use of filters, and allows information to be presented as summaries, as trends, or graphically. These products are discussed in Chapter 10. Other products include decision support tools, boardroom graphics and executive information systems (EIS), which are discussed in Chapter 12, and knowledge management tools, which are discussed in Chapter 14.

Information overload seems to be less of a concern than it used to be, perhaps because of the widespread availability of products of this type. A 1999 survey by Reuters shows that concerns about information overload have fallen since their previous survey. Managers' attitude to the Internet has shown a marked change – in 1997 almost half predicted it would make information overload worse whereas the 1999 survey shows that about the same proportion think it improves things with only 19% thinking it has made things worse.

1.6   Internal and external information sources

External sources of information include news and information services (teletext, Prestel), prices (Bloomberg, Bridge, Reuters) and reference information (postal addresses, company information). There are a number of different ways of delivering this:

- Television, including satellite and cable television services;

- Computer networks;

- Magnetic disk, magnetic tape or optical disk.

The most important of these are computer networks. Internet information providers such as Compuserve and Delphi, and network-based information systems such as Tel-me, are important sources of reference information. Such information is now usually provided as a 'feed' that can be read by the financial services organization's own systems.

Information may also be provided on optical disk, which can almost always be read directly by the financial services organization's own systems. This method is most often used for reference information that needs to be updated infrequently. An example is Reed Elsevier's Books On-Line. Networks – especially the Internet – are increasingly replacing optical disk for information of this type, although the very high storage capacities offered by low-cost digital versatile disk (DVD) may change this.

Managers use external pricing information to keep an up-to-date picture of the value of the assets of the organization or its customers. Reference information might be used in planning marketing campaigns or in developing new products, perhaps based on public reference information such as the Census.

Customer and product information

During the first generation, most financial services organizations held information about accounts rather than about customers. This approach was very efficient for batch processing of transactions but meant that these organizations had little idea of the overall financial positions of their customers. Financial services organizations received adverse publicity when they referred cheques for customers who had substantial balances on their accounts. This became even more important during the second generation, when on-line enquiry terminals became available, and staff made such decisions at the counter.

Therefore most financial services organizations built customer databases during the third generation. We shall discuss database technology – which was the enabling technology – in Chapter 10, but these databases created a relationship between information about the customer and information about the account. We can show this as a diagram:

Figure 1.1: Entity-relationship diagram

This is called an *entity-relationship diagram* (ERD). The boxes are *entities* – these are types or *classes* of data. The lines show the relationship between these entities: the fork at the right of the line (called a *crow's foot*) shows that one of the entity on the left can have a relationship to many of the entity on the right – one customer can hold many accounts but (in our example) each account can only be for one customer. ERDs are often used as a convenient way of showing the main types of data and the relationships between them.

Customer information will typically include the following:

● Demographic details such as date of birth (age), sex, marital status;

● Contact details such as salutation, address, telephone number;

● Employment details such as employer, type of employment, salary;

● Marketing information such as market segment, television region, propensity to buy;

This will be linked to account information, which will typically include the following:

● Account details such as sorting code, balance, currency;

● Statement details such as statement address, frequency, whether cheques should be returned;

● Sometimes historic information such as average balance, number of referred cheques, number of missed repayments;

Each account will be linked to details of the individual transactions, such as date, amount and statement narrative.

Financial services organizations also hold a much wider range of information about products held by customers. This may include both account-based products and non-account-based products such as insurance.

Market research and marketing information

Financial services organizations apply increasingly sophisticated marketing analysis techniques to their customers. These include propensity scoring, discussed in Chapter 3, and market segmentation.

Market segmentation looks at how customers' buying behaviour is affected by their characteristics. The most important types of segmentation include the following:

- *Demographic segmentation* segments customers on social class. This is the most common type of segmentation.

- *Geographic segmentation* segments customers on where they live. This is important in reflecting regional differences and has the advantage that regional advertising media can be used to target customers.

- *Geodemographic segmentation* segments customers on a mix of demographic and geographic factors. A well known form of geodemographic segmentation is the MOSAIC system.

- *Psychographic segmentation* segments customers on their attitudes and values.

- *Lifestyle segmentation* segments customers on their lifestyle and aspirations. This has been used as a basis for building global brands, most notably Martini.

- *Technographic segmentation* segments customers on their attitude to technology. This is discussed in Chapter 3.

As financial services organizations obtain more information about their customers they are able to refine this segmentation, and the objective is sometimes described as a 'segment of one' by which each customer is treated as unique and the customer's needs are fully understood by the organization.

Financial services organizations segment customers based on their own information supplemented with information taken from sources such as the Census.

Another important source of marketing information is competitor intelligence. Sources of competitor intelligence include:

- Customers;

- Consultants;

- Competitor information, including marketing brochures, press releases and annual reports;

- Industry surveys from sources such as Keynote, Jordan, Mintel, and the Economic Intelligence Unit.

Credit reference agencies

Financial services organizations use credit reference agencies as part of the credit scoring process (discussed in Chapter 11). Credit reference agencies take information from various sources:

- The electoral roll (for checking addresses);

- County Court judgements (CCJs);

- Credit Account Information Sharing (CAIS);

- Credit Industry Fraud Avoidance System (CIFAS).

CCJs

CCJs record legal proceedings taken to recover debts. These are centrally recorded in the Register of County Court Judgements, run by the Office of Fair Trading.

CAIS

CAIS is the credit providers' trade organization. Members, including the financial services organizations, can choose to provide only 'black' information (for example missed repayments) or to also provide 'white' information (accounts with a good repayment history). Organizations can only look at white information if they also provide white information. There are privacy issues around this, and most financial services organizations provide only black information.

Credit Reference Agency Equifax also operates a system called Insight, which is similar to CAIS.

CIFAS

CIFAS is a company run by the UK credit reference agencies, and records fraud attempts. In order to look at CIFAS information, credit providers must also provide information to CIFAS and must follow these up by taking criminal proceedings against suspected fraudsters.

Bloomberg, Bridge and Reuters

The most important sources of external information for financial services organizations are Bloomberg, Bridge and Reuters. All of these provide:

- Price information for stock markets, exchange rates, securities markets, derivatives and commodity markets;
- Brokers' and research reports;
- News feeds, business briefings and financial television services.

They also provide dealing products.

Economic and company information

Sources of economic and company information include:

- Reports from brokers and economic research groups;
- Companies House;
- McCarthy;
- Extel;
- The ICC;

- Jordan;
- Dun and Bradstreet.

News feeds

Bloomberg, Bridge and Reuters supply news feeds, as do many of the organizations we have already discussed, such as McCarthy. Other important sources include the newspaper and television groups.

2

THE IMPACT OF INFORMATION TECHNOLOGY ON STAFF

2.1   Convergence

The development of the financial services industry is shaped by many factors. One of these is convergence, which is occurring within both the financial services industry and technology.

First let us consider convergence within the industry. Traditionally the various types of financial services organization were kept separate. Different patterns of regulation and agreements resembling cartels reinforced the separation of function. At this stage there was a very clear distinction between banks, building societies, insurance companies and other financial services organizations such as hire purchase companies, friendly societies and credit unions. Retailers and other non-financial services organizations had no presence in the retail financial markets, although companies such as GE Capital had a long-established presence in the capital markets.

This started to break down with the entry of foreign banks into the UK market in the 1960s. This was supported by regulatory changes such as Competition and Credit Control (1971) and the 'big bang' (1986). These led to a process of deregulation and convergence between financial services organizations. This has been reinforced by globalization, disintermediation and the entry of non-financial services organizations into the market.

Globalization is the tendency for markets to be global in scope. In financial services this is most obvious in the wholesale markets, but credit cards – dominated by the global Visa and MasterCard networks – provide a retail financial services example. Globalization tends to open local markets to international competition.

Disintermediation is the tendency for the removal of intermediaries or 'middlemen'. Again this is most obvious in wholesale financial services, where the growth in the securities market has greatly reduced multinational companies' dependence on bank lending. The main driver for disintermediation in retail financial services is the Internet.

Technology also seems to be converging. Previously separate technologies such as computers, television and telecommunications are converging into what is increasingly called *information and communications technology* (ICT). The main feature of this is the growth in digital technology and its extension from computers into telecommunications and, more recently, television and radio.

Digital technology means that information is carried as discrete pieces, as opposed to analogue technology in which information is carried as continuing varying quantities. We can see this by comparing a digital watch with an analogue watch. The digital watch shows discrete numbers between 0 and 9, and will show an exact time. The analogue watch has sweep hands that, in theory, change continuously. We shall return to digital and analogue technology in Chapter 11.

The rate of change in the financial services industry over the past 20 years has been unprecedented, and has been the result of the increase in competition due to these factors.

2.2   Impact on staff numbers and career paths

Information technology has acted as an 'enabler' allowing financial services organizations to respond to this change by making significant changes to their structure and method of operation. For example:

● There has been a change in financial services organizations' cost structure from variable costs (staff costs) to fixed costs (investment in equipment). This has allowed these organizations to handle increased business volumes without increasing staff numbers in the same proportion.

● Financial services organizations' senior managers are increasingly able to access the information needed to run the business directly through computer systems. The traditional role of middle managers in 'filtering' information between the front line and senior management is increasingly irrelevant.

● Financial services organizations are increasingly reducing or eliminating the traditional back office. These functions are being transferred to the front office, eliminated through the use of automation, or centralized in 'factory' environments.

● All organizations, including financial services organizations, are increasingly recognizing the value of knowledge as a corporate asset. A separate but related development is a focus on teamwork and self-managed teams as a method of work organization.

Motivation

Before we look at the impact of such changes on staff numbers and career paths we need to consider motivation. Motivation produces the expenditure of effort, energy and excitement that contributes to performance. One of the most important models for motivation is that of Abraham Maslow, which includes five layers:

Figure 2.1: Maslow's Pyramid of Motivation

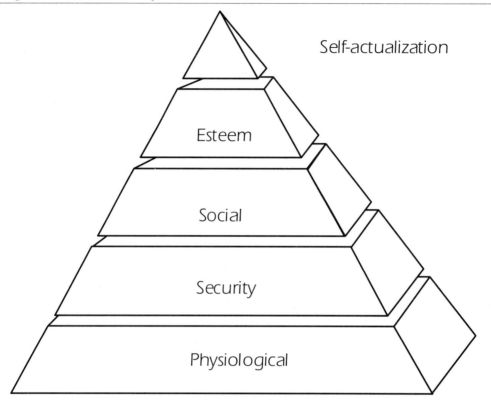

The lowest layer includes physiological needs such as food and shelter. When these have been satisfied, they no longer motivate. The next level of the model – security needs – becomes the main motivator. We continue up through social needs and esteem needs to the highest level of all, the self-actualization layer.

Traditional career paths – the 'job for life'

Financial organizations traditionally offered a 'job for life' – a career with a steady progression through the organization until the employee reached the limit of his or her abilities or ambitions. The reasons for this included:

- The organizational culture of financial services organizations, many of which were large bureaucracies that placed a high value on staff loyalty.

- The type of skills required. As these did not change – lending assessment now is practically the same as it was 100 years ago – an employee would become more valuable over time because he or she would be using the same skills but would be improving them through experience.

Therefore staff retention was a major issue for senior management. If we consider the way 'traditional' financial services organizations operated:

- Physiological needs were met by above-average pay and an extensive package of benefits.

- Security needs were met by a culture of lifetime employment and by generous sickness and retirement benefits.

- Social needs were met through social interaction in the workplace and the financial services organizations' support for social activities.

- Esteem needs were met through regular promotions (supported by a very hierarchical structure) and status symbols such as larger offices and company cars.

- Self-actualization needs were met by development schemes and support for professional updating such as that provided by The Chartered Institute of Bankers.

All of this has changed. The 'job for life' has gone, and staff cannot be sure that their skills offer them any security in a financial services sector that has cut its staff numbers so drastically. Social opportunities are reduced, with fewer staff, longer hours of work, and more time spent working with the computer rather than with other people. Many of the traditional status symbols have been removed, with offices being turned into interview rooms.

The large-scale introduction of IT has completely changed the nature of the work. Tasks such as lending assessment are now largely carried out through credit scoring. Employees are finding that the skills for which they were recruited and trained are increasingly unimportant.

The effect on staff numbers is readily apparent. Consider the following table showing the change in the number of staff employed by the four main high-street banks between 1990 and 1994:

	1990	**1994**	**%age change**
Barclays	84,700	63,500	– 25.03
Lloyds	58,600	43,500	– 25.77
Midland	47,100	41,900	– 11.04
NatWest	85,900	67,200	– 21.77
TOTAL	278,290	218,094	– 21.63

This trend towards a fall in the number of staff employed continues.

Effect of changes

We can consider the effect of these changes under six headings:

- Job security;
- Reward systems;
- Nature of work;
- Skills changes;
- Career paths;
- Empowerment.

Job security

The most obvious effect is on job security. Financial services organization staff no longer feel that their jobs are secure. Managers need to consider the effect of introducing IT on staff motivation and to find ways to motivate staff who are worried by the future.

Reward systems

There has been a major change in reward systems, with across the board pay rises replaced by a mix of bonuses and performance-related pay rises. The importance of information as a basis for such systems is obvious.

Most transaction systems produce basic work measurement information such as the number of transactions processed and sometimes error rates. Workflow systems, discussed in Chapter 10, produce a much wider range of statistics, and can give very precise information about job performance. An additional benefit of this is that it can help to increase the objectivity of the appraisal process.

Nature of work

Another effect is on the nature of jobs staff are being asked to do. This is often called the change from 'teller to seller', which describes how the job of branch staff increasingly involves selling products to the customer, rather than simply waiting for the customer to ask what is available. The emphasis now is on selling skills rather than the traditional skills of the teller.

This change has a major effect on employee perceptions. It is a change to the 'psychological contract' between employer and employee. We shall return to this theme later in this chapter.

Skills changes

As well as the need for selling skills, the introduction of IT has had other effects on the skills required of staff.

One such effect is the requirement for computer skills. These range from basic keyboard skills through the use of electronic office products to programming, either using macro languages (to program spreadsheets and word processors) or possibly using programming languages.

Staff need to be able to handle a wider range of transactions with less routine work. This might suggest there is a need for a wider range of skills. An alternative view would be that the skills required of most staff have narrowed. Although they are handling a wider range of transactions, much of the processing is being carried out by the computer, and only a narrow range of computer skills are actually required.

IT has also removed the need for some skills. The large typing pools maintained by financial services organizations in the past have been replaced by word processors, which can be used directly by staff and managers. Lending assessment has been automated through the use of credit scoring systems.

Career paths

Another effect is *delayering* – taking away layers of middle management. One of the main functions of middle management used to be processing information – deciding what information was sufficiently important to be passed on to higher management. IT can now do this. This has produced a flatter organization, with fewer opportunities for promotion. Employees looking for promotion now need to be willing to move 'sideways' – broadening their experience in other areas of the organization – as they can no longer rely on a regular series of promotions within the same branch or department.

Empowerment

Fewer staff are now handling more complex transactions for larger numbers of customers with less supervision. Clearly this has increased staff responsibilities. IT has been an important – though not the only – factor in making these changes possible.

IT has made more information available to staff, allowing them to take decisions without referring them to higher authority. Another reason for delayering is that first-line managers and supervisors are now better able to take routine decisions. Although this has a beneficial effect on motivation it can also lead to stress (strain).

The term *empowerment* is used to describe this increase in responsibilities.

2.3　Impact on roles

IT has had an enormous effect on the roles and responsibilities of staff working for financial services organizations. Let us start by reviewing how some of the main IT developments have affected staff. Developments over the past quarter century affecting staff have included:

● Back-office automation;

- Front-office automation;
- Alternative methods of service delivery.

Back-office automation

Back-office automation started in the early 1970s with the automation of the cheque-clearing process. The process has continued since, receiving a boost with the microcomputer revolution of the late 1980s and the introduction of electronic office products. The most recent development has been the centralization of back-office functions into processing centres, many of which are using technologies such as document image processing (DIP) and workflow automation (discussed in Chapter 10).

Many traditional back-office jobs in financial organizations were very labour intensive. This had two consequences. First, the amount of work that could be handled depended directly on the number of people available to do it. Second, supervisors were needed to check the quality of the work.

Back-office automation has greatly reduced the relationship between the amount of work and the number of people required. This has allowed the financial organizations to greatly increase the number of transactions they carry out using the same number of staff. The clearing system provides a good example of this.

Back-office automation has helped to reduce the amount of supervision needed because IT can be used to carry out some of the checks. Even so, computers could not eliminate all errors while the back office remained dependent on forms completed manually in the front office.

Automation has also changed the way in which the back office is organized. Prior to automation there was a clear distinction between 'clerks' and 'typists'. Clerks filled in forms, which were handed to someone else for typing. Not only was this a very inefficient process, there was also the possibility of mistakes. Automation has removed this distinction. Most staff and many managers would now be expected to use a workstation in the normal course of their work.

Front-office automation

Front-office automation is more recent. It started with the introduction of enquiry terminals at the counter. The functions available through the counter terminal have gradually expanded to provide much more information and to allow staff dealing with customers to enter transactions directly, without needing to pass these to back-office staff. These systems also provide sales support, prompting tellers with information about customers' needs.

This has had considerable effects not only on staff themselves but also on the layout of branches, where less space now needs to be set aside for back-office functions.

Front-office automation had another important effect. Forms could be passed from the front office to the back office as information, not as paper. This meant that it was no longer necessary for back-office processing to be carried out in the same building as the front office, and allowed the introduction of process centres.

Automation of the front office also reduced the errors that resulted from forms being completed manually and passed to the back office for processing. The computer could check forms as they were entered and allow errors to be corrected immediately, instead of the form being rejected in the back office and having to be returned for correction. Any problems with the information given could be confirmed with the customer.

Alternative methods of service delivery

Alternative methods of service delivery range from the automated teller machine (ATM – introduced in the 1970s) and electronic funds transfer at point of sale (EFTPOS) through telephone banking (introduced in the 1980s) and PC banking to Internet banking. These methods allow customers to carry out many routine transactions without going into a branch.

This has allowed branch staff to deal with more complicated and interesting business. Against this, it has also reduced the economic justification for branches, and has resulted in branch staff being under more pressure to generate increased sales. A *service ethic* has been replaced by a *sales ethic*.

Providing financial services organizations with an alternative to traditional branch networks raises the question: what happens to those branch networks and to the people who work in them?

One possibility is simply to use branches as shops – to get new business, to provide existing customers with limited services, and to advertise products. An alternative is to use them as a means of building a local franchise by providing a wider range of services. Both approaches have been tried but both have two things in common:

- The need for branch staff to take more of a selling role;
- The need to control branch costs by controlling staff numbers.

2.4   Job design

IT has had an effect on the way jobs are designed. Good job design attempts to ensure employee job satisfaction as well as an efficient process. The five principles of good job design are as follows:

- *Task identity* is concerned with whether the person carrying out the task can see the end product. Is he or she just 'another cog in the machine'?

- *Task significance* is concerned with whether the person sees the task as making a contribution to society. Nursing is an example of a job with high task significance.

- *Skill variety* is concerned with whether a person needs to use a wide variety of skills or whether the task is monotonous.

- *Autonomy* is concerned with how much choice the person has about how he or she carries out the task.

- *Feedback* is concerned with whether the person is told how well he or she has done the job, or whether he or she finds out only if something goes wrong.

The car assembly line is an example of poor job design. People work on a single task (low skill variety), which does not greatly contribute to the finished product (low task identity). They are forced to work at the speed of the assembly line (low autonomy) and get little feedback unless they fall behind. They may feel they are contributing to air pollution and traffic jams (low task significance).

Note that this does not mean that car assembly lines are inefficient means of producing cars, merely that they do not result in job satisfaction for employees. This increases costs through poor industrial relations, absenteeism and sickness. Some car firms (such as Volvo at their Kalmar plant) have attempted to improve job design in car manufacture through the use of autonomous work groups.

IT is often accused of de-skilling jobs, reducing skill variety. This is true in some cases, but IT can also be used to make jobs more interesting. IT can provide one person with enough information to carry out a process such as account opening on his or her own – increasing task identity and job satisfaction. This also usually results in a more efficient process as 'hands offs' (where work is transferred from one person to another) can introduce delays and the risk of information being lost or misunderstood.

A useful model here is the 'levels' model developed by Robert Dilts. This identifies five levels, all of which need to be considered:

Figure 2.2: Robert Dilts' Levels Model

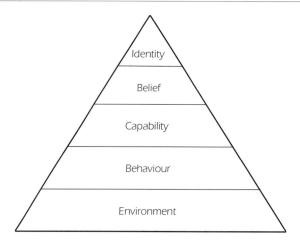

- The *identity* level is concerned with individuals' basic sense of purpose. One of the issues with the teller to seller change is that it required a change at the identity level that many people were unwilling to make.

- The *belief* level concerns the beliefs that affect individuals' actions. These will relate to the reward system, the individual's psychological contract with the organization, and the individual's belief about how his or her actions will be perceived by colleagues and customers.

- The *capability* level concerns what the individual is capable of doing.

- The *behaviour* level concerns what the individual actually does. This may be more or less than he or she is capable of doing.

- The *environment* level concerns how individuals react to their environment, both physical (for example working conditions) and social (for example colleagues and customers).

Organizations usually apply changes at the capability level (training), the behaviour level (changes to process or job descriptions), and sometimes the environment level (changes to working conditions and the introduction of support mechanisms such as decision support systems). They do not always address the need to make changes at the belief and identity levels.

2.5   New IT-related responsibilities

As financial organizations have begun to make more extensive use of IT in branches, staff have taken on additional responsibilities related to IT. For example:

- Branch staff have new responsibilities to carry out basic security and maintenance functions for workstations and local area networks (LANs) located in their branches.

- Staff must be aware of the Data Protection Act, the Computer Misuse Act and intellectual property legislation, which affect all staff.

- Some branch staff may have responsibilities including training, 'troubleshooting' and installing new hardware and software.

2.6   Training

Training is very important if we are to realize the benefits IT offers:

- IT systems are an investment, and staff need training to understand how to use and get the best out of the systems available to them.

- Training is important in staff motivation. It increases employees' skills, and represents a real and obvious investment by the employer in the employee.

  Motivation is important as career expectations have changed. The traditional 'job for life' expected by financial organizations' employees has been replaced by greater uncertainty. The trend is for a focus on lifetime *employability* to replace a promise of lifetime employment.

On-the-job training

We can classify training methods as *on the job* or *off the job*.

On the-job-training is conducted in the workplace. The most important on-the-job training methods are:

- Coaching;
- Computer-based training (CBT);
- Videos;
- Training databases;
- Books and manuals;
- Circulars.

A number of these methods, including CBT, videos, training database and manuals, can be used either on the job or off the job.

Coaching

Coaching, also called 'sitting next to Nellie', involves an experienced member of staff sitting next to a trainee and showing him or her what to do. The trainee will go through the incoming work, and the coach will intervene when the trainee comes across a new type of work or an unusual situation.

The advantages of coaching are that it is cheap and it makes good use of staff knowledge.

The disadvantages are that the trainee may learn bad habits, that the coaching may not cover all situations (as only situations that come up during the coaching period will be covered), and that it disrupts the experienced staff member's work.

With financial services organizations investing more heavily in staff training, coaching is now not usually the main method of training. A variation on coaching called *buddying* is increasingly common, with the buddy providing a reference point for questions or work problems.

Mentoring is used in management development. The mentor's role is rather different, being concerned less with the technical aspect of the work and more with developing an understanding of how the organization works (for example the politics).

Computer-based training (CBT)

Computer-based training (CBT) uses a computer program that takes the trainee through the material, with exercises to assess progress. CBT is often used to train staff in using the financial services organization's computer systems and may be built into these systems, possibly as an electronic product support system (EPSS), which is discussed in Chapter 10.

The advantages of CBT are that it is cheap to deliver and it is comprehensive, covering everything.

The disadvantages are that it is expensive to develop and update as computer systems change. CBT may not be seen as relevant to work if the examples used are unrealistic or out of date.

The Internet is increasingly being used by distance learning providers to deliver CBT commercially. Two examples are the Ziff Davies University (which delivers computer courses) and Duke University's Fuqua Management School (which delivers its MBA programme).

Videos

Videos may be used to deliver training material. These may also include exercises, and are often used with a workbook.

The advantages of videos are that they are cheap to develop and deliver. They are comprehensive, covering everything.

The disadvantages are that they are one way, not providing the trainee with any feedback, and that the trainee may get bored. If workbooks are used these can include self-assessment material, providing the trainee with feedback. Videos may be used with a discussion group, which can overcome these disadvantages.

Training databases

Training databases are separate databases used only for training. They allow trainees to try out computer system facilities without affecting the 'real' database.

The advantages of training databases are that they are cheap to develop and deliver, and they are usually cheap to update.

The disadvantage is that they do not give trainee guidance or feedback, unless they are supplemented with computer-based training.

Books and manuals

Books and manuals are published training material written by a teacher or a 'technical writer'.

The advantages of books and manuals are that they are cheap to deliver, they cover everything, and they can be used for reference as well as for training.

The disadvantages are that the trainee may get bored, and books and manuals have poor visual impact.

Circulars

Circulars include information circulated by the employer containing updating information. They are used mainly for advising of small changes to procedures or computer systems.

The advantages of circulars are that they are very cheap to deliver and quick to produce (and therefore up to date).

The disadvantage is that they are not suitable for large amounts of information.

Off-the-Job training

Off-the-job training is conducted outside the workplace, often in a specially designed training centre. The most important off-the-job training methods are:

● Lectures;

● Briefings;

● Seminars;

● Interactive video disk (IVD);

● Business games.

Lectures

Lectures ('talk and chalk') involve the lecturer standing up in front of a class and talking. The lecturer can use a variety of techniques to involve the trainees and maintain their interest.

The advantages of lectures are that the notes provide reference material, and they are good for large amounts of information. The lecturer can adjust the delivery to meet the needs of the trainees, and can test their understanding of key points.

The disadvantages are that trainees may get bored, if the class has a varied level of understanding it is difficult for the lecturer to adjust the pace to meet the needs of individuals, and the feedback the trainees receive depends on the lecturer's knowledge.

Briefings

Briefings are similar to lectures but less formal, usually presenting only a summary of the material.

The advantage of briefings is that they are good for updates on very recent material.

The disadvantages are that they can lack depth and they may be incomplete or biased.

Seminars

Seminars usually involve a seminar leader making a presentation, followed by discussion in small groups.

The advantage of seminars is that detailed discussion improves understanding.

The disadvantage is that they are time consuming, and therefore expensive, for the amount of training material delivered.

Interactive video disk

Interactive video disk (IVD) uses case study material delivered through a special reader.

The trainee goes through part of the material and is then required to choose a course of action. The IVD system assesses the trainee's course of action and shows what would have happened if the option chosen had been selected. The disk is a 12 inch optical disk using different technology from CD-ROM and cannot be delivered through a standard PC.

The advantage of IVD is that the trainee can choose between several actions, allowing the consequences of mistakes to be shown.

The disadvantages are that it is expensive to develop and update, and that it requires special equipment and therefore is expensive to deliver.

Business games

Business games are simulations of business situations, usually played against other people using a computer system as referee.

The advantages of business games are that they keep trainees' interest and provide an opportunity to practise techniques.

The disadvantages are that the competitive element may take precedence over learning, and the games may be seen as irrelevant to the work environment.

Comparison of methods

Generally, on-the-job methods are cheaper than off-the-job methods. Not only are the methods themselves often cheaper, staff also do not have to be taken away from work (which increases costs as these absences need to be covered). On-the-job methods can also be scheduled to fit in with the normal working day – using CBT during quiet periods, for example.

Against this, on-the-job methods can often be disruptive - trainees asking questions, for example. On-the-job methods such as coaching can result in the trainee picking up bad habits from the coach. Off-the-job methods are much better for training complicated skills because there are no distractions and because the trainer can be an expert in the subject. Off-the-job methods are also often better for new skills, where there is no one in the workplace who could answer questions and the trainee might feel lost if on-the-job methods are used.

Training programmes

Training is more than sending people on courses! Training should be part of an overall training programme, the development of which involves the following steps:

- Identify training needs.
- Set training objectives.
- Decide training methods.
- Draw up a training plan.
- Validate the training.

- Evaluate the training.

Identify training needs

The first stage is to identify that an individual has training needs. This usually comes about as a result of a shortfall in performance, as a result of a change in the nature of the job, or as part of a planned development programme.

IT has a role in identifying performance shortfalls. It can be used to identify individual error rates and also for monitoring. A good example of the latter is in call centres, where supervisors are able to monitor agents' calls. The agent's performance can be assessed against a checklist of good practice and any training needs identified.

A change in the nature of the job may arise as a result of changes to systems or procedures, or changes to legislation. An individual's job may also change as a result of a transfer or promotion. These give rise to a *skills gap* – the gap between what the employee can do and the needs of the job.

Training needs arising as a result of a development programme anticipate future changes in the nature of the job. Individuals receive training to equip them for potential future jobs. Again there is a skills gap, but in a development programme it is bridged before the future job arises.

An alternative approach is to look at *competencies*. These are underlying characteristics and behaviours that affect an employee's ability to do the job. An example of a competency might be written and verbal communication. Competency assessment is most common as part of a development programme.

Set training objectives

The next stage is to set objectives to be met by the training. Although these will be based on the training needs we must recognize that there are some needs that cannot be fully met by training. Lending is an example of this – we can teach the basic techniques, but the character judgement that is a key part of it needs to be developed by experience.

Training objectives need to be *SMART* – specific, measurable, achievable, relevant and timebound.

Decide training methods

The next stage is to decide on which training methods should be used. We discussed the options earlier in the chapter. Selection of training methods should consider:

- The requirements of the material (for example, complex material is best delivered off the job);

- Any constraints on delivery (for example, whether staff can be released to allow off-the-job training);

● The individual's learning style.

The concept of learning styles was developed by Honey and Mumford and is related to the learning cycle of David Kolb. This shows there are four stages in the learning process – experiment, experience, reflect and understand. Trainees have to go through all four stages before they are fully trained. Training methods generally give an opportunity to try things out (experiment) and describe how they are meant to work (understand). Trainees also need a chance to think about what they have learned (reflect) and to see how it works in a real-life situation (experience).

Figure 2.3: The four stages in the learning cycle

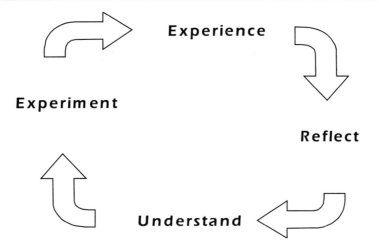

The four stages in the learning cycle correspond to the four learning styles. Activists prefer to learn by experiment, theorists prefer to understand the basic principles, reflectors prefer to observe and reflect on the material, and pragmatists prefer to experience the material in a work situation.

Therefore the selection of training methods needs to take account of the trainee's preferred learning style, as the trainee will be most interested and will absorb most information when that style is used. However, the trainee still needs to go through the entire cycle to complete the training.

Scheduling training is very important. In general, training should be given shortly before the new skills are needed, perhaps with refresher training a few weeks or months later. If training is given too early, the trainee will forget important parts before he or she gets the chance to use them. If training is given too late, the trainee will not have time to complete the learning cycle and to fully understand the training before using the new skills.

Validate training

The next stage is to validate the training. This involves checking that the trainee can meet all the training objectives after completing the training programme. Note the importance of setting SMART objectives to ensure that the training can be validated.

Evaluate training

The final stage is to evaluate the training. This involves ensuring that the value to the organization of meeting the training objectives is greater than the cost of the training programme. This is not usually a problem for IT training, as people need to know how to use the system in order to take advantage of the facilities it offers them. Evaluating training is also useful for comparing different training methods – is it worth using a cheaper method that gives slightly less thorough training?

2.7   Health and safety issues

Potential health and safety issues posed by information technology include:

- Repetitive strain injury (RSI);
- Back and neck problems;
- Radiation from screens;
- Danger from trailing cables;
- Exposure to hazardous chemicals;
- Risk of electric shocks;
- Injuries through moving equipment.

Long though this catalogue may be, problems are usually the result of avoidable factors such as poor posture and inadequate support. Most organizations issue guidelines that will help to avoid any health and safety issues. Rest breaks are recommended where staff use computer screens intensively.

Repetitive strain injury

Repetitive strain injury (RSI) is damage to the tendons of the hand that has been associated with keyboard work. A wrist support can be used to ensure that the hand and fingers are at the correct angle to minimize the risk of RSI.

Back and neck problems

Back and neck problems can result from incorrect posture. Screens should generally be at eye level, and chairs should give sufficient back support.

Radiation from screens

Concern has been expressed in the past about radiation from screens. Modern screens emit very little radiation, and filters are also available to further reduce this.

Other problems

Other problems are relatively rare, and fall within the standard health and safety practices operated by financial services organizations. Computers require a lot of cabling, and trailing cables are dangerous. This is usually minimized by boxing in cable runs. Cleaning materials may contain hazardous chemicals, and these must be controlled. There is a risk of electric shocks from faulty equipment, and all electrical work must be carried out by qualified electricians. There is a risk of injuries when equipment is moved, and any equipment that may need to be moved on a regular basis should be mounted on a trolley.

2.8   Teleworking

Teleworking involve employees working away from the office. *Telecommuting* is an alternative term for teleworking. We can identify three main forms:

● Homeworking;

● Knowledge working;

● Mobile working.

We need to look at these together with the related topics of telecottaging and hot desking.

By *homeworking* we mean relatively simple processing tasks carried out by employees at home. Data entry tasks such as entering details from application forms provide a common example. Another example is a *virtual call centre*, by which calls into a call centre can be routed to agents working at home. BT ran a virtual call centre pilot for their directory enquiries service in Scotland.

The technology required is relatively simple. A workstation with a built in modem will be connected to a server in the financial services organization's data centre, usually through a dial-up line. Where fast response is required a digital line may be used. Security is very important, and the workstation will have passwords for users to get into the workstation, to use the application software, and to access the data centre. Messages will usually be encrypted to prevent their being intercepted, and there may be a firewall between the workstation and the server to prevent attempts at 'hacking'. These security measures are discussed in Chapter 4.

We can show the technology as follows:

Figure 3.4

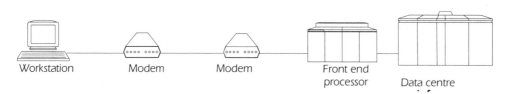

By *knowledge working* we mean more complex roles such as consultancy and research. Management – especially project management – is possible on a teleworking basis. The requirement is usually to use a range of software tools such as word processors, spreadsheets, databases, presentation tools and Internet browsers.

The technology required is very similar. The workstation will be a powerful PC with a wide range of software. Knowledge workers may require access to customer or commercially sensitive data, in which event there may be additional security devices attached to the PC.

We can show the technology as follows:

Figure 3.5

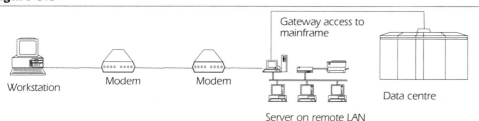

Mobile working refers to employees who travel for a large part of their working day and need to process information while on the move. This is becoming increasingly important as financial services organizations deliver services to their customers rather than expecting customers to visit them.

A number of technologies can be used, including the following:

- The simplest option is to use a stand-alone laptop or notebook computer. The employee will return to a central office from time to time to transfer the data into the organization's systems. The main disadvantage of this approach is that the data may be lost or damaged before it is transferred.

- An alternative is to transfer information from the portable computer to the organization's systems using a dial-up connection over the public telephone network. Messages will need to be encrypted because of the risk of interception. A variation on this is to use a mobile phone link to transfer the information. These are probably the most common forms of mobile working.

● Another alternative is to transfer information over the Internet. The security issues associated with the Internet are discussed in Chapter 15, but messages will need to be encrypted, and a virtual private network can be used to provide a higher level of security.

Teleworking has both advantages and disadvantages. If we consider the advantages and disadvantages for the organization first:

Advantages	Disadvantages
Savings on premises costs	More difficult to control
Employees do not have to travel	Higher equipment costs
Access for employees who cannot travel	Higher telecommunications costs
	Security issues
	Health and safety issues
	Perceived as 'skiving'

There are *savings on premises costs* as employees are providing their own place of work.

Employees do not have to travel to work. This reduces the risks of lateness or disruption due to travel problems. Some organizations expect employees who are teleworking to work longer hours to reflect the saving in travelling time.

Access for employees who would not find it easy to travel to work. These include carers and the disabled.

It may be more *difficult to control the work* being done. Control must be in terms of what is produced rather than the way the employee works, and this is not suitable for all jobs. Employees may suffer from distractions, affecting the quality or quantity of their work.

There are *higher equipment costs*. If employees are sick or on holiday, the equipment is idle and cannot be used by others. The equipment may be more likely to suffer damage either accidentally (for example from children or pets) or through environmental factors (dust and humidity levels may be higher in domestic premises). The cost of supporting and repairing equipment will be higher as the equipment will need to be brought in to a centre or an engineer will need to be sent to the employee's home.

There are *higher telecommunications costs* as employees must connect to the office over public telephone lines.

There are *security issues*. Data confidentiality may be difficult to guarantee as family members, visitors and others may have access to the equipment. There is a risk of viruses being introduced. It is difficult to ensure that backups are taken. There may also be data security issues associated with documents and forms sent to or produced by the employee.

The are *health and safety issues*. It is difficult to ensure that employees use appropriate office furniture providing adequate support. Problems may be more difficult to detect as employees may change their pattern of work to hide problems.

Other employees and managers may *perceive working at home as 'skiving'*, which can damage morale.

The advantages and disadvantages for employees are:

Advantages	Disadvantages
Control over working hours	Isolation
Reduced travel time	Overwork
Control over working environment	Access to support services

Better *control over their working hours*. Employees are not restricted to 9 – 5 working and can choose to work predominantly early in the morning or late at night. They can also split their work – this can be useful for parents with school-age children, who may choose to work (for example) 10 – 3 together with a two-hour period either early morning or late evening. This is also useful for staff who work predominantly 9 – 5 but have the option to stretch their day by doing additional work in the evening or at weekends.

Reduced travel time. As we have discussed, this benefit may need to be shared with the organization. Teleworking is also useful for employees who spend a lot of time travelling as part of their job, as it provides them with a base for administrative tasks without additional travelling.

Better control over their working environment. Employees can organize their working environment in the way that best suits them, without the constraints provided by the office. This freedom must be used with care to minimize distractions and avoid health and safety risks.

Isolation. Employees can feel very isolated. This is partly physical – they are no longer part of a team – but it is also partly an isolation from information. Employees do not know what is going on in the office; they have no access to the grapevine or to their network of colleagues and mentors. Employees who telework can find it difficult to secure promotion simply because they are never in the office – their achievements are less noticeable than those of their peers. It may also be more difficult to secure access to training as training needs may be less apparent.

Overwork. Because employees can work extended hours they may be under pressure so to do. This pressure may come from the organization although it is more usually self-imposed. This can lead to stress (strain) as discussed above.

An anecdote appeared in the *Financial Times*. A senior manager in an organization sent out an email at midnight. He started to receive replies *immediately*. Although the ability to work at unusual hours is one of the main benefits of teleworking, it is unhealthy should this start to be regarded as normal practice.

Access to support services. Employees do not have access to support services such as photocopying.

Telecottaging is a variant on teleworking. Instead of employees working at home they work in office premises close to their homes. Financial services organizations can use spare space in branches for this purpose, or local business centres can be used.

Telecottaging overcomes many of the disadvantages of teleworking. Although the organization still incurs costs the premises are often cheaper than the premises released (for example out-of-town sites rather than city centre) and may be in buildings that are underutilized. They have disadvantages of their own, of which the most important is probably the need for the telecottager to conform to the culture of the premises in which he or she is located.

Hot desking allows employees to work away from the office much of the time but to book a desk (and sometimes an office) when they need to come in. Again this overcomes many of the disadvantages of teleworking.

In practice, hot desking is often done badly. Successful hot desking requires:

- An effective system for booking desks, offices, meeting rooms and equipment;

- Storage space for employee's possessions, which can be moved into position quickly and easily;

- Equipment set up in a standard way so that it does not need to be individually reconfigured for each employee.

3

THE IMPACT OF INFORMATION TECHNOLOGY ON THE CUSTOMER

3.1   Relationship and transaction banking

It used to be that 'the banker knew his customer', and this assumption is the legal basis of the banker – customer relationship. The term *relationship banking* implies this level of knowledge as well as a relationship of trust – a fiduciary relationship – between banker and customer.

The relationship banking model proved unsustainable for mass market customers. Competitors with lower cost bases prevented the banks from charging high enough margins to support relationship banking. The banks found staff costs growing faster than their income and were forced to introduce automation to allow them to service larger numbers of customers in order to remain competitive.

The automation resulting from the first two generations of information technology allowed banks to handle increased numbers of customers without increasing staff numbers. However, this increase in numbers and other changes in banking practice such as the more frequent rotation of managers between branches made it impossible for banks to have the personal knowledge of their customers implied by relationship banking.

This resulted in a switch to *transaction banking*. The fiduciary relationship was replaced by a simple buyer/seller relationship and the application of the principle of *caveat emptor* ('let the buyer beware').

Transaction banking had its disadvantages:

- Courts were not always willing to accept that financial services organizations had no fiduciary duty towards their customers.

- Transaction banking has undermined traditional customer loyalty. This has allowed new entrants to the financial services market to cherry pick the most profitable customers and products, reducing financial services organizations' ability to subsidize less profitable operations.

- There is an increasing recognition that financial services organizations need to reinvest in the communities in which they operate, and the model of transferring deposits out of poor areas to finance lending in wealthier areas is under challenge. Legislation similar to the US Community Reinvestment Act is a possibility should organizations fail to address these issues.

3.2   Re-personalizing the relationship

Has the traditional banker/customer relationship gone for ever? Although we may not know our customer in the traditional sense we can use information to behave as if we do. We can describe this as 're-personalizing' the relationship. Instead of relying on staff knowledge, financial services organizations are increasingly relying on capturing this knowledge in computer systems.

One of the earliest examples of this is the *customer view*. Early computer systems often viewed the banker/customer relationship as based on the account. There was no attempt to connect different accounts held by the same customer. This led to absurd situations such as customers with thousands of pounds in their deposit accounts having cheques referred if they exceeded agreed limits by a few pounds. The customer view gives us the ability to take an overall view of the relationship with the customer.

A more sophisticated approach is to take account of customer preferences. Customers do not want to be offered insurance products every time they enter a branch, nor do they want to receive large amounts of unsolicited mailings and telephone calls. Financial services organizations can maintain contact histories for their customers, allowing them to avoid repeated offers to the same customer. In addition, customers can specify that they do not want to receive unsolicited mailings or telephone calls.

We have gone from a simple view of the customer's affairs to the ability to react to past events. The next stage is to anticipate future developments.

One example is the extension of credit scoring techniques into propensity and attrition scoring:

- *Propensity scoring* predicts the probability of a customer's buying a particular product. It uses historic information to develop a profile of those customers who are most likely buy this product in the next 1 – 2 years. This profile can be used to target marketing activity on these customers.

- *Attrition scoring* predicts the probability of customers' closing their accounts or allowing their accounts to go dormant. The high cost of recruiting new customers often makes it beneficial for financial services organizations to take action to retain existing customers.

It is important to understand that propensity and attrition scoring do not attempt to *predict* the future actions of individual customers. What they do is to indicate customers with a *higher probability* of buying a product or ending their account relationship.

Another example is the use of technology for customer identification. This includes:

- *The use of smart cards*. Private banking customers can be issued with smart cards. These give access to branch premises but also identify the customer to staff, who can greet him or her by name and call up all the necessary details as the customer enters the premises.

This has been used in the Middle East.

- *Caller line identification*. Call centre technology can identify the number from which a call has been made, unless it is withheld for privacy reasons. This can be used with computer telephony integration (discussed in Chapter 8) to call up the customer's details on the agent's screen when the call is put through. This must be used with caution – there are privacy issues and the caller must be positively identified before any information is given – but it can reduce the delay in call handling.

- *The use of biometrics*. Biometrics are discussed in Chapter 4 and are physical characteristics used to identify an individual. Where biometrics give positive identification they can eliminate the need to ask customers for forms of identification such as a driver's licence and they can also be used to identify customers to staff.

All of these can produce benefits in terms of customer service. They give us a better understanding of our customers' financial affairs and needs. They produce a more personal feel, both by showing customer knowledge and in avoiding sales approaches that the customer may regard as aggressive. They also benefit customers by improving security – providing customers with more effective means of identification without a requirement for papers, identification numbers and verification information which may get lost, forgotten or stolen.

There are also disadvantages. IT reduces individual responsibility as credit scoring systems have replaced the lending officer and centralized direct mailing has replaced personal contact as a way of generating business. Competition and the use of IT to deliver services have led the banks (in particular) to close branches, reducing the service available to customers in the immediate area.

IT has also introduced new problems for customers. Errors may be harder to detect in fully automated systems such as standing orders, and problems with these remain one of the main sources of customer complaints. ATMs offer convenient encashment facilities but they can run out of cash or, more rarely, the ATM network may fail. Errors in direct mail can be embarrassing – a major bank is reported to have sent a letter to a deceased customer commiserating with him on his death!

There are areas where IT has clearly improved customer service. The popularity of EFTPOS and debit cards proves that customers are quite happy to use services provided through IT. The effect of IT on the business market, with office banking systems, has greatly improved the service available to these customers.

Perhaps the biggest benefits lie in the future. Customer information systems allow the banks and building societies to personalize their service again. If staff may not know the customers by sight they can still know all about them though IT.

3.3 Technophobia

There is a general perception that customers suffer from *technophobia* – a fear and dislike of technology. It is not clear that there is any real evidence for this (some surveys have suggested that many customers prefer using ATMs for balance enquiries and withdrawals), but financial organizations need to take care when they introduce new methods of service delivery.

Customers are cautious about innovations. There are a relatively small number of 'early adopters' and a significant minority of 'laggards'. This applies to any form of innovation and does not necessarily imply any fear of technology as such.

Consultants Forrester Research have developed an approach to market segmentation that specifically considers attitudes to technology. They classify customers according to:

- Whether they are 'technology optimists' or 'technology pessimists';

- Their income;

- Whether their primary motivation is career, family or entertainment.

From these categories they develop ten market segments.

In this model high-income technology optimists represent the primary market for technology innovation, corresponding to the early adopters. Low-income technology optimists generally wait for prices to fall but follow as quickly as their economic circumstances allow. High-income technology pessimists will buy new technology but spend less time using it. They also place high importance on ease of use and reliability. Low-income technology pessimists are disconnected from technology.

Low-income technology pessimists correspond to technophobic customers. Forrester data is based on a survey of US consumers and shows this group representing about 30% of consumers – a significant minority but less than a third of the potential customer base. High-income technology pessimists are willing to use technology – Forrester shows PC ownership in excess of 50% – provided they have confidence both in it and in their ability to use it.

If technophobia exists, it is probably a result of bad experiences with technology. We need to be aware of the problems that can arise and to treat customer concerns sympathetically.

The main sources of concern include:

- ATMs that are not available;

- Phantom withdrawals;

- Fraudulent EFTPOS transactions;

- Fraudulent Internet transactions;

- Errors in standing orders.

ATM failure

Customers rely on ATMs for cash, and can find ATM non-availability very irritating. There are three possible reasons for ATM failure:

- The failure of the ATM itself. This is quite rare. ATMs are very robust devices, and it is unusual for them to fail.

- The failure of the telecommunications links to the main computer or of the main computer itself. This is rather more common.

- Running out of money. This is the most common reason for ATM unavailability.

Financial services organizations manage these risks by providing customers with information about alternative ATMs. Stickers can be used to remind customers of those other organizations whose ATMs they can use through reciprocity arrangements, or to direct customers to the location of alternative ATMs.

The amount of money loaded into an ATM depends on the anticipated demand, but financial services organizations also need to consider the cost of using money in this way. Money held as notes in an ATM cannot earn interest. Financial services organizations can reduce the risk of ATMs running out of money by:

- Developing models to predict the expected pattern of demand for ATM withdrawals. The systems that control the ATM maintain statistics about the actual pattern of demand, which can be used to refine the models. This allows ATMs to be loaded with the minimum amount needed to ensure that the ATM will not run out of money provided there is no major departure from normal patterns of demand.

- Using the controlling software to check that the ATM still has money and is still functioning. If the ATM runs out of money a local branch can be notified and instructed to fill it. This can also be carried out by a central group. Other sources of failure can also be notified and an engineer sent.

Phantom withdrawals

Phantom withdrawals are ATM withdrawals that the card holder denies making. There is concern that either the system is making an error and debiting the wrong account or a fake card has been produced.

The majority of phantom withdrawals have been traced to unauthorized use of the card by a family member or friend. There are no instances where the system is known to have made an error.

Fake cards are reasonably easy to make and, if the PIN is known, can be used to withdraw cash. There have been some elaborate fraud attempts including:

- Using fake ATMs to steal the card and to get the customer to type in the PIN;

- Attaching a device to an ATM that will read the magnetic strip (to be copied later) and ask the customer to type in the PIN.

Financial services organizations have been slow to answer customer concerns on phantom withdrawals. The use of video cameras hidden in ATMs and improved methods to prevent cards from being forged or copied make it easier to prove that phantom withdrawals do not happen, but it is the responsibility of the staff to deal with complaints in a helpful and informed way.

Fraudulent EFTPOS transactions

Fraudulent EFTPOS transactions may be due to fake, lost or stolen cards. There is also the possibility of collusion between the retailer and the fraudster.

Precautions against fraud fall into three main categories:

- Card-based precautions;
- System precautions;
- Procedures.

Card-based precautions are designed to make cards more difficult to counterfeit and to make stolen cards more difficult to use. The main card-based precautions are:

- Tamper-proof signature strips, which prevent a signature from being erased;
- Holograms on the card, which make it more difficult to counterfeit;
- Photographs on the card, which make stolen cards more difficult to use;
- Card verification value (CVV – Visa) or card validation code (CVC – MasterCard), additional information making the card difficult to counterfeit.

The first two of these are already widely used. Photocards and CVV/CVC are relatively recent developments that have been shown to be effective in cutting fraud.

The use of signature verification as the primary means of confirming the customer's identity means that personal identification numbers (PINs) are rarely used to protect EFTPOS transactions in the UK.

Smart cards, discussed in Chapter 11, are more difficult to counterfeit and contain more identification information. They are currently used in countries such as France and Japan, and it is likely that they will eventually replace magnetic strip cards.

System precautions are designed to prevent counterfeiting of cards or to detect when a card is stolen. The main system precautions are:

- Hot card files, held either locally or centrally, which record lost or stolen cards and prevent their being used;
- On-line authorization, preventing cards from being used beyond the funds and credit available;
- Expert systems, which detect patterns of use that may indicate fraudulent behaviour.

All of these are widely used. Expert systems used in the UK include Fraudwatch (Barclaycard) and Falcon (MasterCard).

Procedures are designed to ensure that stolen cards are not misused. The main procedures include:

- Floor limits, which can be used to force authorization of all transactions in retailers particularly likely to be targeted by fraudsters;

- Advising customers that they will shortly be receiving a new card and to contact the issuer if it does not arrive by the validity date;

- Requiring customers to validate cards before use;

- Card collection from branches, which prevents cards from being intercepted in the post.

The first three of these are widely used. Card validation is common for new issue of a card but not for renewals. Requiring customers to collect cards from branches has service implications.

Fraudulent Internet transactions

The risk of fraudulent Internet transactions and the measures used to protect against them are discussed in Chapter 15.

Standing orders

Errors in standing orders are a common cause of customer complaint. The main problems are standing orders being paid twice, standing orders not being paid at all or cancelled, or expired standing orders being paid.

This is an example of a problem that was less common when standing orders were processed manually because the standing orders clerk would notice if the payment was incorrect. With IT used to automate the process, an error made when the standing order is set up will not be detected until after the payment has been made. This means that it is particularly important to ensure that care is taken when standing orders are set up and that the application software carries out all reasonable checks.

3.4　Overcoming technophobia

How do we overcome technophobia?

Advertising can help. One American bank advertised its new ATMs as 'Tillie the Teller' to make them seem friendlier to its customers. More recently the emphasis has been on the convenience technology offers – in particular, the availability of 24-hour banking.

We need to ensure that our systems are easy to use. This applies to all computer systems, of course, but is particularly important for systems that customers are expected to use without assistance.

Systems designed to be used by customers must be very easy to use. This includes the following:

- Screen designs must be clear, there should not be too many colours and colours should contrast well. The screen should be legible even if sited in sunlight or where there are reflections from internal lights.

- The screen should give clear instructions to the customer. Courtesy words such as 'please' and 'thank you' may be used at the start and end of a transaction where appropriate.

- It should be clear when the customer is expected to enter something. If there is likely to be a delay while the system carries out some processing a message such as 'busy – please wait' should be displayed.

- Navigation – the way the customer moves from one screen to another – should always be clear. The customer should always be able to cancel a transaction if he or she wishes.

- Transactions should not take too long. Not only is there a risk of the customer forgetting what he or she wants to do, the effect on other customers who may be queuing to use the system also needs to be considered.

New technology such as touch-sensitive screens and multimedia has made it easier to design systems that are customer-friendly.

Staff should be willing and able to help customers – if staff do not understand how to use the equipment, how can customers be expected to? If equipment is located in branches, staff should be trained to deal with enquiries and problems. If possible, staff should be available to assist customers who are not happy to use the equipment unaided.

We must never lose sight of the fact that financial services organizations exist to provide services to their customers. Even where technology is introduced for reasons such as cost control, it should not undermine this fundamental customer service ethic.

4

INFORMATION SECURITY AND DATA PROTECTION

Introduction

We have discussed the view of information as one of financial services organizations' most important assets, so the need to safeguard information should be self-evident. In practice we are concerned with safeguarding data as this automatically safeguards the information, which we have already defined as data in context. This subject is called *data protection*, and includes data security and data privacy.

Data security is concerned with ensuring that our data is protected from loss or damage, and that we can access it when required. We usually consider data security under two further headings:

- *Data availability* is concerned with protecting data from loss and ensuring that data can be accessed.

- *Data integrity* is concerned with protecting data from damage and ensuring that the data held is accurate, up to date and consistent.

Data privacy, also known as data confidentiality, is concerned with ensuring that data about customers and data that is commercially sensitive to the financial services organization is not seen by anyone not properly authorized.

A related subject with which financial services organizations are concerned is intellectual property rights, in particular copyright protection and compliance with software licensing agreements.

4.1 Legal basis

Until recently, financial services organizations' legal responsibilities have been concerned mainly with data privacy. This was based on case law (*Tournier v. National Provincial and Union Bank of England* 1924) and the Consumer Credit Act 1974.

UK government legislation to implement European Directives led to the strengthening of data privacy provisions, and imposed on financial services organizations a legal responsibility for data security. These obligations were specified in the Data Protection Acts of 1984 and 1998 and the Computer Misuse Act 1990. The Criminal Justice Act 1984, the Police and Criminal Evidence Act 1984 and the Civil Evidence Act 1995 also imposed data security responsibilities on financial services organizations.

Intellectual property rights are protected through the Copyright Act 1956 and the Copyright (Computer Software) Act 1985. Contract law provides additional protection for software purchased from external vendors.

Case law

Tournier v. National Provincial and Union Bank of England 1924 defined the banker's obligation not to disclose information about customers without their consent. This applies to all information the bank may obtain provided that this arose out of the banking relationship: for example, it includes records of interviews and telephone calls as well as financial records. It continues after the closure of the account or accounts, although any new information obtained after closure would not be covered.

This protects information banks hold about customers both on computer systems and as manual records. It has now been largely superseded by later legislation, in particular the Data Protection Acts of 1984 and 1998.

Consumer Credit Act 1974

The Consumer Credit Act 1974 (CCA) was designed to control organizations involved in the granting of credit, with the particular objective of protecting borrowers from unfair lending practices.

The main relevance of the CCA is with regard to the use of credit reference agencies. The Act defines a credit reference agency as a business whose function is to provide information relevant to the financial standing of individuals. This includes both profit-making and non-profit-making organizations such as trade associations. All credit reference agencies must be licensed by the Office of Fair Trading. Although financial organizations also provide financial information, this is not their main business and they are not regarded as credit reference agencies under the CCA.

The CCA covers printed information as well as information held in machine-readable form. The CCA gives individuals four rights:

- It places a duty of disclosure on businesses (including financial services organizations) using the services of a credit reference agency. An individual may apply in writing within 28 days of completion of negotiation of a credit agreement, and has the right to be informed of the name and address of any credit reference agency consulted.

- It gives the individual a right of access to the information held. The individual must request this in writing and pay a small fee. The credit reference agency must supply all information held about the individual (which may include information about other individuals – for example the husband or wife – if this is considered relevant to the individual's credit-worthiness).

- It gives the individual the right to have information deleted or corrected where it is factually incorrect and likely to damage the individual (for example by making it less likely that credit will be granted). The individual may give the credit reference agency written notice requesting removal or amendment, to which the credit reference agency must respond within 28 days.

- If the credit reference agency does not accept the removal or amendment of the information, it may serve a counter-notice of non-action. The individual has the right to add a 'notice of correction' to the information held. This is a short statement to show why the information held is incorrect. The credit reference agency may apply to the Office of Fair Trading to have the notice of correction quashed if it believes it to be incorrect or if it has other reasons for not publishing it (for example if it is libellous or frivolous).

Data Protection Acts 1984 and 1998

The Data Protection Act (DPA 1984) was passed in 1984 to comply with European Union restrictions on cross-border data processing and to meet public concern about the use of data held on computer systems. It protects personal data recorded in a form that can be processed automatically – usually a computer system, although any data that can be identified using computer-readable media (for example a bar code) would be covered.

Personal data is defined as statements of fact or opinion about living individuals. This excludes information about limited companies although information about sole traders – treated as individuals in law – is covered. It does not cover statements of intention.

The DPA 1984 defines a data subject as being the person about whom data is held. It defines a data user as a person or organization holding data. Where people access data as part of their jobs, the organization (rather than the individual) would be the data user.

It defines processing as amending, deleting or adding to data, or processing data into information. The final category might include activities such as matching data from different sources, for example matching spending behaviour data from loyalty schemes against banking data.

The DPA 1984 includes eight basic principles:

- The information to be contained in personal data shall be obtained, and personal data shall be processed, fairly and lawfully.

- Personal data shall be held only for one or more specified and lawful purpose.

- Personal data held for any purpose or purposes shall not be used or disclosed in any manner incompatible with that purpose or those purposes.

- Personal data held for any purpose or purposes shall be adequate, relevant and not excessive in relation to that purpose or those purposes.

- Personal data shall be accurate and, where necessary, kept up to date.

- Personal data held for any purpose or purposes shall not be kept longer than is necessary for that purpose or those purposes.

- An individual shall be entitled:

  a) at reasonable intervals and without undue delay or expense:

    i) to be informed by any data user whether he holds personal data of which that individual is the subject; and

    ii) to request access to any such data held by a data user; and

  b) where appropriate, to have such data corrected or erased.

- Appropriate security measures shall be taken against unauthorized access to, or alteration, disclosure or destruction of, personal data and against accidental loss or destruction of personal data.

There are some exemptions from the non-disclosure requirements of the DPA 1984. These include disclosure to the employees of the data user to allow them to carry out their duties, disclosure to the data subject, disclosure with the data subject's consent, and disclosure necessary to safeguard national security, prevent or detect a crime, as required by law or the courts, and to prevent injury or health damage.

All data users must register with the Data Protection Registrar, who ensures compliance with the DPA 1984. Information to be registered includes: who the data user is, what personal data is held, the purpose for which it is held, where the data subject may apply to look at this data, to whom the data may be disclosed, and any foreign countries to which the data may be transferred.

There are some exemptions from the registration requirements of the DPA 1984. These include data that must be made public by law (e.g. a company's register of shareholders) and data required to protect national security. Personal data held for domestic or recreational purposes need not be registered, and personal data held by unincorporated clubs need not be registered provided the members agree and the data is not disclosed.

There are also exemptions for mailing lists (which can consist of names and addresses only) and for payroll, pensions and accounting data, provided that this data is not used or disclosed for any other purpose. In practice, most financial services organizations would want to be able to analyse this data, and it would need to be registered.

The DPA 1984 gives all data subjects a right of access to data held about them. The data subject must write to the address given in the register and, if the data user has more than one entry, the data subject must say to which entry he or she is requesting access and may be required to submit each request separately in writing. The data user may charge a fee for each request and must respond to the request within 40 days, although this period may be extended if the data user needs time to identify the individual concerned or to get agreement from other people.

If the data user does not respond to the request, the data subject can apply to the Registrar or the courts. The Registrar may serve an enforcement notice, requiring the data user to provide the information, or a de-registration notice, after which it would be illegal for the data user to continue to hold the information. The data subject may make further requests provided they are at 'reasonable' intervals.

There are some exemptions from the subject access requirements of the DPA 1984. The most important of these concern data needed to prevent a crime, data held for tax purposes, data held by financial regulatory bodies, data held only for statistical purposes (where it is impossible to identify any of the data subjects from the data held), and data covered by legal privilege – such as information about third parties given by a client to a solicitor. Data held purely for back-up (copies that can be used to replace other data if it is destroyed) is exempt, as is data already covered under the CCA.

As well as the right of access, the data subject has three other rights. These are the right to compensation for any damage caused by the data being inaccurate; the right to compensation for any damage caused by loss or unauthorized disclosure of the data, and the right to have factually inaccurate data corrected or removed.

Compensation can only be awarded if the data subject suffers damage – compensation will not be awarded for embarrassment unless damage is also suffered. Compensation will not be awarded if the data user can show that all reasonable care was taken to ensure the accuracy of the data, or if the data accurately records information received from the data subject or a third party and its source is clearly indicated.

If compensation has been awarded, the courts can also order data to be removed if there has been unauthorized disclosure and the courts are satisfied that this is likely to recur. This is possible even if the data is factually correct. If a computer bureau is responsible for the disclosure, the customer on whose behalf the data is held must be notified before the data is deleted.

Financial services organizations have appointed compliance officers responsible for ensuring that their obligations under the DPA 1984 are met.

The main changes under the Data Protection Act 1998 (DPA 1998) are:

- It has been extended to cover 'structured storage systems' including paper filing systems and microfiche.

- The principles now include a requirement that personal data shall not be transferred outside the European Economic Area except to countries that ensure an adequate level of data protection.

- Individuals can give notice in writing that the data user must not use their data for marketing purposes.

- There are restrictions on the use of automated decision systems. They can still be used as a condition for entering or performing a contract (therefore credit scoring a new loan application is still permitted) but in other circumstances individuals must be informed when a decision is made on this basis and have the right to have it reassessed manually.

DPA 1998 revises the principles of DPA 1984. The first five principles are broadly the same as the first six principles of DPA 1998 (the second principle is a combination of the second and third principles from DPA 1984). The sixth and seventh principles broaden the seventh and eighth principles from DPA 1984. The eighth principle is new and strengthens the restriction on cross-border data processing. The revised principles are as follows:

- Personal data shall be processed fairly and lawfully and, in particular, shall not be processed unless:

  - at least one of the conditions in Schedule 2 is met, and

  - in the case of sensitive personal data, at least one of the conditions in Schedule 3 is also met.

  (Schedules 2 and 3 establish that either the data subject has given consent for processing or that the processing is necessary, for example to fulfil a contract or for legal reasons. Schedule 3 is concerned with sensitive data such as racial origin, religious belief or sexual preference for which a stricter definition of 'necessary' is applied.)

- Personal data shall be obtained only for one or more specified and lawful purposes, and shall not be further processed in any manner incompatible with that purpose or those purposes.

- Personal data shall be adequate, relevant and not excessive in relation to the purpose or purposes for which it is processed.

- Personal data shall be accurate and, where necessary, kept up to date.

- Personal data processed for any purpose or purposes shall not be kept for longer than is necessary for that purpose or those purposes.

- Personal data shall be processed in accordance with the rights of data subjects under the Act.

- Appropriate technical and organizational measures shall be taken against unauthorized or unlawful processing of personal data and against accidental loss or destruction of, or damage to, personal data.

- Personal data shall not be transferred to a country or territory outside the European Economic Area, unless that country or territory ensures an adequate level of protection for the rights and freedoms of data subjects in relation to the processing of personal data.

Computer Misuse Act 1990

The Computer Misuse Act was passed in 1990 after some highly publicized cases of *hacking*

– unauthorized access to data held on computers. The Act introduced three new criminal offences:

● Unauthorized access to computer programs and data;

● Unauthorized access with intent to commit or facilitate the commission of a further crime;

● Unauthorized modification of computer material – that is, programs and data held in a computer.

The first offence is relatively minor and allows the prosecution of people who simply want to look at data to which they have no right of access. If convicted, such people can be fined up to £2,000 and/or imprisoned for up to six months. The other two offences are far more serious and cover actions such as industrial espionage, attempted fraud and the introduction of computer viruses. People convicted of these two offences may be imprisoned for up to five years and/or may be given an unlimited fine. Prosecution for these offences does not prevent someone also being prosecuted for the first offence, where the requirement for proof is lower.

Criminal Justice Act 1984 and Police and Criminal Evidence act 1984

For a conviction under the CMA, the person must be aware that he or she was not authorized to access or modify the data. This is why financial services organization systems now display warning messages when people log on to use them. It must also be shown that the person's actions caused the computer to carry out some function – even if only to reject the access attempt.

The computer's own records (for example a list of attempts to log on to a system) can be used as evidence provided it can be shown that the recording system is proven and the computer was operating correctly. This must be certified to the court by an expert witness in order to meet the requirements of the Criminal Justice Act 1984 and the Police and Criminal Evidence Act 1984.

Civil Evidence Act 1995

The Civil Evidence Act 1995 extended the acceptability of computer records as evidence into civil law. The Act was particularly concerned with the acceptability to a court of law of images of documents stored on microfiche or optical disk.

The Act requires that the recording system is proven and the computer was operating correctly. It also requires that a complete audit trail is kept and that the recording medium is of a form that cannot be altered undetectably. For example write once read many optical disc (WORM) and compact disc-recordable (CD-R) are acceptable whereas compact disc-rewritable (CD-RW) is not. Provided that the requirements laid down in the British Standards Institution's code of practice are met, images are acceptable although they are considered less good than the original documents.

Copyright Act 1956 and the Copyright (Computer Software) Act 1985

Computer programs are the *intellectual property* of the author, and copyright law exists to protect the author's rights. Under the Copyright Act 1956 and the Copyright (Computer Software) Act 1985, original works such as computer programs cannot be copied without the permission of the author for 50 years after publication.

As far as computer software is concerned, the author is usually the organization that produced or commissioned it. The individual or software house who wrote the computer programs usually waives any rights in favour of the organization.

These Acts not only prevent the programs from being copied but also prevent the production of programs that do the same thing as the originals. This is important in IT where the identification of requirements and design of the system accounts for much of the cost of systems development.

Law of contract

Software purchased from external vendors is also covered by contract law. This takes the form of a licence agreement, which the purchaser accepts as part of the purchase of the software, limiting the purchaser's rights to copy or to sell the software.

As an example, consider the purchase of 'shrink wrapped' package software for a personal computer. The floppy disks (or, increasingly, CD-ROMs) that contain the software are usually in a sealed envelope. By breaking the seal the purchaser agrees to the terms of the licence. This restricts the number of copies that can be made, and if the purchaser makes more than the licence allows him or her can be sued for breach of contract.

In the UK, an organization called the Federation Against Software Theft (FAST) represents the interests of the software producers, and has prosecuted some very large companies for breaches of copyright and contract law. The Business Software Alliance (BSA) is the US equivalent.

Bank rules

Bank rules were originally written to ensure that banks complied with the *Tournier v. National Provincial and Union Bank of England* case. These were then modified to meet the requirements of subsequent legislation. They typically cover areas such as:

● Who is responsible for data and what controls need to be put in place in order to ensure that data remains confidential and available and retains its integrity;

● Measures to protect computer equipment from damage or theft, and to ensure that any equipment failure does not result in a loss of data;

● Measures to protect telecommunications links from unauthorized access, including rules relating to accessing and receiving data from the Internet;

- Rules governing relationships with suppliers to ensure competitive tendering, to protect the organization against unfair contracts, and to ensure that the organization's intellectual property rights and rules of non-disclosure are respected.

4.2 Threats and risks

It is useful to draw a distinction between a threat and a risk:

- A threat is anything that could compromise the security or privacy of data.
- A risk is loss or damage to the business.

In risk management we are concerned with the *threats* to data protection. How we manage these threats will depend on the potential loss or damage to the business – the *risks* associated with the threat. We also need to be aware of the particular threats posed by the nature of IT:

- Much more information can be produced, which will need to be stored and disposed of securely.
- Information can be produced in a portable form, for example floppy disks, magnetic tapes and portable computers, which will need to be protected against theft.
- Transactions can be entered and enquiries made by anyone with access to a workstation attached to the computer network provided that they know the passwords. Physical security is important to limit access to workstations, and automated security checks such as passwords must be kept secret.
- Offices and branches are now almost totally dependent on IT to provide an acceptable level of customer service, so hardware, software and data need to be protected against damage, and plans need to be in place to restore service as soon as possible in the event of failure.

We shall look at threats first. We shall focus on three main categories of threat:

- Malicious action;
- Disaster;
- Hardware or software failure.

Malicious action

Malicious action is carried out deliberately, with the intention either of doing damage or of committing another crime. The most important types of malicious action are:

- Hacking;
- Introduction of a computer virus;
- Fraud.

Other forms of malicious action are less common and include sabotage.

Hacking

Hacking is unauthorized access to data or computer systems. The main types of hacking are:

- Use of the Internet to gain access to systems and data;

- Use of dial-up telecommunications links to gain access to systems and data;

- Electronic eavesdropping including tapping telecommunications links;

- Internal hacking.

Most people would associate the word 'hacking' with illegal access through the Internet, and this is the most common form of external hacking.

With the increase in the use of the Internet, dial-up telecommunications links are perhaps less common than they used to be. They are still used to provide customers with access to PC banking services (although the Internet is increasingly taking a more prominent role). They are often used to provide a secondary communication link in case the main link fails. They are increasingly used to allow staff working outside the office to access organizations' systems and data through a cellular telephone link.

Hackers can use a 'demon dialer' to call telephone numbers randomly. When the response comes from a computer system the demon dialer will stop and the hacker will attempt to gain access to the system, perhaps using a dictionary program to try passwords. Another approach is to try to cause an error in the system that will give the hacker access to the operating system. Once the hacker has identified a telephone number that gives access to a computer this may be shared with other hackers.

Electronic eavesdropping can use a wire tap on a telephone line. If wireless telecommunication or a cellular telephone link is used this can also be intercepted. The eavesdropper can listen to the message and potentially alter its content. A variant on this is to intercept the image of a computer screen. Computer screens emit radiation, which can be detected using a tuneable monitor, which can recreate an image of the original screen.

A lot of hacking is internal. Staff access data and systems for which they are not authorized, either taking advantage of poor security systems or using stolen passwords. This is sometimes associated with fraud.

Although hacking is seen mainly as a threat to data confidentiality it can also threaten the integrity of the data. Hackers using the Internet or dial-up connections are not always content just to look at the data but may also want to leave messages to announce what they have done. These messages may change the value of (or 'corrupt') data used by the system. Hackers may also change Web sites.

Computer viruses

Computer viruses are computer programs that can duplicate themselves. They 'infect' other programs by adding a copy of themselves to the end of the program. Some viruses are harmless but others can destroy data held on disk or even physically damage the computer.

There are a number of different forms of virus, the most important of which are executable viruses, macro viruses and worms.

Executable viruses affect computer programs – for example .EXE and .COM files on PCs. These are the original and best-known type of computer virus.

Macro viruses affect the macros used with office automation software, especially word processors. They usually create an AutoOpen macro that will run automatically when the document is opened. The threat of macro viruses is growing faster than any other type of virus, because of the ease with which they can be spread using email and because the older generation of virus checkers was unable to detect them.

Worms affect networks. Although they are relatively rare they are capable of causing considerable disruption.

All types of virus work in much the same way:

● When an infected program is run, the program's first action is to write a copy of itself into memory. It will then go on to complete the program's normal functions.

● The copy of the virus in memory is actually a small computer program of a type called 'terminate and stay resident'. It does not do anything until another computer program starts.

● When another program starts, the virus will first check to see whether it has already been infected. If it has, the virus will not do anything. If not, the virus will attach a copy of itself to the end of the program and will change the first instruction in the program so that the virus is run before the program does anything else. It will then write the program back to disk with the copy of the virus attached.

Viruses check to see whether the program has already been infected because they want to stay hidden for as long as possible. If a virus kept re-infecting the same program, the program size would increase (remember that viruses infect programs by *adding* a copy of themselves to the end) and it would soon be obvious by the increase in size that the program was infected.

To see whether programs have already been infected, viruses look for a 'signature'. This is a part of the virus that has an identifiable pattern. Some viruses (called 'polymorphic' viruses) continually change the pattern, which makes it harder for virus checker programs to identify them.

● Most viruses will not take any other action until a certain amount of time has passed or until they have infected a number of other programs. This gives the virus the chance to spread as widely as possible. Once this has happened, the virus will wait for a trigger – usually a date, such as Frodo's birthday (22 September) for the Hobbit virus or Friday 13th for the virus of the same name.

● When the trigger arrives, the virus will take whatever action it is designed for. Despite the publicity attracted by viruses, many of them do little damage (the Hobbit virus simply displays the message 'Frodo Lives').

Viruses such as this cause no damage to the data on the computer, or they may simply hide files (they are still stored on disk but the operator cannot see them). Other viruses delete files, but the operator can recover the data fairly simply provided he or she realizes what has happened. However, there are viruses that do more substantial damage, overwriting the contents of files with meaningless data or causing physical damage in some way.

Fraud

In most 'computer frauds' the computer is used only to create the documentation – the fraud takes advantage of weaknesses in the organization's procedures and controls rather than in its computer systems. For example, the computer can be used to record the receipt of false invoices, but this relies on a failure to reconcile invoices against orders and delivery notes.

Another type of fraud is the misuse of the organization's computer resources. Hugo Cornwall in *Datatheft* gives the example of two employees who used their office computer to run a music rescoring business. They were using three-quarters of the available storage space before they were detected.

Disaster

Disaster includes various categories such as fire, smoke, flood and explosion.

The effects of fire are obvious, and usually result in the complete loss of everything in the affected area – not only the computers but also magnetic disks, optical disks and magnetic tapes. Smoke can also produce damage over a much wider area, causing electrical short circuits and damaging magnetic disk drives.

Water also causes damage by short-circuiting electrical equipment. Water damage can be the result of flooding, burst pipes or sprinkler systems designed to combat fire. In many small office fires the threat of damage to computers from the sprinkler system is greater than the threat due to the fire!

Explosions can be due to gas leaks, chemical explosions, bombs, or disasters such as crashes. An explosion can cause great damage to computer equipment in the vicinity, warping disk drives and breaking circuit boards. Debris spread by the explosion as shrapnel may cause further damage. The explosion may be followed by a fire, resulting in additional damage due to the fire and smoke. Water damage may result from pipes fractured by the explosion and from sprinkler systems activated if there is a fire.

Hardware or software failure

The most common causes of hardware failure are wear and tear, and environmental factors such as variations in power supply. Wear and tear includes connections becoming loose, circuit boards cracking, and disk drive read-write heads getting out of alignment. Variations in power supply include both electrical 'surges' and power cuts.

Peripheral equipment is equipment attached to the computer, and is subject to a wide range of temporary failures including paper jams on printers and 'parity checks' on storage devices. Ionising radiation (such as X-rays or ultraviolet radiation) or magnetic or electric fields can corrupt data held on magnetic storage devices such as disk or tape.

Telecommunications links are subject to various types of failure including lines being cut and electrical interference. Even if interference does not prevent messages being received the amount of 'noise' may make it impossible to interpret the signal correctly, or the message received may not be the same as the message sent. Telecommunications components such as modems and multiplexers are also subject to the same causes of failure as other hardware devices.

Software failure is often the result of errors made when the software was written. The software may not have been designed to cope with a particular set of conditions, and when these occur there will be an error. The 'millennium bug' is a good example of this. Alternatively the software may not work on the particular hardware (perhaps because there is insufficient storage space) or with other systems software components.

4.3   Risk management

To convert threats into risks we need to consider the probability of the threat being realized and the expected cost to the organization if it is. One method is *Courtney risk analysis*. The probability of the threat being realized in the next 12 months is multiplied by the expected cost to give an annualized loss expectancy or ALE.

The expected cost itself depends on the possible consequences of the threat being realized and the cost of those consequences. Many threats have a range of possible consequences, some of which are very low risk because their financial implications are small or because the probability of that particular consequence is very small.

Another approach is called *failure mode effect analysis* (FMEA). This involves the following stages:

● Identify the potential 'failure modes'. We have described these as the risks above.

● For each risk, identify the potential effects of failure.

● For each risk, identify the potential causes of failure. We have described these as threats above.

● For each threat, identify how likely it is to occur. This is expressed as a number between 1 (low) and 10 (high).

● For each threat, identify how severe a problem it will cause if it does occur. This is expressed as a number between 1 (low) and 10 (high).

● For each threat, identify how likely it is that the threat will be detected. This is expressed as a number between 1 (high probability) and 10 (low probability).

- Multiply the likelihood of occurrence, the severity and the likelihood of detection to calculate a risk priority number (RPN). A high RPN indicates a major threat for which there must be counter-measures.

Having quantified the risk, the next stage is to manage it. Lane defined four general approaches:

- Eliminate it.
- Reduce it.
- Ignore it.
- Transfer it.

Eliminating the risk involves reducing to zero the probability that the threat will be realized. This is rarely possible, although some threats may materialize in a number of ways, and it may be possible to eliminate some of these.

For example we can eliminate the risk of computer viruses being introduced through infected floppy disks by using PCs that do not have floppy disk drives. It is still possible for computer viruses to be introduced over the network, however.

Reducing the risk involves either reducing the probability of the threat being realized or reducing the cost, or both. This is a common approach to risk management.

Ignoring the risk is feasible provided that the ALE is small and the cost is not excessive. This approach is common for small risks.

Risks can be transferred, either to a supplier or to an insurer. Should the risk be realized a supplier may have to put things right or pay compensation, or both. This approach is common, with suppliers being expected to provide warranty against failures.

Where a service is provided, for example where a supplier runs the financial services organization's computer systems (facilities management, discussed in Chapter 5), service level agreements allow the risk of poor service to be transferred in much the same way.

Corporate assurance is similar to a warranty, except that a guarantor (rather than the supplier) provides the assurance. This is common where the supplier is a relatively small organization and the guarantor has a relationship to the supplier, for example in providing marketing support.

An insurer would simply pay the organization's loss. This is common, particularly where the probability of the risk being realized is low but the potential cost is high.

4.4   Risk prevention

Before we look at specific responses to the types of threat we considered earlier, we need to consider the most important approaches to risk prevention. These are:

- Contingency sites;

- Fault tolerance;

- Backups and checkpoints;

- Passwords and access security;

- Encryption.

Two additional topics we shall consider at this stage are business continuity planning and audit trails.

Contingency sites

Contingency arrangements allow financial services organizations to use alternative computer equipment if they have a problem. Most such organizations have spare equipment of their own, but it is also possible to make contingency arrangements with equipment suppliers or computer bureaux. There are two types of contingency arrangement, hot site and cold site.

Hot site contingency means that the spare computer equipment is fully set up and loaded with the data needed to run the organization's systems. This may be up to date as at the start of the business day, or data may be copied to the contingency site on a regular basis. If the main computer system fails, the hot site computer can be ready to take over.

This may not be immediate. Unless completed transactions are immediately copied to the contingency site there will be a need to re-process or re-enter data lost when the main system failed. Even so, it should be possible to restore access to systems and data within a relatively short time.

Cold site contingency simply means that spare computer equipment is available. If the main computer system fails, the cold site computer will need to be loaded with the programs and data required to run the organization's systems. Data lost when the main system failed will need to be re-processed or re-entered. This may take several hours.

Hot site contingency is much more expensive than cold site. In effect the financial services organization needs to pay for two computers, only one of which will be fully used. Some organizations exploit this by splitting their workload between the two computers. If both are working neither is fully utilized, but they are able to carry out additional, lower-priority work. If one computer fails, all work is switched to the other and low-priority work is discontinued. Even if this approach is not used, some systems are so important that the extra cost of hot site contingency can be justified. An example is a dealing system, where the organization could lose large amounts of money if it is unable to react to exchange rate changes.

Fault tolerance

An alternative to contingency sites is the use of *fault tolerant computers*. These are designed so that important components are duplicated – if the original fails the duplicate can take over. Fault tolerant computers are used where it is very important that computer systems do not break down, such as the payment systems CHAPS and SWIFT.

We can also apply the idea of fault tolerance to magnetic disk storage. RAID, which stands for a 'redundant array of inexpensive disks', can be used to store data. The data can be 'mirrored', with copies stored on two or more separate disks, so that the failure of one disk will not result in the data being lost. RAID allows data to be stored on cheap disks and to be at least as safe as data stored on more expensive, higher-quality disks.

An alternative to mirroring is 'striping'. Three disks are used, and the data is split between two of the drives. The data on the two drives is compared and the *difference* is written to the third drive. If one of the drives holding the data fails, this can be reconstructed from the other data drive and the drive holding the difference. Striping is possible because the computer can treat data as if it were a series of numbers, and this is important for a number of risk prevention techniques.

Backups and checkpoints

Taking a backup involves copying data and programs to a removable storage medium such as magnetic tape, magnetic disk or optical disk. If the data or programs are later lost, the backup copies can be reloaded. This will not completely prevent the loss of data – transactions entered since the backup was taken will still have to be re-entered – but it will minimize the loss. All data and programs must be backed up regularly.

The usual approach is the three generation (or 'grandfather – father – son') backup. Let us use this approach to see how we might take backups over a typical week:

● Monday's work will be processed. At the end of the day all data will be copied to magnetic tape (tape 1) and stored in a fireproof container.

● Tuesday's work will be processed and the data copied to tape 2, which will be stored in a fireproof container. Tape 1 will be sent to another location for safekeeping.

● Wednesday's work will be processed and the data copied to tape 3, which will be stored in a fireproof container. Tape 2 will be sent to another location for safekeeping. Tape 1 will be retrieved from storage and returned to the building.

● Thursday's work will be processed and the data copied to tape 1, overwriting Monday's work. Tape 1 will be stored in a fireproof container. Tape 3 will be sent to another location for safekeeping. Tape 2 will be retrieved from storage and returned to the building.

● Friday's work will be processed and the data copied to tape 2, which will be stored in a fireproof container. Tape 1 will be sent to another location for safekeeping. Tape 3 will be retrieved from storage and returned to the building.

If the data on the computer is found to be corrupt there are three backups available for recovery – the previous day's work (the 'son', stored on site in a fireproof container), the work from the day before that (the 'father', stored off site), and the work from the day before that (the 'grandfather', on site after retrieval from off site storage). This allows for two types of problem:

- The backup tapes themselves may be corrupt. Three-generation backup provides three chances of finding a readable tape, although if the father or grandfather backups are used some data will have been lost and will have to be re-entered or re-processed.

- The problem may have arisen earlier in the week but may only just have been discovered. Three-generation backup allows the organization up to three days to discover any problems.

We have said that backups can be made to any removable storage medium. The choice of backup medium depends on a number of factors, the most important of which are cost, robustness and the quantity of programs and data that needs to be backed up.

- *Cost.* Cost can be expressed in terms of cost per megabyte (a megabyte is one million characters of information).

- *Robustness.* Robustness is the probability of the backup medium getting corrupted, so that the stored information cannot be read. Robustness can be expressed as the mean time between failures (MTBF) – the average number of hours' usage before the medium fails.

- *Quantity of programs and data.* This is also called *volume,* and is the storage capacity of the medium.

Magnetic tape is one of the oldest media used for backup, and is still one of the most important. It is very cheap, quite robust, and can store very high volumes.

During the first and second generations of IT, magnetic tape was usually in the form of a reel of tape, which had to be loaded manually and was suitable only for mainframe and minicomputers. This has now largely been replaced by magnetic tape cartridges, similar to video cartridges, and a smaller version is used for backing up personal computers. More recently, digital audio tape (DAT) has been introduced.

The main disadvantages of magnetic tape are that reloading backed-up data is slow, and that data stored on magnetic tape can be corrupted, especially when the tape itself is heavily used. However, low cost and high capacity still make magnetic tape the most important medium for long-term storage of backed-up information.

An important alternative is optical disk. This can be 'write only', which is cheaper and can hold more information, or rewritable. The price of optical disk has fallen greatly over recent years, and it is now little more expensive than magnetic tape. It is robust, and can store very high volumes.

A major advantage of optical disk is that it can be read randomly, like magnetic disk, and reloading backed-up information is much faster than for magnetic tape. Optical disk backup is often provided through 'jukeboxes' having a number of optical disk drives and a mechanism allowing optical disks to be loaded into the drives from an expansion rack.

Integrated storage units are becoming increasingly important. They will usually store current information on magnetic disk, older information to which access is still needed on optical disk, and information for which access is rarely needed on magnetic tape. A particular feature of these units is that the user does not need to know where the information is stored to get access to it – the information can be requested using the standard database access language SQL, and the unit will work out where it is stored and will retrieve it.

Removable magnetic disk storage is still often used, especially for personal computers. Floppy disks have been used for many years, but their capacity is too low to be used for backing up significant amounts of information. More common is the *zipdrive*, a high capacity floppy disk unit that uses data compression to allow it to store large amounts of data.

Data compression uses patterns in the data to reduce the amount that needs to be stored. The phrase 'the cat sat on the mat' contains 22 characters. If we replace 'the ' with '*' and 'at ' with '#', we can store this phrase as '*c#s#on *mat', which contains 12 characters (note that we have to put 'mat' rather than 'm#' because there is no final space). We have reduced the amount of storage needed by almost 50%.

Removable hard disk storage is also found, especially in the form of PC cards designed to fit into slots in portable computers. This is usually too expensive to be effective as backup, and its main benefit is the ability for individuals to hold personal data and transfer this to any computer to which they have access. PC cards are discussed in Chapter 10.

Magnetic disk storage is generally more expensive than magnetic tape, and only zipdrives offer cost or capacity comparable to optical disk. It is also less robust than the major alternatives. Information backed up onto floppy disk or removable hard disk can be read directly, with no delay while the data is reloaded, and this can be of benefit.

In spite of their low capacity, floppy disks continue to be used for backup because:

- Floppy disk drives are installed as standard in personal computers, and can be used to back up programs and data at no additional cost.

- Data compression software such as WinZip allows them to be used for backup provided the amount of information to be stored is not too large. Note that the capacity of a floppy disk with data compression is still much lower than that of a zipdrive.

- Differential backup, which backs up only the program and data files that have changed, can be used to reduce the amount of storage required. The disadvantage of differential backup is that reloading the computer requires every differential backup to be applied in turn – a very time-consuming process and vulnerable to corruption affecting any backup in the series.

A more sophisticated version of the differential backup, which is used on mainframe computers, is *checkpointing*. Instead of copying the whole of a data file, only the items of data that have changed are copied. This is much faster than copying the entire file, and checkpointing can be used to recover from errors while processing individual transactions.

Compare this with other forms of backup, where we have to recover from the start of the business day (or a previous business day if differential backup is used or there is a problem with the most recent backup). This would mean that almost an entire day's work might need to be re-entered if there was a problem towards the end of the business day. Checkpointing avoids this problem.

Passwords and access security

We can restrict access to systems by asking for a code to gain access. Each user will typically have a *user ID* (which defines who the user is) and a *password*.

The user ID is not necessarily secret. John Smith, employee number 12345678, may have a user ID of JohnSmith, SmithJ, SmithJ1 (if there is another J Smith in the organization) or 12345678. The user ID will not change, and its long-term secrecy cannot be guaranteed.

The password must be kept secret. The user chooses a password, and must change it regularly, usually on a monthly basis. The password must typically include between 6 and 32 characters, and the system may check to see that the new password is not too similar to the previous password. To gain access, the user must enter both the user ID and the current password correctly. To protect the secrecy of the password, the system will not show the characters of the password on the screen but will usually show a character such as '*' instead to prevent onlookers from identifying the password.

If the password is wrong the user will usually be allowed to enter it again, but many systems allow a maximum number of tries (typically three), and may prevent the user ID, the workstation itself or both being used after this maximum has been reached.

For each user ID, the system will store a security profile saying what the user can do and what data he or she can access. This usually gives a level of authority. For example, branch staff may be classified as tellers (who can only make enquiries), clerks (who can enter transactions or make changes), supervisors (who *cannot* enter transactions but *can* authorize them) and a manager (who can do anything, including change security profiles).

Variations on passwords include test keys, as used in telex messages, and code books. The code book can be used to validate messages sent over a network. Each branch has a unique list of codes. Whenever the manager wants to send a message he or she will use the next code in the list. The computer processing the message has a copy of the list of codes and will check that the correct code has been used for the branch. The code book itself is kept securely under lock and key.

Passwords can also be used to restrict access to hardware, for example workstations or terminals. Most personal computers have a *power on password* which must be entered correctly to use the PC. Power on passwords apply to the computer itself, and are not specific to a user or associated with a user ID. Workstations or terminals can have a security profile, for example to restrict which terminals can enter certain types of transaction. This is useful for ensuring that transactions such as money transfers can only be entered in secure areas. We can combine terminal profiles with individual profiles to provide a further level of security.

It is usual to automatically *log off* terminals from any systems to which they are attached if a period of time passes without anything being entered. This ensures that staff do not leave terminals in a position to enter transactions when they go to lunch or go home, for example. We can also restrict who is allowed to use certain terminals by checking the terminal against a list of valid user IDs.

Alternatives to user IDs and passwords include badges and biometrics. *Badges* can be required in order to activate terminals – this could be combined with a system where staff need badges to gain access to the premises. The badge is usually a magnetic stripe card, which is swiped through or placed in a reader attached to the terminal. Smart cards can also be used, and another alternative is the active badge or radio badge, which activates the terminal when it is within a certain distance of a sensor attached to the terminal.

A variation on this is often used for office banking. The customer uses a smart card, which not only proves his or her identity to the system but also provides a key for coding and decoding messages sent to and from the bank. A new smart card is sent to the customer on a regular basis, changing the key used for encrypting messages.

Biometrics have started to gain acceptance as a means of identification. The most important methods currently are fingerprint recognition, iris recognition and voice recognition:

- *Fingerprint recognition* relies on the pattern of a fingerprint or thumbprint. Personal computer manufacturer Compaq now sells a fingerprint reader as an optional attachment. This is perhaps the most likely approach to using biometrics for identifying individuals in an office environment.

- *Iris recognition* photographs the pattern of the iris. This has largely replaced the older method, which used a laser to scan the pattern of blood vessels on the back of the retina. Nationwide Building Society has used iris recognition in an automated branch pilot in Swindon since mid-1998, and surveys suggest that 94% of customers would recommend its use. Three other European banks have plans to test this technology.

- *Voice recognition* can be used in telephone banking, and recognizes the pattern of the voice. Do not confuse voice recognition with speech recognition (which interprets speech) or voice response (which recognizes the tones from a touch tone telephone). Voice recognition systems achieve an accuracy of about 95%, and are less reliable than fingerprint or iris recognition.

Encryption

Encryption is used to encode messages or data, and is another technique that relies on the computer's ability to treat data as a series of numbers. When the computer encrypts data, it carries out a mathematical operation using the data and an encryption key.

The mathematical operation usually used is the *exclusive OR* (XOR), but we can illustrate the principles using multiplication. If our encryption key is 67 and the data we wish to encrypt is 12345 we can multiply these to get 827115. It is impossible to get back to the original data without knowing the key.

In practice, encryption keys are much larger than 67! 'Weak' encryption uses a key of 40 binary digits – allowing numbers of over one *million* million to be used. 'Strong' encryption starts at 56 binary digits – 72 thousand million million – and systems used to encrypt financial transactions may use 128 binary digits – three hundred million million million million million million.

Financial services organizations have two main requirements for encryption:

- To encode data held on portable computers. This is important as staff increasingly use portable computers when visiting customers' premises, to store information about both the customer relationship and any new business. This protects sensitive information if the portable computer is lost or stolen.

- To encode messages containing confidential information or carrying instructions for the transfer of value.

The difficulty with using encryption to encode messages is that the sender needs to have access to the encryption key. If a financial services organization provides thousands of its customers with the key, how can this be kept confidential?

We have already discussed the use of smart cards to provide customers with encryption keys. However, issuing new smart cards every month is too expensive to be practical for the retail market. Another approach is to use different keys for encoding and decoding the message. The key used for encoding is called the *public key* and the key used for decoding is called the *private key*. Together the public and private keys are called the *key pair*, and there is a mathematical relationship between them. This is called *asymmetric* or *public key encryption*, while the use of a single key is called *symmetric* or *secret key encryption*.

One issue with encryption is that it can be used to conceal illegal activities, and governments have restricted access to encryption technology as a result. For example, the US government classifies 'strong' encryption as a weapon and restricts its export. One approach that has been considered is *key escrow*, by which a copy of the decoding key is left with a trusted third party, and the police can retrieve it only with a court order. Another approach, used in the 'clipper' chip developed for encryption by the US government, uses a second key to which only the government has access. This is becoming particularly important in the context of the Internet.

We can encrypt data using either hardware or software. Hardware encryption uses a special computer chip that automatically carries out the encryption process. It is faster than software encryption and is used where large amounts of data need to be encrypted. Software encryption is more flexible, and keys and algorithms (the method of encrypting the data) can more easily be changed.

Business continuity planning

Business continuity planning attempts to answer the question: if any part of our IT systems fails what will we do? It is also called contingency planning, disaster planning or recovery planning.

The answer will depend to a large extent on the likely cost of the failure to the organization. There is no point in making elaborate plans to recover from systems failure if these cost more than the failure would. Techniques such as Courtney risk analysis are important to quantify the various risks and to identify how much should be spent on counter-measures.

Organizations need to be aware of the time value of different types of information. For example, the loss of information about the organization's foreign exchange position, even for a few minutes, can be very expensive if rates change. The loss of information about customer balances for a very short period would generally be less expensive.

Most organizations will have recovery plans that cover a large-scale failure, perhaps the loss of a data centre or of a major part of the organization's telecommunications network. There is ample evidence that companies that suffer catastrophic failure such as fire can go out of business if they do not have adequate recovery plans.

Organizations may not bring the same level of planning to more localized failures. Offices and branches are often left to make their own plans for the failure of local components such as workstations and even LAN file servers. Although this approach is valid (a centrally imposed plan may be costly to develop and inflexible to implement) there do need to be checks to ensure that offices and branches have drawn up adequate plans. Although the immediate financial costs of failure within a branch may be small, the effect on customer service and satisfaction needs to be considered.

Audit trails

Audit trails keep a record of everything that happens in the course of processing a transaction. The most common form of audit trail is a system *log* that records all attempts to access systems and data. Attempts that are unsuccessful may well be shown on a separate security report for later investigation.

In addition to the system log, most systems in financial services organizations maintain their own audit trails. These systems usually require different people to enter and authorize transactions, and maintain an audit trail by recording who entered and authorized each transaction, when it was entered and authorized, and sometimes the terminals on which it was entered and authorized.

Audit trails do not prevent breaches of data protection, but they make it easier to detect and to identify who is responsible. Audit trails may also be needed to comply with the Police and

Criminal Evidence Act 1984 and the Civil Evidence Act 1995.

4.5   Specific responses to threats

Let us return to our three main categories of threat:

- Malicious action;

- Disaster;

- Hardware or software failure.

How can we apply the risk prevention methods we have discussed to these, and what other methods can we use?

Malicious action

Some of the approaches to risk prevention we have discussed above apply to the threats due to malicious action. For example:

- Backups allow programs and data to be recovered to their state before the malicious action took place.

- Passwords and access security prevent access to systems by hackers or by those intending to introduce a computer virus.

- Encryption prevents hackers from intercepting messages, either to breach data confidentiality or to alter the message with the intention of committing fraud. Encryption also prevent thieves from reading the data stored on a stolen portable computer.

In addition to these general measures, there are some specific measures that financial services organizations can take to protect themselves against malicious action. These include:

- Eavesdropping detection;

- Virus protection measures;

- Authorization.

Electronic eavesdropping on telecommunications links can sometimes be detected, either because the signal received is not as strong as normal or because of increased static on the line. If either of these happens, the message can be delayed or switched to another line. As well as helping to counter eavesdropping, this ensures that messages are sent over the clearest possible line, which reduces the chances of message corruption. This does not apply to wireless links as there is no loss of signal.

The Tempest standard defines the shielding required to ensure that the radiation from a screen cannot be picked up on a tuneable monitor.

Virus protection measures include restrictions on sources of software, controls over microcomputer floppy disk drives, firewalls and virus-checking programs.

Restrictions on sources of software usually require that all software is obtained from reputable sources and is still sealed in its original packaging when it is delivered. Cheaper sources of software such as shareware are sometimes infected with computer viruses. If software media are not sealed in their original packaging there is a risk that they will have been used on a computer infected with a virus and will have picked up an infection that way (there are also licensing implications, as we discussed earlier).

A common source of virus infection is the use of floppy disks containing infected files. We can prevent this entirely by using workstations that do not have floppy disk drives. A more common but slightly less effective approach is to lock the floppy disk drives.

Firewalls are used to reduce the risk of infection over networks, especially the Internet. We discuss firewalls in Chapter 15.

There are two main types of virus-checking program:

- One type looks for the signatures of known viruses. This has the advantage of allowing a virus to be detected before the program is run, but it cannot detect new viruses (where the signature is not known to the virus checker) and it usually cannot detect polymorphic viruses, which change their signatures.

  All new microcomputer software should be checked using this type of program.

- The other type records information about all the programs on the computer. When it is run, it will check that the programs have not changed (remember that the virus adds a copy of itself to the end of the program).

  We cannot use the change in file size to identify virus infection. Viruses can change the information held about the file to hide the change in size. Instead we again rely on the ability of the computer to treat a computer program as a number. The virus-checking program carries out mathematical calculations to produce a distinctive *checksum* which is then stored in a file. The next time the virus-checking program is run the checksum is recalculated and the value compared with that stored. If they are not the same this suggests a virus infection.

Another approach is to prevent any data being written to the area where computer programs are stored. This may take the form of setting up a separate area on the hard disk for software and preventing any changes to this data, or at least warning if such an attempt is made. This approach is often used to protect programs stored on the file servers of local area network.

Authorization involves another person – often a supervisor – checking the data back to the original input instructions and authorizing it. Authorization is used for transactions such as payments and new accounts where an error could be expensive for the organization.

Disaster

Some of the approaches to risk prevention we have discussed above apply to the threats due to disaster. For example:

- Contingency sites allow rapid recovery of the most important systems and data in the event of disaster.

- Backups allow programs and data to be recovered to their state before the disaster took place.

In addition to these general measures, there are some specific measures that financial services organizations can take to protect themselves against disaster. These include:

- Fire prevention;

- Flood prevention.

Fire prevention measures include the use of smoke detectors, fire alarms and fire doors. Fire extinguishers should be available, and should use carbon dioxide or powder instead of water-based foam. Copies of backup data stored on site should be kept in firesafes or fire-resistant cabinets.

Sprinkler systems should not be used near computer equipment as the water will cause damage. Halon gas systems, which spray gas to smother a fire, are usually used near mainframe computer equipment.

Flood prevention measures include the use of false floors provided with drainage to allow small amounts of water (for example from a burst pipe) to drain away. Computer facilities such as data centres should not be sited where they are likely to be subject to flooding.

Hardware or software failure

Some of the approaches to risk prevention we have discussed above apply to the threats due to hardware or software failure. For example:

- Fault tolerance allows hardware to continue to operate even if some components fail.

- Backups and checkpoints allow programs and data to be recovered to their state before the failure took place.

In addition to these general measures, there are some specific measures that financial services organizations can take to protect themselves against hardware or software failure. These include:

- Uninterruptible power supplies;

- Preventive maintenance;

- Parity checking and data correction.

Computers are very sensitive to variations in power. Some of the most sensitive equipment is protected by capacitors. In the event of power failure these supply power for long enough for the equipment to close down safely, preventing any damage. Another method is the use of surge protectors to prevent a power surge causing damage.

Uninterruptible power supplies are more sophisticated and can be used to ensure that voltage does not go outside the range acceptable to the computer. Large data centres will usually also have a standby generator, allowing rapid restoration of power in the event of power loss.

Computers, like cars, need regular maintenance to detect and sort out problems. This is called *preventive maintenance* because it helps to prevent the computer from failing when it is processing the organization's work.

Parity checking is used to identify corruption in data read from magnetic disk or tape, or received over a telecommunications link. It again relies on the ability of the computer to carry out mathematical operations on data. The results of these operations are stored as additional characters with the data. When the data is read or received, the computer repeats the calculations to see if it gets the same answer. If not this shows that the data has been corrupted.

Errors in data sent over telecommunications links can be corrected automatically. When the receiving device gets a block of data it checks the parity. If this is correct it will send an acknowledgement (ACK) back to the sending device. If the parity is incorrect it will send a negative acknowledgement (NAK) back, and the sending device will send the block again. A system of this type is called an automatic repeat request (ARQ) system.

4.6   Protecting intellectual property

Software producers can protect themselves against illegal software copying in two main ways. The first is to make the user run a special computer program to install the software before using it. This can include a number of measures against copying:

●   It can show the registered user's name whenever the software is used. This does not stop further copying but it makes it easier to identify software that has been illegally copied.

●   It can keep a count of the number of times the software is installed. For a piece of software designed to be used by one person, two copies are usually allowed (one copy is for backup, in case the main copy is destroyed), and the install program cannot be run more than twice.

●   It can record some information about the machine on which it is installed, which makes it impossible to install the software on any other machine.

The second method is to make the user run the software with either a 'key disk' or a 'dongle'. A *key disk* is a floppy disk that contains information about the software. When the software is run it will check to see if the key disk is there and, if not, it will stop. A *dongle* is a small device that is attached to the back of the computer (where a printer would be attached). Again, if there is no dongle the software will not run.

The most common method is a requirement to install the software. Software pirates commonly use 'clone' programs in an attempt to copy floppy disks and CD-ROMs prior to installation, but these can be made difficult to copy exactly. Dongles are usually found only with special-purpose software.

5

CONTRIBUTION OF THE INDIVIDUAL

Introduction

This chapter is concerned with how we, as individuals, contribute to the development of information systems. We can identify four main roles, each of which may contribute differently:

- Business users;

- Power users;

- Managers;

- IT professionals.

Power users are information system users who are able to use query languages to request information and to develop systems and databases. The role of power users in end-user computing is discussed in Chapter 12.

In particular, users and power users will be involved in specifying the requirements and in testing for information systems. They may also be involved as managers in agreeing to ('signing off') the various stages in the development process.

During the first generation, computing was a highly specialist skill, and the role of business users was confined to providing information about their requirements. This was effective for the relatively simple requirements of the time, but as business requirements became more complex a 'disconnect' between what the business required and what was delivered became increasingly apparent.

Users started to get more involved in the process during the second and third generations. The development of the PC at the start of the third generation allowed the business to develop systems without the involvement of the information systems function. Although this improved responsiveness to business requirements it resulted in a loss of control over data and a serious threat to data protection.

This resulted in organizations losing control over their information. Mission-critical information was spread over a large number of mainframe, minicomputer and PC systems, and no-one had an overall picture of what was available. Compliance with the Data Protection

Act 1984 and the Computer Misuse Act was almost impossible. Organizations began to take greater control over the development process, and a more equal relationship between the business and IT emerged.

The fourth generation is again increasing the power of the business to develop systems independently of IT. It is unlikely that this will cause problems similar to those of the mid-1980s because the Web is a network – the problem in the mid-1980s was of information being held on stand-alone PCs where there was no way of identifying what was stored where.

We can summarize this as a diagram:

Figure 5.1

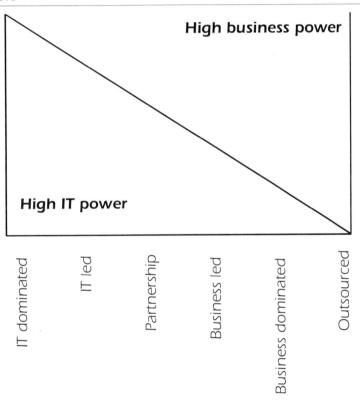

- High IT power can lead to an *IT dominated* model of systems development. The business gets what IT thinks it needs. This is generally unhealthy although may be essential for some very complex technical areas.

- As business power increases this leads to an *IT led* model. This may be appropriate where technology is changing very rapidly and the business does not have the time to develop an understanding of how to exploit it.

- Where business and IT power are equal this leads to a *partnership* model. The business and IT work together to solve the organization's problems.

- As business power increases this leads to a *business led* model. The business decides what is required and IT identifies how.

- A further increase in business power can lead to a *business dominated* model. The business takes total control of the systems development process. This may be essential, for example if the business is fighting for survival, but leads to a short-term view of technology and is generally unhealthy.

- *Outsourcing* removes the IT function completely. We shall discuss outsourcing later in this chapter.

5.1   The business and systems development

There are two main views of what the relationship between the business and the systems development function should be:

- One view is that the relationship is *contractual*. Systems development is a supplier like any other supplier and should be managed according to terms agreed in a contractual document.

- The alternative view is that the business and systems development should operate in *partnership*. Systems development is not a zero sum activity and both parties benefit by cooperating rather than competing.

Both approaches have their advantages, and most financial services organizations fall somewhere between them, moving closer to one or the other as recent experience and management fashion dictate.

The main advantage of the contractual relationship is that of certainty. Both parties are committed to take certain actions and are liable should they fail so to do.

The main disadvantages of the contractual relationship are interpretation and the risk of the systems development function not going beyond the narrow view of the contract:

- Interpretation is a source of problems for all complex contracts. During the early stages of the systems development process it is often very difficult to define a precise contract, as the objectives of the development and the method of work may be difficult to specify with any certainty.

- We have already shown that changes occur naturally during the course of a project. A contractual relationship needs to consider how such changes are accommodated and who will bear the cost. Contracts must specify how responsibility for changes is to be allocated.

- A contractual relationship implies that the systems development function will deliver exactly what is specified. This is a disincentive for systems developers to use their knowledge and experience to suggest improvements beyond the contracted minimum.

One approach that relies on a contractual relationship is to use an external supplier for systems development. This is called *outsourcing*. External suppliers can also be used for operating computer systems, where it is called *facilities management*.

The contractual relationship is the preferred approach for most financial organizations at the time of writing, and many are considering facilities management and outsourcing.

Outsourcing has the disadvantage that the organization loses control over its development process. If we regard information as a tradable commodity and source of competitive advantage (as discussed in Chapter 6) we can readily see the disadvantages of outsourcing. There are a number of examples of organizations outsourcing the systems development process and then buying this back to recover control. Further, studies show that 80% of outsourcing contracts do *not* save the organization money – the usual rationale for outsourcing.

Facilities management does not have this disadvantage, and the main issue with facilities management is security of supply – can the supplier guarantee the service levels that the organization requires?

5.2   What is a project?

We usually talk of activities such as developing a computer system as a *project*. This is 'a group of connected activities with a defined starting point, a defined finish and a need for a central intelligence to direct it', carried out in order to achieve a business objective. Features of projects include the following:

- They have defined start and finish points.

- Each project is unique.

- The project organization is temporary and may change during the project.

- There is an element of risk and uncertainty.

- The project team may need to interact with other groups within and outside the organization.

It is worth noting that this is different from the way in which most of us work. Most work in financial services organizations is driven by the customer – we do not start the day with the specific objective of serving exactly 500 customers before the branch closes! Nor is there any obvious relationship between tasks such as cashing a cheque, looking up an account balance and amending a standing order.

There is a recent trend for 'business as usual' to be run on a project basis. This has always been true for activities such as marketing campaigns, new branch openings and product launches. Events of this type are becoming more common, and project management techniques are being applied to new activities requiring organizational change. Therefore it is likely that there will be a greater transfer of project management skills into the business over time.

5.3   The systems development context

Systems development is one activity in a broader business and information context. We can show this as follows:

Figure 5.2

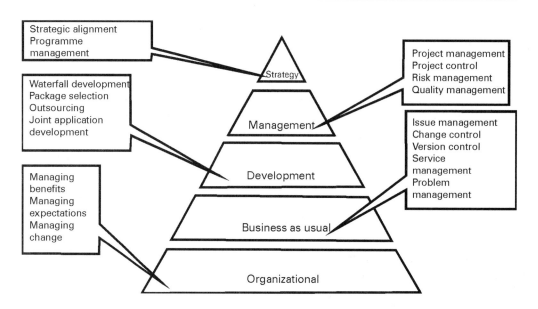

The *strategy* layer includes:

● Strategic alignment. This is the process of ensuring that the systems developed are consistent with the overall objectives of the organization. This is outside the scope of this book.

● Programme management. This is the overall management of a number of interdependent projects to achieve a single overall purpose. This is outside the scope of this book.

The *management* layer includes:

● Project management and control. These are discussed in detail later in this chapter.

● Risk management. This is discussed below.

● Quality management. This is discussed below.

The *development* layer is discussed in detail later in this chapter.

The *business as usual* layer includes:

● Issue management. This is discussed below.

● Change control. This is discussed below.

- Version control. This is discussed below.

- Service management. This is discussed below.

- Problem management. This is discussed below.

The organizational change layer includes:

- Managing benefits. This is discussed below.

- Managing expectations. This is discussed below.

- Managing change. This is discussed below.

Risk management

We discussed threats and risk in Chapter 4, but we need to take a slightly different approach to risk management when we are looking at projects.

There are two reasons for this. First, organizations have no choice about incurring risks in the normal course of business – it is the price of entry to the financial services industry. Projects are an investment, and organizations must balance the risk against the expected reward before deciding whether to undertake the investment.

The second reason is that projects are very much more risky than normal business. There have been various studies on project success rates, and these indicate the extent of the problem:

- Only 2% of projects are implemented without changes.

- Fewer than 16% of projects are implemented to time and budget.

- Only one-third of projects are judged 'successful' by business management.

- 31% of projects are cancelled before completion.

- 15% of projects deliver absolutely nothing.

We must be careful not to read too much into these figures. Business requirements do change, so we should expect projects to change or even to be cancelled to reflect this. However, it does illustrate the uncertainties associated with projects.

We can think of normal business risk as having one dimension – we know what our business is but we do not know which of the various threats may materialize. With projects we have two additional dimensions:

- *Process uncertainty.* Each project is unique. Although the lifecycle gives us some guidance there is usually some uncertainty about the best way to do things.

- *Control uncertainty.* The control processes associated with projects are not always reliable. Whatever methods are used to ensure quality, it is impossible to be certain that the project will meet the requirement until it is implemented.

Consultants Gartner Group have suggested a model for classifying projects that looks at *team risk* and *technical risk*. *Team risk* looks at the knowledge and experience available within the project team. *Technical risk* looks at factors such as the size of the system and the familiarity of the project team with the technical environment in which the system will operate.

One approach to managing risk is *potential problem analysis*. This builds on some of the ideas of FMEA (discussed in Chapter 4), and some of the stages are identical:

- Identify the potential problems (potential effects) of failure.

- For each potential problem, identify the possible causes of failure. We have described these as potential causes (FMEA) or threats.

- For each threat, identify how likely it is to occur. In potential problem analysis this is expressed as a number between 0.1 (low) and 1 (high).

- For each threat, identify how severe a problem it will cause if it does occur. This is expressed as a number between 1 (low) and 10 (high).

These are stages 2 – 5 in FMEA. The remaining stages in potential problem analysis are:

- Multiply the likelihood of occurrence by the severity to calculate a risk assessment. A high risk assessment indicates a major threat, for which there must be counter-measures.

- For each threat, identify the possible preventive actions. Identify the cost of the preventive action.

- For each preventive action, identify the probability of its failing. This is expressed as a number between 0 (none – the preventive action is certain to succeed) and 1 (high).

- Multiply the risk assessment by the probability of the preventive action failing. If no preventive action has been identified the probability of its failing is 1.

- For threats where the risk assessment multiplied by the probability of failure is not zero, identify contingency plans to mitigate the effect of the threat. Identify the cost of contingency plans.

Potential problem analysis provides a structured framework for identifying preventive actions and contingency plans. However, the decision as to which actions and plans to put in place will depend also on the cost if the threat is realized.

Quality management

The concept of quality is poorly understood. It may help to start with three definitions:

- Quality is defined as 'fitness for purpose' – how good something is at doing the job for which it is intended. If you want a family runabout, you buy a Vauxhall Astra in preference to a Rolls Royce. For this particular purpose, the Vauxhall Astra is the 'quality' car.

- Quality assurance (QA) is concerned with ensuring that all the checks in a defined process have been completed. The systems development lifecycle, for example, usually has checks at the end of each stage, and QA ensures that these have been carried out.

- Quality control (QC) is concerned that the tasks in the process are carried out to standard. This is measured by the checks built into the process.

QA can be validated externally, and quality standards such as BS5750 and ISO9000 are QA standards. QC can only be validated from within the project, and the main QC techniques are:

- Walkthroughs;
- Inspections;
- Testing.

A *walkthrough* is a meeting at which the developer presents his or her work to an audience that may include other members of the project, IT staff from other projects, business users and IT staff with relevant technical knowledge. The purpose of the meeting is to give the audience the opportunity to ask questions or make suggestions.

An *inspection* also takes the form of a meeting and has a very similar audience. However, proceedings are controlled by an independent inspector, instead of the developer. The inspector will usually be either a quality assurance specialist or an IT specialist, and will have studied the developer's work carefully in advance of the meeting.

Inspections should be more thorough than walkthroughs, both because a second person has had the opportunity to examine the work carefully and because the inspector is accountable for any problems that are found.

Walkthroughs and inspections are usually carried out at the end of each stage of the systems development cycle before system testing. It is common to break large developments down into 'sub-projects' and to carry out separate walkthroughs or inspections on these.

Testing takes place during the development process, and is discussed in more detail later in this chapter. We can distinguish between:

- *Unit testing*, which takes place during the construction stage and checks that individual system components work as specified. Unit testing is carried out by the developer.

- *System testing*, which takes place as a separate stage and checks that the system works as a whole and that it will not adversely affect other systems. System testing is usually carried out by a designated system tester, who may be independent of the project team.

Issue management

An issue is anything that arises during the project that needs to be resolved before project completion. Issues may include items such as:

- Possible new legislation, which could have an impact on the project;
- Changes to the organization's strategy, which could change the project's priority;
- Competitor activity to which the project may need to respond.

The distinctive feature of issues is that they cannot be resolved by the project team or the sponsor alone. They will usually require a decision from executive management, and may require outside opinion – for example from the Inland Revenue, regulatory bodies or legal opinion from counsel.

The issue management process is as follows:

- Record the issue on an issues log.

- Identify the impact of the issue and the date by which it must be resolved.

- Identify the appropriate escalation route and allocate responsibility for resolution.

- If necessary, seek the sponsor's approval for any budget required (e.g. for external legal opinion).

- Escalate the issue.

- Monitor the issue resolution process and, if necessary, follow the issue up to ensure that it is resolved in time.

Change control

Changes can arise during the development process as a result of:

- Changing business requirements. Major changes to market activity will affect the system, and competitive activity or customer pressure may well change the functional requirements.

- The issue management process. Resolution of issues may change the scope of the project.

- Problems encountered during the development process. A common example of this is where a system component from an external vendor does not work in the way expected. The system may need to be changed to use a different component or to perform additional tasks to remedy deficiencies in the component. More rarely, the component may have capabilities beyond those anticipated, allowing it to perform tasks that the system would otherwise have to perform.

- Changing technology. Changing technology during a project is not usually recommended but it may be necessary. One example is where the intended technology is becoming obsolete. The project team may have to choose between changing technology and proceeding in the knowledge that competitors will be able to leapfrog them by using the new technology.

Change can also arise after the system has been implemented as a result of either changes in business requirements or problems with the system.

The change control process starts when a change request is raised. The stages are as follows:

- Record the change request.

- Link the change request to any corresponding issue or problem record.

- Analyse the impact of the requested change.

- Review the change. This is usually carried out by a Change Control Board of senior managers, who will decide whether the change will go ahead and allocate a priority to it. Small changes can sometimes be approved under a small changes budget without approval by the Change Control Board.

- Schedule the change.

- Small changes will often be bundled together into a software 'release' to avoid staff being subject to constant minor system changes. Large changes such as the implementation of a new system will usually form a release on their own.

Release management is a part of change control. Releases are often designed so that small changes can be individually switched on or off, allowing them to be switched off if we want to go back to the previous version.

This ability to switch changes on and off is also important in implementation, and is discussed later in this chapter.

Version control

When we make changes to a system, we do not simply replace the old system component with a new one. Instead we create a new version of the system component and change the system to use the new version rather than the old one. There are two main reasons for this:

- We may want to go back to the old version. The new version may not work, or may cause problems with another part of the system, or we may find that the change does not achieve our objectives. Creating a new version and keeping the old one makes it easier to go back.

- We want to keep an audit trail of changes to the system. If we did not do this, it would be easy to commit fraud by changing the system, putting through a fraudulent transaction and then changing the system back again.

Version control involves the following:

- If a system component is to be changed it needs to be 'checked out'. This avoids problems where several people are trying to change the same system component simultaneously.

- The change is made and tested.

- The system component is 'checked in', assigned a new version number and scheduled for release into the production environment.

Service management

Service management controls the performance of the system. This is specified in a service level agreement, and a failure to meet the agreed level of service may be reported as a fault. Service level agreements cover aspects such as response times to enquiries entered through the screen, when the service will be available for use, and the proportion of time the system should be working. Service level agreements may also cover fault correction, setting maximum times for the investigation and correction of faults by type and priority.

Problem management

Problem management starts with a problem report (fault report) being raised, and allows users to report perceived problems for resolution. The user will also indicate the priority allocated to its correction. The stages in the problem management process are:

- Record the problem and allocate responsibility for dealing with it.

- Check that it is a problem. Problem reports are sometimes raised because the user is not fully trained in the use of the system or has not consulted the system documentation.

- Analyse the causes of the problem and identify what changes need to be made to rectify it.

- Progress the changes through the relevant stages of the change control process.

- When the problem has been rectified, mark the problem report as closed.

Managing benefits

Managing benefits is an increasingly important part of systems development. Benefits management involves the following steps:

- Identify anticipated benefits as part of the initial business case (this is discussed later in this chapter).

- Identify how to measure whether the benefits have been achieved, and allocate responsibility for realizing each benefit to the relevant senior manager in the business.

- Ensure that the information required to assess the achievement of the benefits is collected, and monitor progress towards it.

- Assess whether the benefits have been achieved as part of the post-implementation review.

This is best practice, and many organizations still make little systematic attempt to assess whether the benefits anticipated are realized in practice. Note that measures such as number of staff employed are not good for benefits measurement as they are affected by other factors such as changes in business volumes.

Managing expectations

One reason why project sponsors are often disappointed by the results of systems development is a failure to manage expectations. Business cases may present an optimistic assessment, which may not be realized in practice.

One way of investigating this is to compare the actual *net present value* (NPV) of benefits realized with the NPV forecast by the business case. For projects intended to produce cost savings the benefits realised are 110% of the benefits forecast. For projects intended to produce increased sales the benefits are 60% of forecast. For new products they are only 10% of forecast.

Stakeholders may also develop unrealistic expectations. The development process involves finding out what the business wants. This may create the expectation that all the requirements identified will be satisfied.

Those involved in systems development must set realistic expectations and manage these actively. This includes:

● A clear distinction between the 'vision' of what is expected in the long term and what will be delivered initially;

● A focus on the 'must have' requirements rather than those that are less important;

● Open acknowledgement that not everything that is requested will be delivered;

● A means of 'parking' requirements that are identified as important but which fall outside the scope of the development.

Managing change

In this context, managing change is concerned with organizational change and not with change control. We can look at managing change through the transition curve:

Figure 5.2

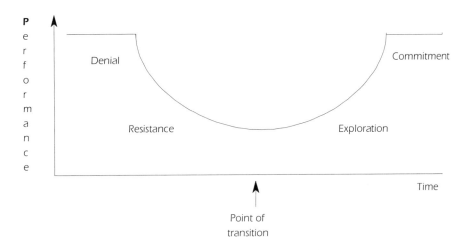

The stages are:

● *Denial.* The first stage is a denial that the change will happen, or that the change will affect the individual.

- *Resistance.* The second stage is resistance to the change, which often takes the form of non-cooperation with those implementing the change.

- *Exploration.* The third stage is an acceptance that the change is going to happen and exploration of its possible consequences for the individual.

- *Commitment.* The fourth stage is the individual's commitment to the change.

The objective of managing change is to ensure the fastest possible progression through the stages to commitment.

Managing change is a complex subject that deserves a book of its own. Two important models of change are:

- *The force field model.* This looks at change as a balance of driving forces and restraining forces. Change will only occur if the driving forces are stronger than the restraining forces. This can be achieved by strengthening the driving forces or weakening the restraining forces.

Figure 5.3

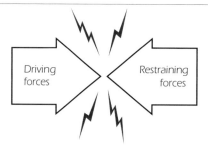

- *The unfreeze – change – refreeze model.* This looks at the process of change. The first stage is to 'unfreeze' the current situation. This includes making people aware that change is inevitable. The second stage is to make the change. The third stage is to 'refreeze' the situation into the new pattern. This includes reinforcing the change and making sure that people do not revert to their old pattern of behaviour.

In the context of information management the key processes are:

- *Communication.* The project team should communicate with all stakeholders throughout the process.

  Communication is essential to manage expectations. If this does not take place, stakeholders will be influenced by the grapevine and 'fear, uncertainty and doubt' (FUD). Communication helps to weaken the restraining forces, and is important both in unfreezing the current situation and in refreezing the changed situation.

- *Consultation.* As far as is possible, all affected stakeholders should be consulted and involved in the process. Some groups, such as the unions, may need a formal communication structure.

Consultation gives a sense of ownership of the change. Those consulted may also be able to identify possible problems with the change and suggest improvements. Consultation helps to weaken the restraining forces, and can improve the quality of the change.

- *Training.* Those expected to work with the system will need to be trained in its use.

  We discussed the benefits of training in Chapter 2. Training is critical to the refreezing process.

- *Support.* Those affected by the change need both technical and personal support.

  Technical support usually takes the form of helplines. Personal support may be provided through counselling and assistance, especially for those whose jobs will be adversely affected by the change. Even where people are not directly affected they may still need support – 'survivor syndrome' is a bereavement reaction found in organizations where large numbers of staff have been made redundant. Support is important to the refreezing process.

- *Continuous improvement.* Major changes are rarely perfect when they are first implemented, and a programme of continuous improvement is of benefit in eliminating any problems. It has the further benefit of transferring ownership of the new system to those who are using it.

  Continuous improvement is part of the refreezing process. It is likely to produce further changes to the system to support or implement the changes made, and weakens the restraining forces for these subsequent changes.

5.4   Project organization and accountability

Any project will have a number of 'stakeholders' who will be affected by its outcome. If we consider a large IT project within a financial services organization the stakeholders will include:

- The management of the user department that is commissioning the project;
- The staff of the user department;
- Staff in other departments who will be affected by changes in the user department;
- The financial services organization's senior management;
- The financial services organization's shareholders;
- Those customers who may be affected by the changes;
- The development staff who will be developing the project;
- The senior management of the information technology function;
- Finance department;
- Inspection/audit department;

- Legal department;
- Compliance department;
- Those suppliers who may be affected by the changes;
- Those suppliers who are participating in the project.

Given the number of stakeholders, it is hardly surprising that project organization is very complex. The interests of stakeholders can be represented through:

- Formal involvement in the project;
- 'Sign off' of the relevant parts of the project;
- Participation at the implementation stage.

The method of representation varies, but a typical pattern might be:

	Formal involvement	Sign off	Participation at implementation
User department management	Yes	Yes	
User department staff	Yes		Yes
Other affected department staff			Yes
Senior management		Yes	
Shareholders			Yes
Customers			Yes
Development staff	Yes		
IT senior management		Yes	
Finance department		Yes	
Inspection/audit department		Yes	
Legal department		Yes	
Compliance department		Yes	
Affected suppliers			Yes
Participating suppliers	Yes		

It is worth noting how few of the stakeholders will usually have formal involvement in the project. In particular, it would be unusual for key stakeholders such as shareholders and customers to have any involvement prior to implementation.

The formal project structure may be as follows:

Figure 5.4

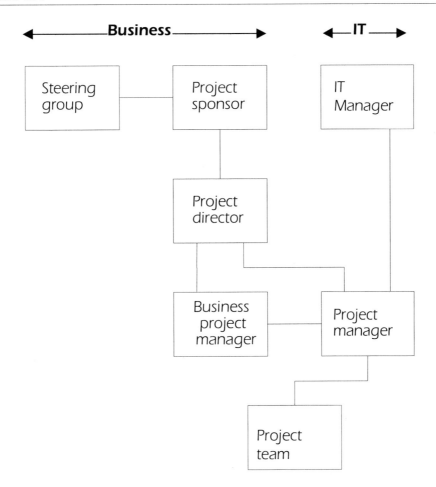

The roles that will always be present are:

- Project sponsor;
- IT manager;
- Project manager;
- Project team.

Other roles that may be present include:

- Steering group;
- Project director;
- Business project manager.

The project sponsor will commission the project and define its objectives. If there is no steering group the project sponsor will discharge its responsibilities. The project manager will report progress to the project sponsor, typically on a monthly basis.

The IT manager will have overall responsibility for providing IT resources for the project. The split of management responsibilities by which the project manager reports to the project sponsor for project issues and the IT manager for resources and staffing issues is an example of the use of matrix management in project work.

The project manager will manage the project on a day-to-day basis. The project manager will produce the project plan, allocate work and monitor the plan.

The project team will carry out the work necessary to complete the project.

There will be a steering group for large projects and projects affecting different parts of the organization. The steering group will be drawn from senior business management, and will be responsible for ensuring that the project meets the requirements of the stakeholders. The steering group will authorise changes to the project budget and will sign off major deliverables.

There will be a project director for large projects. The project director will represent the interests of the business but will be involved on a much more regular basis than the project sponsor or steering group. The project director will be the first point of reference for issues, and will decide how these will be resolved.

There is sometimes a business project manager. The business project manager represents the interests of the business and will be involved on a day-to-day basis. Responsibility for the project may be split, with the business project manager responsible for business issues such as training, procedure manuals and implementation while the project manager is responsible for the development of the system.

It is important to understand the difference between project management and project direction:

- Project management is concerned with *how* the project is managed on a day-to-day basis. Project management is a specialist skill and is completely different to 'business as usual' management in a functional organization. Project managers must be trained specialists, and managers drawn from the business often find it difficult to make the transition to project management.

- Project direction is concerned with *what* the project is doing and whether this will meet business needs. Project direction should usually come from the business, and there are a number of approaches including the appointment of a project director and/or a steering group. Where a business project manager is appointed, the role will often be providing project direction rather than project management.

The project team includes people with a variety of skills (a *multidisciplinary team*) who can contribute towards the current stage of the project. During the systems analysis stage, for example, the project team might include a business analyst (who has a good understanding of the business problem), some systems analysts (who can describe the processes needed to solve the problem in logical terms), and a data analyst (who understands how to describe the data in logical terms).

During the systems design stage this would change. Some of the systems analysts might be replaced by designers, and the data analyst would be replaced by a database designer. These people's skills are in deciding how the logical description produced at the systems analysis stage should be turned into a physical system.

This raises the issue of continuity. As membership of the project team changes, how can we ensure that the project as implemented will meet the intentions from the problem definition? One approach is for the same people to occupy the key roles of project manager, project director and project sponsor throughout.

5.5   Project management and control

Project management and control involves drawing up a project plan to estimate the time and resources necessary to complete the project and then monitoring progress against the plan. We shallnot cover this in any detail but the main stages are as follows:

- The project is broken down into *tasks*, each of which is a self-contained piece of work, and the time and resources needed to complete each task are estimated. The most important resource is usually people, and the estimate made at this stage shows the number of people and the skills required. Other resources that might be shown on the plan include special equipment.

- Any relationships or *dependencies* between tasks are identified. The most common type of dependency occurs when one task must be completed before another starts, but there are other types of dependency such as two tasks needing to either start at the same time or finish at the same time. From the tasks and dependencies a *network diagram* or *precedence diagram* can be produced.

- The next stage is to identify the actual resources the project will need – to replace numbers and skills with the names of the developers who will work on the project. At this stage it may be necessary to revise the dates on the network diagram to prevent resource contention. Resource contention occurs when an individual is scheduled to work full time on more than one task simultaneously.

The project manager will use the revised network diagram to estimate the time and cost to complete the project. The time estimate is based on the *critical path* – the *longest* path through the network diagram which is also the *shortest* time in which the project can be completed. The cost is based on the cost of resources (including people).

A project budget may be produced but this is not always the case. The main cost element for most IT projects is staff costs, and projects are often controlled on the basis of people's time rather than a budget. Developers working on the project use timesheets to record how their time is allocated between tasks.

Some approaches to project management require a *statement of work* to be drawn up for each task. This is a precise definition of exactly what is required to complete the task and of the measures of quality that will be applied to the results. This may form the basis of a legal contract, especially if the task is to be subcontracted to an outside organization.

Two other terms you might come across are Gantt charts and PERT networks.

Gantt charts are named after Henry Gantt (a management theorist from the nineteenth century). They are bar charts showing the activities down the left side and the project dates across the top. Next to each activity, a line is shown from the scheduled start date to the scheduled end date. Gantt charts are particularly useful for project control. If the project manager draws a vertical line down the page from today's date this will show all tasks that should have been completed to the left of the line; all tasks that should be in progress will cross the line, and tasks that are scheduled to be started in the future will be shown on the right of the line.

PERT networks are a more complicated form of network diagram developed by the US Navy. We shall not discuss PERT charts in any detail, but they are used to show the maximum amount of time a task can be delayed (the *float*) without affecting the planned completion date. PERT stands for Program Evaluation and Review Technique.

Project management systems are computer programs that support the project manager. These assist with the planning of the project, and allow the completed plan to be shown as a network, as a Gantt chart or as a breakdown of tasks.

The program will identify the critical path and calculate the float for each activity. It will identify whether resources have been overscheduled. It can produce individual work plans for every member of the project team.

These programs are particularly useful for project control. They usually allow staff to enter their timesheets (often based on the individual work plans), and can apply *charge-out rates* to calculate staff costs. Some programs can bill users for staff time if necessary.

They can be used to record when individual tasks are complete. If a task runs over schedule, they can forecast a new estimated completion date for the project as a whole. These programs generally also allow a 'percentage complete' figure to be entered against tasks in progress (although people's estimates of how much work remains to be done should usually be treated with extreme caution!).

By capturing all the information about the project, including the initial plan, any revisions and the actual time and cost of the project, these programs can be used to improve planning and estimating for future projects.

5.6   Deliverables and sign-off

One of the main forms of project control is deliverable sign-off. Deliverables that need to be signed off include the terms of reference and the key outcomes from the development stages.

The lifecycle used in the systems development process may also say which deliverables should be produced and signed off for each development stage. This sometimes takes the form of a project deliverables catalogue or a project responsibility matrix.

Once a project has completed a development stage it should not continue until the deliverables have been signed off. Without sign-off, the project team does not have the authority to continue. In practice this rule is sometime waived as it would lead to all work on the project being halted, but organizations must ensure that sign off takes place as quickly as possible.

Terms of reference

Terms of reference are the contract between the project sponsor and the project manager. They are essential because:

- They set the sponsor's expectations for the project.

- They define the project manager's mandate and authority.

- They provide a framework for the development process.

The acronym BOSCARDI is sometimes used for the contents of the terms of reference. This stands for:

- Background

- Objectives

- Scope

- Constraints

- Assumptions

- Reporting

- Deliverables

- Issues

Background is the background to the project.

Objectives says what the project is trying to achieve. The objectives section of the terms of reference will be used to assess the overall success of the project, and they need to be SMART (specific, measurable, achievable, relevant and trackable).

Scope says what the project will and will not consider. The scope may relate to a business process or a functional area. One approach that is sometimes used is to draw up a table of what is and is not included in the scope.

Constraints are any restrictions within which the project team must operate. The most common constraints are project cost and time taken.

Assumptions document any assumptions made by the project team. Common assumptions include access to senior management within the organization.

Reporting defines to whom the project team reports.

Deliverables define what the project team is expected to produce. The terms of reference will specify only the key deliverables that are subject to sign-off.

Issues include anything that still needs to be resolved. All issues should be resolved before the terms of reference are finally signed off.

Terms of reference for IT projects will usually cover the entire project up to implementation. They may need to be revised during the development as conditions change. Alternatively, separate terms of reference may be produced for individual stages within the development.

Business case (cost–benefit analysis)

The business case is the financial justification for the project. It considers the costs and benefits of the project, and uses accounting techniques to determine whether the project should go ahead.

We can classify costs as one-off or recurring. One-off costs can be classified as capital or development costs. Recurring costs can be classified as maintenance or operating costs:

- *Capital costs.* These include the cost of new hardware (processing power, storage and peripherals) and telecommunications. They may also include the costs of additional office equipment. Additional space might be needed (for example to house a new computer), and this would be included.

- *Development costs.* These include the costs of the staff involved in building the new system. They may also include overhead costs for managing the project and for non-IT staff (for example the user department or internal audit staff). They include one-off costs associated with any new software that may be needed.

- *Maintenance costs.* Where new software or hardware is purchased these will be specified in the contract. There will be an allowance (typically 10% of the development costs) for changes and improvements to the system.

- *Operating costs.* These include the cost of additional resources required to run the system – for example, the annual cost of any additional processing or storage requirements. They will also include any annual licensing costs for new software or hardware. They will include the predicted costs for *consumables* such as additional telecommunications line charges, paper and floppy disks.

We can classify benefits as tangible or intangible. Tangible benefits result in a direct financial return, for example in reduced costs or increased income. Intangible benefits are less easy to quantify. Common sources of benefits include:

- *Benefits due to cost savings.* These include any projected savings due to being able to use fewer staff or lower-graded staff, together with any associated premises cost savings. They may include one-off cost savings through not renewing equipment leases or contracts with suppliers.

- *Benefits due to increased earnings.* These usually arise when the new system provides an additional business opportunity. For example, EFTPOS not only saves financial organizations the high cost of processing cheques, it also provides opportunities to earn fees from the retailers for processing EFTPOS transactions.

- *Benefits due to better quality.* In principle, better quality can improve customer loyalty and market share, reduce the costs associated with correcting mistakes, and lead to better decisions. In practice it can be difficult to quantify these in money terms.

- *Benefits due to reduced risks.* Reduced risks can reduce the costs needed to manage those risks. These are usually intangible, but calculations such as the annualized loss expectancy (discussed in Chapter 2) can be used to get an indicative saving.

In assessing cost benefit, we need to apply two tests. First, is it a good investment? We need to estimate all the costs and all the benefits from the solution in money terms and use an investment appraisal technique in order to decide whether spending money on this particular solution is a good investment. Second, is it within the overall IT budget? Most organizations limit their overall budget for IT to prevent costs growing faster than the overall growth in earnings. If the cost of an investment is greater than the available budget it will only be approved under exceptional circumstances – for example, if it is necessary to meet a legal obligation or if the return on the investment is exceptionally high.

Cost-benefit analysis uses standard accounting techniques to decide whether the investment in the project will be justified. The most important of these are:

- *Net present value.* This looks at the amounts that will be spent (costs) or earned (benefits) over the expected life of the project. These are discounted by a notional interest rate to allow for the fact that interest needs to be paid on money spent now, so future earnings need to be at least as great as the lost interest if the project is to be financially justified. The value of all the discounted costs and benefits is added up to find out what the total would be now – the net present value. If this is greater than zero, the amount the project will earn is more than the amount of lost interest and the project is financially justified.

- *Internal rate of return.* This works on the same principle as the net present value calculation (this principle is called 'discounted cashflow' or DCF). However, instead of setting a rate for discounting cashflows, it calculates the actual rate required to produce a net present value of zero – the internal rate of return. If this is greater than the organization's target rate for return on investments the project is financially justified.

- *Payback.* This works by comparing the project's initial costs (capital costs plus development costs, less any one-off savings due to sale of surplus equipment or premises) with the future earnings (benefits less maintenance and operating costs). The amount of time that will be needed before the benefits pay back the initial investment is calculated and compared with a target. If the investment will be paid back in less than the target the project is jusitifed.

DCF calculations rely on a notional interest rate, which in theory is the cost of capital for the organization. In practice financial services organizations often use 'hurdle rates', which compare the investment with the opportunity cost of using the capital elsewhere.

Net present value is generally accepted as the best technique but the others are widely used. Internal rate of return is often used to compare projects, but this can be slightly misleading (for reasons of interest to those studying accountancy, which we shall not go into here). Payback is a very crude technique, which has the benefit of providing a simple way of assessing risk – the longer the payback period the more likely it is that changes in the nature of the business or in technology will make the system obsolete.

We can show the variety of techniques used in the UK:

	Year		
Method used	**1975**	**1981**	**1986**
Payback	73%	81%	92%
Accounting rate of return	51%	49%	56%
Internal rate of return	44%	57%	75%
Net present value	32%	39%	68%

The accounting rate of return is an older technique that was mainly used by firms who did not use computers. This table illustrates both the persistence of payback for cost-benefit analysis and the fact that firms often use a number of different measures as part of the analysis process.

5.7   Systems development

How do we develop an IT system? There are four common approaches:

● The traditional approach is called *waterfall development*. This defines the development process as a series of stages through which the project moves. It is called waterfall development because it is not possible to go back up the waterfall – once a stage has started it is not possible to go back to an earlier stage, as shown in the diagram:

Figure 5.5: Waterfall development

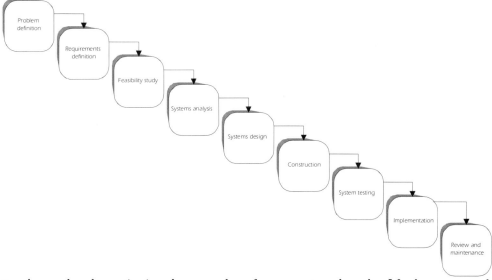

- A popular alternative is to buy a *package* from an external vendor. Vendors can supply software ranging from full service packages covering industries such as banking and insurance to specialist niche packages covering areas such as payroll or derivatives trading.

- Another alternative is *outsourcing*. This uses an external vendor to meet some or all of the organization's requirements for systems. Again, this can range from full outsourcing of all systems provision to the more limited provision of 'turnkey' systems in niche or non-strategic business areas.

- Another approach is *joint application development*, also called prototyping or iterative development. Unlike waterfall development this does allow us to go back to earlier stages during the development process – this is called *iterative development*.

Before we look at these in detail, we need to consider the difference between a lifecycle and a methodology.

A *lifecycle* is a checklist, telling us what stages we need to go through in developing a system and what we are trying to achieve in each of these stages. It tells us *what* to do during the systems development process. Lifecycles were originally developed to support the waterfall approach to development, for example the National Computer Centre's Systems Development Lifecycle (SDLC).

The word *methodology* really means the study of methods. In IT, we use this word to describe a comprehensive approach that covers *how* to develop systems as well as what must be done. The main characteristics of a methodology are as follows:

- It covers the whole of the systems development process from the initial identification of the problem to the period after implementation.

- It includes its own lifecycle, and it may allow alternative lifecycles to take account of the difference between types of project.

- It includes a set of techniques, and it may have its own distinct 'notation' for describing parts of the system. The same techniques will usually be used throughout the development process, with additional levels of detail being added during the later stages, and will form the basis for most of the documents produced during the development.

- It may include project management techniques, and some methodologies, such as PRINCE (Projects In Controlled Environments), are mainly concerned with project management.

- It may include a set of computer-aided software engineering (CASE) tools specifically designed to support the methodology, possibly also including project management tools.

- Training and consultancy in using the methodology will usually be available.

Waterfall development

Developing a system using the waterfall approach involves going through a series of stages – the lifecycle – in order. Before we can go on to the next stage we should have completed the previous stage and had it signed off.

We shall use a ten-stage lifecycle as a basis for considering waterfall development as follows:

- Problem definition;

- Requirements definition;

- Feasibility study;

- Systems analysis;

- Systems design;

- Construction;

- System testing;

- Implementation;

- Review;

- Closure.

Problem definition

The problem definition stage answers the question: what problem are we trying to solve? Although this may seem obvious, it is common to find symptoms and possible solutions confused with the real problem. For example a manager may define the problem as 'I need this report on my desk at 8:30 every morning' when what is *really* needed is access to the information the manager requires to take decisions. This could be the report asked for, it could be a different report giving more relevant information, it could be on-line access to the information, or it could be access to a decision support system (as discussed in Chapter 12).

It is the responsibility of the business user to define the problem clearly and correctly. This raises two problems. First, the business user may take a parochial view – considering only the effect on the particular department and ignoring other possible users of the system. Second, the business user may not have the skills to analyse the root causes of the problem or the knowledge to understand what IT can achieve.

Business analysts – IT specialists with a good understanding of the business – can play a useful role here, bringing analytical skills and an understanding of what IT can (and cannot!) achieve to the problem definition. IT specialists may also need to be involved where solutions to the problem are likely to affect other systems or to involve a requirement for additional hardware, system software (discussed in Chapter 10) or telecommunications.

Others who may need to be involved could include organization and methods specialists and internal audit staff. External consultants may be able to advise on approaches that other organizations have taken to the same problem.

A short conference or 'workshop' usually forms an important part of the problem definition stage, allowing all the relevant groups an opportunity to discuss the problem and its impact on them. The outcome of this stage will be a problem definition report, which will be used as input to the feasibility study stage.

Requirements definition

Requirements definition looks in detail at what the new system is expected to do. This will include the functions carried out by any existing system (whether it is manual or on a computer) together with any new requirements.

Interviews and questionnaires are used to identify the requirements. New requirements may be identified using techniques such as brainstorming, workshops and throwaway prototyping (discussed later in this chapter under joint application development).

Observation and participation may be used to build up a description of the current system. Workflow within the office is documented and copies taken of forms and reports. Published documentation such as procedure manuals is an important source of information. Business analysts will sometimes work in the department for a period to observe and participate in the business processes. The current system is often documented using techniques such as process maps and flowcharts, as these can be easily used in the later stages of the development.

The business analyst carries out the requirements definition, working closely with the business users. At this stage, additional IT staff – systems analysts who will work on the next stage – may also be involved.

The outcome of this stage is a requirements definition report containing a list of requirements and charts describing how the current physical system works. These are supported by examples of forms, copies of relevant documentation and statistics about the number of transactions carried out.

Other lifecycles use the term *systems investigation* for this stage.

Feasibility study

The feasibility study stage looks at possible solutions to the problem, and considers whether they are feasible and how much they might cost. Feasibility includes:

- *Technical feasibility* – can the problem be solved given the current availability of technology?

- *Fit with existing systems* – how will the technology required fit with our existing systems? In particular, how do we get the information we need into and out of the various possible solutions?

- *Fit with strategy* – does solving the problem fit with the organization's business strategy? Does the technology fit with the organization's technology strategy?

- *Technology risks* – what risks are associated with the technology? How will the organization manage these risks? 'Leading edge' technology in particular is prone to risks including whether it will work and the risk of obsolescence if it is overtaken by a different technology.

- *Cost-benefit* – do the expected benefits offer a satisfactory return on the investment required? We discussed cost-benefit analysis earlier in the chapter.

The feasibility study starts by identifying different options for solving the problem. This will consider factors such as whether the problem can be solved using a package, how much of the solution should be delivered using technology, and what technologies are available. This stage must also include the identification of evaluation criteria and the assessment of the options against these criteria.

The feasibility study stage is usually carried out by a business analyst. If additional hardware, telecommunications components and/or software form part of the solution it is likely to involve discussions with potential suppliers and also with the technology strategists within the organization. Internal audit staff may be involved if there are any security issues.

The outcomes from this stage will include a feasibility study report (outlining options and making recommendations), a cost-benefit analysis, and (if outside suppliers are likely to be involved) a draft request for information.

A request for information describes the work the supplier will be required to do and asks for an estimate of time and costs – either on a fixed price basis (once the tender is accepted the agreed price is fixed) or on a time and materials basis (the price may change if the supplier completes the work cheaper or more expensively than estimated). Requests for information are discussed in more detail later in this chapter.

Systems analysis

The systems analysis stage produces a full description of *what* the system will need to do. This is based on the description of the current system and additional requirements developed during the requirements definition stage. It does not consider *how* the system will do it or the constraints under which the system will operate. This is described as a logical model of the system.

The analysis of an existing process usually starts by removing the constraints that affect the physical system. For example, physically it is usually impossible for two different people to work on the same document at the same time. This constraint would be ignored during analysis. The analysis of new requirements often starts by identifying how they fit into the existing process. A detailed discussion of systems analysis techniques is outside the scope of this book.

This stage is carried out by systems analysts, some of whom may have been involved in the requirements definition stage. The business analyst will usually continue to be involved and may work as a systems analyst – the skills required are similar. A specialist data analyst may be involved in producing a logical model of the data.

The business users will be involved in checking the analysis and confirming that the system would meet their requirements. The analysis stage usually involves specifying screen and report layouts, and the business users would be involved in this.

The outcome from this stage will be a systems requirements definition containing models of the processes and data to be provided by the new system.

Systems design

The systems design stage looks at how the system can actually be built – it produces a physical model of the required system. This will include deciding which processes will be carried out manually and which by the computer. This is called the *man-machine boundary*. The manual component of the system will need to consider how staff will interact with the computer.

It also needs to identify the constraints under which the new system will operate. These are likely to be different from the constraints of the current system – for example an on-line system, where up-to-date information can be requested at any time, will be less constrained than a batch system, where information is available only as reports printed at the end of the previous day. These constraints are then applied to the logical model from the systems analysis stage to produce a new physical model.

Design of the computer system will depend greatly on technical factors – whether the system will be batch, on-line or real-time, whether a database will be used, etc. It is important that the computer system design is efficient in the particular environment in which it will operate.

The systems design stage may be carried out by specialist system designers or by systems analysts carrying out a design function. The skills required are more technical than in the systems analysis stage, and a common approach is to have one or more specialist system designers working with the systems analysts who worked on the systems analysis stage. One area where a specialist designer is almost always required is database design.

Business users will have limited involvement in this stage, although they may be consulted about the *user interface* – what the screens and reports will look like – if these were not fully defined during the systems analysis stage.

The outcome from the systems design stage will be an overall systems design report and possibly a set of program specifications. Alternatively, the program specifications may be written during the construction stage.

Construction

The construction stage involves writing the computer programs required. It also involves a certain amount of 'unit testing' to ensure that the programs work properly.

This stage is largely the responsibility of IT staff. Unless a prototyping approach is used, the business users' only involvement may be in producing documentation and forms and in preparation for testing the system.

The outcome of this stage is a set of computer programs.

System testing

The system testing stage involves a far more thorough test than that carried out at the construction stage. Not only does it check that the programs work on their own, it also checks that they work together and that they do not cause any problems for other programs that may be running on the computer. This stage may include a number of tests:

- System testing, to check that all the system components work together;

- Regression testing, to check that the system works with other systems that may be running at the same time;

- Volume testing, to check that the system will handle the required numbers of transactions;

- Operational proving, to check that the system will run on the system for which it is intended and that the operating instructions are complete and accurate;

- Acceptance testing, to check that the system will meet the business requirement and that the user manual is complete and accurate.

Which of these tests are carried out depends on the nature of the system, but systems testing (always), operational proving (almost always) and acceptance testing (sometimes) are the most important.

IT staff are often responsible for all of these. Business users are involved in the acceptance test and, in some organizations, may have complete responsibility for it. Business users will be involved in drawing up *test cases* to be system tested and in checking the results.

The outcomes from this stage will be a set of tested programs with operating instructions and user manuals. Many organizations retain the test cases and results to make it easier to test changes to the system or to regression test other systems.

Implementation

The implementation stage involves making the programs available for use. This will include designing any training programmes, writing manuals and designing forms for the users. There are four approaches to implementation:

- Big bang, in which the new system is implemented through the entire organization, all at once.

- Parallel run, in which the new system and the current system are allowed to run alongside each other for a period. The results from the two systems are compared to check the correctness of the new system.

- Pilot run, in which the whole of the new system is implemented in part of the organization – say 2–5% of the branch network for a large retail financial services organization. A pilot run requires that different versions of the software are used in different parts of the organization, and the technique of allowing changes to be switched on and off is usually used.

- Phased implementation, in which part of the new system is implemented in the whole of the organization.

The decision as to which implementation strategy should be adopted is mainly that of the business user. However, IT staff should be involved, and the decision may need to be approved by internal audit.

Review

Reviews are very important to allow the organization to learn from the development. There are two types of review

- Post-development reviews;

- Post-implementation reviews.

Post-development reviews cover the *efficiency* of the development process, and are carried out by IT staff. They are usually carried out by someone who was not involved in the original project team, and look at whether all of the stages in the systems development cycle were completed correctly and what problems were encountered.

Post-implementation reviews cover the *effectiveness* of the system, and may be carried out by

IT staff, business users or external consultants. They look at the original objectives of the project and determine how well the system meets these. They look at whether agreed service levels are being achieved. They also consider how easy the system is to use and look at issues such as cost overruns and late delivery.

Closure

Some types of project have a formal closure or decommissioning phase when the main project deliverable reaches the end of its economic life. Obvious examples include projects to build nuclear power stations and offshore oil rigs, where the cost of decommissioning has a substantial effect on the project's business case.

Although this is rare for information technology projects we must give consideration to when the system will be replaced. As systems get older they incur increasing costs:

- Maintenance costs increase. Changes to the system often have the effect of increasing maintenance costs, and it may be expensive to support obsolete technology. We can use the analogy of an old car where it may be hard to find spare parts or find a mechanic who undertsands how to service it.

- The system may act as a constraint on the business. The limitations of the system may limit the business's ability to enter new markets. This will impose an opportunity cost in terms of lost business opportunity.

- Maintaining the system diverts scarce resources away from the development of new systems to meet business needs. We consider one solution to this – outsourcing system maintenance – later in this chapter.

For an information technology project it would be very unusual to include a specific closure stage in the initial project plan. However, maintenance costs should be monitored and the decommissioning or replacement of the system should be considered when these get too high.

Using a package

The decision to use a package does not mean that we do not need a structured approach to the process. We shall use a ten-stage lifecycle as a basis for package selection. The first three and last five stages are similar to the corresponding stages in the waterfall development lifecycle. The stages are as follows:

- Problem definition (as for waterfall development);
- Requirements definition (as for waterfall development);
- Feasibility study (as for waterfall development);
- Request for information and vendor shortlist;
- Invitation to tender and vendor selection;

- Procurement;

- System testing (regression testing, operational proving and acceptance testing);

- Implementation (as for waterfall development);

- Review (post-implementation review);

- Closure (as for waterfall development).

During the feasibility study stage we shall have used sources such as reference books, the computer press, consultants, competitor information and perhaps customers to identify that a package is a potential solution to our system requirements. We shall also have produced a request for information (RFI).

An RFI is a document that typically contains:

- A brief description of the main requirements. This may be a summary of the requirements definition report.

- A statement of the constraints under which the system will need to operate. These might be quite specific (for example, a description of our hardware and telecommunications environment and a requirement that the package must operate within this environment) or they might be more general (for example, a requirement to be able to analyse information using a spreadsheet – it will be the vendor's responsibility to determine how best to move the information from the package into a spreadsheet).

- A request for information about the company. This will include financial health and standard terms of business including warranties and the availability of support and consultancy.

- An outline of the tender process, including the timescales and the form in which tender documents must be submitted.

Request for information and vendor shortlist

The next stage is to draw up a vendor shortlist from the requests for information, as follows:

- From the systems investigation and systems analysis stages, identify the criteria that will be used to assess the package. These will include the functions that the package needs to be able to perform, and compatibility factors such as whether the package can run on existing hardware.

- For each of these criteria, decide whether it is 'must have' or 'nice to have'. An alternative classification takes the acronym MoSCoW from the initial letters of the classification must have, should have, could have, want. Give each of the criteria a weighting that reflects its relative importance.

- Assess each package against the selection criteria. A common approach is to give a score from 1 (does not meet) to 5 (meets very well) against each criterion for each package.

- Calculate the total score for each package. For each criterion, multiply the weighting by the score. Add up the results to give a total.

- Draw up a shortlist of suitable packages. These will be the packages that:

  - Meet all of the 'must have' criteria – typically having a score of at least 3 for each criterion.

  - Represent good value to the organization, taking account of their cost and overall score.

Before embarking on this process organizations have to be aware of the problems that might arise during selection. These include the following:

- There may be no package that adequately meets the selection criteria. In this event it may be necessary to consider bespoke development.

- Available packages may meet some of the selection criteria but some of the required functions may not be available. Here, bespoke development is an option or it may be possible to tailor the package.

The objective is to reduce the number of potential vendors to a manageable shortlist, usually of between three and six. These will be sent an invitation to tender (ITT), which will typically include:

- A list of specific questions about how the proposed solution will meet the requirements;

- Information about how any changes to the package will be implemented;

- Information about *reference sites* – other organizations that already use the package;

- Specific proposals about costs, training, warranty, consultancy and support arrangements.

Invitation to tender and vendor selection

The next stage is to select the vendor:

- The shortlisted packages will be examined in more detail. Depending on the type of package, this may well involve talking to and possibly visiting reference sites.

- All of the shortlisted packages should provide the main functions required by the organization. The final selection will take more account of other factors such as:

  - Performance and response times;

  - Ability to handle required volumes;

  - Compatibility with existing hardware;

  - Compatibility with system software;

  - Quality of documentation;

  - Availability and quality of support;

- Costs, including operating and maintenance costs;
- Audit trails and security/control features;
- Access to and cost of upgrades and enhancements;
- Access to source code.

Procurement

The procurement stage is not usually the responsibility of the project team. Finance or a central purchasing function is usually responsible for this.

The objective of the procurement stage is to secure the package on the most favourable terms to the organization. This will not necessarily be at the lowest possible price as factors such as support, training and security of supply must be considered.

The procurement stage starts during the vendor selection process.

Outsourcing

Outsourcing transfers responsibility for systems development from the organization to an external vendor. The organization may outsource:

- All of its systems;
- Some of its systems (*turnkey development*);
- Part of the development process;
- The running of its computer systems (*facilities management*).

Even though the organization is handing over responsibility for system development, we must still consider this in terms of a lifecycle. Some stages – problem definition and requirements definition – are common and similar to the waterfall development lifecycle. Also common are the stages required to select an external vendor. Others will depend on the type of outsourcing adopted.

The selection of an external vendor is similar to the selection of a vendor for a package solution, involving request for information (also called a request for proposal), invitation to tender and procurement stages. The evaluation process will consider the ability of the vendor to meet the requirements, rather than a specific solution.

Turnkey development

Turnkey systems development involves the organization's transferring responsibility for the development of some of its systems to an external vendor. Financial services organizations generally use turnkey development for systems that are not strategically important, for example administrative systems such as payroll and property management.

The problem definition and requirements definition stages are as for waterfall development.

The systems resulting from turnkey development will be used alongside the organization's other systems. Therefore the later lifecycle stages are needed:

- System testing (regression testing, operational proving and acceptance testing);

- Implementation (as for waterfall development);

- Review (post-implementation review only);

- Closure (as for waterfall development).

The most important factor is ensuring that all of the requirements – including any methodologies or standards to be used – are clearly documented. Asking the supplier to make changes during the development will be expensive. The completed system, including any documentation, must also be carefully checked to ensure that it complies with the requirements before sign-off.

Although we cannot ensure that the supplier uses our methodology, we can require that they document the system in a way consistent with it and with any other standards we use. An important issue here is: who is going to maintain and support the system? If this is the supplier, it may not be necessary for the technical documentation to meet our standards. If we are, it is important that all the documentation is consistent with our own.

Standards are rules to be used in the development process. Standards include:

- *Documentation standards.* These define what documentation should be produced and in what format.

- *Data naming standards.* These define how data elements should be named.

- *Operability standards.* These define how the system should run in the data centre – for example what action the system should take if it cannot find a file it needs.

Partial outsourcing

We have a number of options for partial outsourcing of the development process. Common approaches include:

- Using contract staff as part of the development process;

- Outsourcing the construction stage;

- Outsourcing the maintenance stage.

None of these approaches has a significant effect on the lifecycle.

The reasons for using contract staff as part of the development process include securing access to skills and knowledge that are scarce within the organization, and coping with temporary peaks in demand for developers.

The reason for outsourcing the construction stage is that it is largely independent of the other stages. One option is to outsource this to another country where computer programmers are cheaper, and countries such as India have developed major software industries through this.

Maintenance typically uses up to 80% of an organization's total spending on information systems, and outsourcing this frees resources to use on the development of new systems. The main disadvantage of outsourcing maintenance is that it requires expertise and knowledge of the organization's existing systems, which an external vendor will need to develop.

Facilities management

Facilities management involves the transfer to an external vendor of responsibility for some or all of the following:

- Operation of the organization's data centres and mainframe computers

  or

  Processing of the organization's work on the vendor's mainframe computers;

- Operation of the organization's telecommunications network

  or

  Transmission of the organization's telecommunications traffic over the vendor's network;

- Support for the organization's telecommunications network;

- Support for the organization's 'desktop' – its PCs and terminals.

Facilities management is becoming increasingly important. A few financial services organizations have outsourced their data centres either by floating them as separate companies or by selling them (and transferring their staff) to an external vendor. Outsourcing the telecommunications network and desktop support are more common.

The advantages of facilities management are:

- The organization does not have to pay for upgrades to hardware and software except through the cost of the service. The vendor will be able to spread the cost over a number of clients and will receive discounts as a large user, so the cost of such upgrades is likely to be lower than the financial services organization would have been able to secure.

- The vendor may be able to operate the hardware and software at a lower cost, both because of economies of scale and because the vendor specializes in this type of operation and should be able to generate savings through process improvement.

The disadvantages of facilities management are:

- It may be expensive if the organization relies on unusual hardware or software. As the vendor cannot easily spread the costs, the organization will not achieve any cost savings. This also limits the organization's ability to delay taking new releases of system software as the vendor may only be willing to support older versions for a limited period.

● The organization loses control over its systems. If a contractual dispute arises the organization's security of supply may be jeopardized if the vendor can withdraw the service offered.

Joint application development

Joint application development (JAD) involves a series of meetings or workshops between the developers and the business users to develop the system. This is an iterative process, with new requirements or changes being identified at each meeting and incorporated in a prototype or model of the system prior to the next meeting.

One approach used for JAD is the dynamic systems development methodology (DSDM). This is a five-stage methodology including:

● Feasibility study;

● Business study;

● Functional model iteration;

● System design and build iteration;

● Implementation.

The feasibility study and implementation stages are broadly similar to the corresponding stages in the waterfall development lifecycle, and the business study is equivalent to the requirements definition (system investigation) and systems analysis stages.

The functional model iteration stage involves several cycles of iteration in developing a functional model of the system. The objective of this stage is to work out exactly what the system has to do. The model can be developed using very simple tools – pen and paper can be used to develop prototypes – but will usually use simple tools such as databases and screen painters (to simulate computer screens).

The system design and build iteration stage again involves several cycles of iteration. The objective is to take the functional model developed in the previous stage and create a system that offers robust and efficient performance.

An important technique used in all JAD approaches is *timeboxing*. Each cycle of iteration is limited very strictly to a period of time. Timeboxing is important because it allows the development to be kept under control – without timeboxing developers might be tempted to keep including additional features without going back to the business user to confirm the requirement. Timeboxing can also be used in waterfall development to maintain control over phases such as requirements definition.

We may start JAD by choosing one clearly defined business function within the system. We will use our prototype-building tools to develop a system that supports that business function. We can then choose another business function and prototype that, adding it to our original prototype.

When we have built a prototype that covers the entire system we shall go through the prototype with the business user to identify which parts need further development. We shall make the necessary changes and go through the prototype again. Only when the user is completely happy that the prototype meets the business requirement can the prototype be considered complete.

There are three things we can do with our prototype. We can implement the prototype as it is. We can throw it away and redevelop the system using waterfall methods. We can 'evolve' the prototype.

Implementing the prototype as it is seems obvious. However, there are disadvantages. The system will have been developed with a single user – will it be sufficiently robust to cope with a large number of users at the same time? Is the system efficient, or will it use very large amounts of computer resources? The system will not have been documented – how easy will it be to identify and correct faults or to make changes as the business requirements change?

Implementing the prototype is a common approach where the risks of failure are low – typically systems with a small number of users. Systems running on a large network or alongside other systems should not be implemented directly without considerable testing.

Throwaway prototyping may sound ridiculous but it is a common technique. We have used the prototype to design a system that meets the requirements of the business. This means that we have completed the most difficult stages of the systems development cycle. Further, we know that the system works. If we redevelop the system using waterfall methods and a 3GL we shall produce a robust and efficient system, usually at lower cost than if we had used other methods.

Throwing the prototype away is most common when the system will need to be implemented across a large network, where robustness and efficiency are critical factors.

Evolutionary prototyping involves 'tuning' the system to increase its efficiency and robustness. Important components may be rewritten if necessary, possibly using a 3GL.

Evolutionary prototyping attempts to combine the benefits of implementation and throwaway prototyping. Its disadvantage is that the two parts of the system (the original prototype and the rewritten components) have been developed in different ways and may not fit together very well. One situation where this will not usually present a problem is in a client/server system, where the original prototype can be used for the 'client' component of the system and the 'server' component can be rewritten for greater robustness and efficiency.

6

INFORMATION FOR COMPETITIVE ADVANTAGE

Introduction

The emphasis on financial services organizations' collecting and managing information is relatively recent. During the first and second generations, financial services organizations were interested mainly in operational efficiency, and made little effort at systematic collection of information about their customers.

This changed with the third generation, where the emphasis moved from efficiency to effectiveness. Financial services organizations began to place more emphasis on marketing and on the collect of information to support these activities. At the same time, the development of large relational database management systems (see Chapter 10) made it possible to store and analyse the information collected.

The fourth generation has placed an emphasis on exploiting the new business opportunities offered by e-cash, e-commerce and the information economy.

The common theme is that financial services organizations' attitude towards information technology was its value as a potential source of competitive advantage. What do we mean by competitive advantage and how can we use information technology to achieve it?

A useful starting point is to define competition. A senior banker has given the following definition:

> *Competition is rivalry in selling among sellers acting completely independently within the same time period: that is two or more suppliers striving simultaneously to achieve the same objective. Their effort is to win business from rivals and in many cases to attempt to extend the total market by influencing the environment in which they operate by marketing activity.*
>
> *Marketing can be described as all forms of competitive activity including both price and non-price competition. Such activities as advertising, public relations, sales promotion, product/service development and sponsorship are all forms of marketing activity.*
>
> *Competition has the effect of limiting process and profits: generally, the greater the*

degree of competition in the market the less the likelihood of abnormal profits being earned in the market.

Although quite long, this describes not only what competition is but also its relationship to marketing and its impact on processes and profits.

Competitive advantage is any means by which we can gain an advantage over our competitors. We can seek to win business from our competitors and/or to extend the market in a number of ways. The simplest classification is that of Xavier Gabriel and Paul Strebel:

- Lowest delivered cost;

- Highest perceived quality.

6.1 Lowest delivered cost/highest perceived quality

Lowest delivered cost is the ability to deliver a product or service at a lower cost than competitors. Organizations that are able to achieve this can either gain market share by reducing prices below those of competitors or charge the market rate and earn additional profits.

Highest perceived quality occurs when customers believe that the organization's products or services are better than those of its competitors. Such organizations are able to charge a price premium and earn additional profits or, more rarely, to price their products and services competitively to build market share.

The price elasticity of the product or service being sold affects how the relative benefits of lowest delivered cost and highest perceived quality can be used as sources of competitive advantage. If its price elasticity is low, an increase in price will not have much effect on the demand for the product or service. Basics such as foodstuffs have a low price elasticity. If its price elasticity is high an increase in price will lead to a large fall in demand, reducing total income from the product or service.

We can classify products and services as commodity or branded goods:

- *Commodities* are seen by customers as virtually the same irrespective of supplier. Nails are an example – they are bought by weight, and the customer does not differentiate between manufacturers. The price elasticity of commodities is high, and the ability to produce the lowest delivered cost creates competitive advantage.

- *Branded goods* are seen as very different. Confectionery bars are an example – the customer will specify a Mars Bar or a Kit Kat rather than simply asking for a piece of confectionery. The price elasticity of branded goods is low, and manufacturers are able to charge a premium that represents the value of the brand.

  Some retailers have succeeded in building universal brands by building an image as a supplier of high-quality goods. Examples of such brands include Marks and Spencer,

John Lewis and Tesco. These firms are able to charge a premium across a wide range of own label products.

Retail financial services in general are now seen as a commodity product, although some areas (most obviously credit cards) are strongly branded. Financial services organizations have attempted to build universal brands in the past but generally without success.

6.2 Cost leadership/Differentiation/Focus

There are other ways of classifying sources of competitive advantage. The best known is that of Michael Porter:

- Cost leadership;

- Differentiation;

- Focus.

Although there are some similarities with the classification we have discussed above, they are not equivalent.

Cost leadership and lowest delivered cost are identical.

Differentiation can be on perceived quality but can also be on other factors such as price. Another differentiation strategy is *undifferentiation* – producing products and services identical to those of competitors. Undifferentiation allows the organization to save marketing and development costs and focus on low-cost production.

Because differentiation can cover so many factors, there are no simple rules as to how best to exploit differentiation once achieved. Differentiation on factors such as perceived quality, quality of support, quality of design or brand image is usually exploited by charging a premium price.

Price differentiation can include charging a higher price to build an image. A well known example of this concerns a perfume manufacturer who increased sales by *raising* prices, attracting buyers who were interested in buying the most expensive perfume available as a special present. This is unusual, and the usual reason for price differentiation is to build market share by undercutting competitors.

Undifferentiation usually involves using the demand for the original product created by competitors' marketing activity. Competitors may have created a niche market or may have developed a unique product position. The organization can exploit this by charging a lower price to build market share – the supermarkets have been accused of this by marketing own label products similar in appearance to leading brands. An example from financial services might be the development of gold and platinum cards. These created niche markets, which were entered by competitors and have now become standard products.

The idea of *focus* allows us to choose to compete only in parts – or *segments* – of the market. A financial services organization expects to compete more effectively by concentrating on a small part of the market.

The benefits of focus are:

- *Specialization*. By specializing in a single market segment the organization expects to have a better understanding of the segment's needs and to be able to tailor the way it works to this segment.

- *Possession of complementary assets*. Complementary assets include anything which may add value to transactions involving customers in the market segment.

Some years ago, financial services organizations entered the estate agency market in the belief that a national network of property outlets would support their activities in marketing insurance and mortgages. Although this strategy was unsuccessful it illustrates what complementary assets are.

6.3   Financial services

Before we continue let us consider the characteristics of services. These are:

- Intangibility. Services do not involve the sale of a physical object.

- Simultaneity. Services are created and consumed simultaneously.

- Heterogeneity. The way in which a service is delivered is different every time.

- Perishability. Services have a limited shelf life.

Intangibility means that customers are unable to see the product. This places much more emphasis on the need to market and promote services, and this is particularly important for new products. Another result of intangibility is that we cannot use packaging to draw the customer's attention to the product – the packaging is the environment through which we deliver the service. Bank branches used to be very solid to emphasize the safety of the organization. Branches now are much more customer friendly. The image of the organization is an essential part of its packaging.

Simultaneity means that the product is affected by changes to the process and by the competence and attitudes of the staff performing it. This highlights the importance of staff selection, training and support.

Heterogeneity means that there is a natural level of variation in service delivery. This is difficult for managers to control as it involves making judgements about how much variation is acceptable. Again, staff selection, training and support are important in securing competitive advantage.

Perishability means that customers rarely buy financial services in advance. The only obvious exception is that customers may secure lines of credit such as overdraft limits before they need them. For most financial services the customer wants the service immediately, and convenience is a source of competitive advantage.

6.4   Moving the goalposts

These models assume that the market size is limited and we can only gain competitive advantage by taking market share away from our competitors or by charging a premium price. An alternative way of securing competitive advantage is to create a completely new market.

Say's Law states that supply creates its own demand. Developing a new product can create a market for it. This is a high-risk strategy – most new products fail – but can be a powerful source of competitive advantage.

One reason for this is 'first mover' advantage. Organizations that are the first to enter a market can create an enduring market lead. Obvious examples – where the brand became synonymous with the product – are Hoover and Biro.

Another reason is that the creator of the market can impose standards on the market. This is harder in financial services than in some other industries, as standards are usually agreed by industry-wide bodies or by regulators, but it is possible. Perhaps the clearest example is the introduction of electronic funds transfer at point of sale (EFTPOS), where the industry-wide initiative EFTPOS UK failed to achieve a viable standard and was overtaken by Switch, introduced by Midland Bank. Switch became the standard for EFTPOS in the UK until the introduction by Visa of the Electron and Delta cards.

The characteristics of services we discussed above allow scope for creating new markets. For example:

● Because services are intangible it is relatively simple to create a new service or to modify an existing service to better meet the needs of the customer. Manufacturing industries need to set up expensive factories to make new goods before they gain any commercial return. Service industries can roll out new services relatively quickly.

● Because services are simultaneous any change to the process of creating the service directly affects the customer's experience of having the service delivered. Service industries can use this to differentiate themselves on the basis of the quality of the experience offered. Some industries – notably leisure – are selling the experience as a product in its own right.

● Because services are heterogeneous service industries can customize the service to meet the exact needs of the customer. The ability to offer a bespoke service is itself a new product.

● Because services are perishable the ability to deliver the service to where the customer needs it when the customer needs it is a source of competitive advantage. The rise of telephone banking and the emergence of PC banking and Internet banking are examples of new markets created as a result of this time- and location-based competition.

The role of information in the creation of new markets is ambiguous. Traditional market research and market forecasting techniques are notoriously unreliable when applied to new markets. In the early days of the computer industry, the head of IBM forecast that the *worldwide* demand for mainframe computers would be no more than 25 units. There were similar errors in forecasting the demand for personal computers and home computers.

On the other hand, organizations rely on information to reach potential customers. A profile can be developed based on the marketing concept and customers for 'similar' products. This is difficult for any really innovative products, and test markets and focus groups are important to understand the buyers' behaviour.

The video format 'wars' between VHS and Betamax are instructive in this. The proponents of Betamax relied on the technical superiority of their product. Sony believed that the software was important and secured rights to the distribution of major films, and the success of the VHS format is often attributed to this strategy. However, some commentators have pointed out that Betamax tapes did not have sufficient recording time to record an American football game. The use of video cassette recorders to 'time shift' television viewing required that major sporting events could be recorded, and this resulted in the success of the VHS format. On this view, although Sony was successful in establishing its format it still misjudged its target market.

Many recent innovations in the financial services industry have relied on information technology. A good example is the 'electronic wallet' smartcard such as Mondex or VisaCash. It is worth noting that although these smartcards are physical objects, the services they offer are getting (electronic) cash and payment for goods and services. Therefore they do not break our rule about services being intangible.

It has proved very difficult for financial services organizations to protect their competitive advantage by protecting the underlying technology. There are two reasons for this:

- Financial services organizations usually need to develop these services in partnership with organizations who can provide the technology. For example, Mondex was developed by the National Westminster and Midland banks in partnership with BT. It is in the technology partners' interests to promote and license the use of the technology, even though the financial services organization may prefer the technology to remain proprietary.

- New financial services need to achieve a general level of acceptance before they can be used. For example, Mondex only becomes useful once a significant number of retailers are prepared to accept it. However, retailers are only willing to accept Mondex if a significant number of customers are likely to use it. Therefore National Westminster Bank, who originally developed Mondex, allowed a competitor, Midland Bank, to join the consortium to ensure a sufficiently large number of potential customers to make it attractive to retailers.

To achieve this general level of acceptance, Mondex have been prepared to license their electronic wallet technology. Systems of this type are an example of an open system. We can distinguish between:

- *Open systems*. These are systems about which sufficient information is published to allow others to use them and to develop complementary products. A licence fee may be payable. Note that a system can be open without everything about it being published. Mondex and VisaCash do not publish information about how their security systems work as this would increase the risk of fraud.

Because open systems allow others to enter the market with complementary products this increases the acceptance of the system.

- *Proprietary systems*. These are systems about which no information is published and which only the vendor is allowed to develop. Most early IT systems were proprietary.

  Proprietary systems lock customers in to the vendor. This protects the vendor's competitive advantage provided that customers are prepared to accept being restricted to a single supplier.

- *Public domain systems*. Public domain systems are a form of open system in which the specification is freely published and can be used with no restrictions and no licence fee. The Internet is an example of a public domain system.

We can take examples from PC operating systems. Despite its reputation for playing competitive hardball, Microsoft publishes the details of how to operate with its Windows operating system. This allowed vendors to develop application software that would run under Windows. Apple Computer originally refused to publish details of its operating system or to license its use. Therefore the only application software available was that written by Apple. AT&T developed the Unix operating system and published the specification without requiring a licence fee. A standard version of Unix called Linux is emerging, and the source code for the Linux operating system is freely available.

The consequences of these approaches for market share are clear. Microsoft established its current dominance because its open operating system encouraged the development of a wide range of applications, including the original 'killer application', the spreadsheet VisiCalc. Despite the superiority of its hardware and operating system, Apple failed to establish market dominance, and commands a comparatively low share of the world market. Publication of the Linux source code has allowed enthusiasts to improve the operating system, and its market share is rising rapidly.

In terms of competitive advantage, Microsoft has achieved market dominance in the following ways:

- The original decision to adopt an open strategy produced a short-term advantage through the availability of a wide range of application software.

- By selling very large amounts of software at a relatively low cost Microsoft produced a high level of income, which it reinvested in improvements to the software.

- The Windows operating system also created a complementary asset as a basis for selling other software products.

Apple Computer achieved dominance in niche markets (such as publishing), where the superiority of its product was sufficient to overcome the disadvantage of being restricted to a single supplier. Even in these niche markets Apple was forced to adopt a more open approach.

The problem with the Linux approach is that it is very difficult to make a return on a product that is free. Although Linux has achieved a significant market share its developers have not profited from this. Some companies are attempting to use Linux expertise as a complementary asset by selling support as a service.

6.5   Supply chain

The supply chain is the link between the original supplier and the ultimate customer. For example we can show a simple supply chain for advances:

Figure 6.1: Supply chain

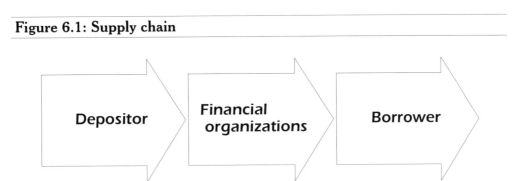

Another way of gaining competitive advantage is to gain control of the supply chain. Organizations can achieve this benefit in a number of ways:

- They may be able to transfer costs or risks from themselves to suppliers or customers. Manufacturing techniques such as just-in-time delivery (JIT) or zero defects achieve this by transferring inventory and inspection costs to suppliers.

- They may achieve process efficiencies by automating part of the process. Links between the WalMart and Proctor & Gamble computer systems mean that products are automatically re-ordered when stocks reach re-order point. This saves on administration costs.

- They may benefit from greater information. We shall discuss this when we discuss Egg in Chapter 9.

- They may be able to lock customers or suppliers into their systems. If customers use personal financial management products such as Microsoft Money or Quicken they are unlikely to switch to a supplier of PC banking services that does not offer that option.

- They may be able to increase product penetration. By making it easier for customers to buy additional products, it is more likely that they will continue with their existing supplier.

Direct banking is the main method that financial services organizations are using to control the supply chain.

7

LOWEST DELIVERED COST

Introduction

One of the main reasons why financial services organizations invest in information technology is to reduce costs.

The approach used in the first and second generations – automation of existing processes – produces only limited cost savings. Bill Gates makes the point in his book *The Road Ahead* that 'automation entrenches inefficiency'. If a process is inherently inefficient, automation will have the effect of making it more difficult to change. This is supported by academic research. The real savings come when information technology is combined with re-engineering the business processes, discussed later in this chapter.

7.1   Clearing system

The clearing system illustrates both the benefits and the weaknesses of automation.

In 1989, a senior banker suggested that staff numbers would have had to rise by at least 50% to cope with the growth in the number of transactions had the system not been automated. As the number of cheques has continued to grow (although more slowly) over the last decade and staff numbers have fallen we can see that financial services organizations would find clearing prohibitively expensive without automation.

The result was a very efficient cheque-clearing system but an *inefficient* payment system. It relied on expensive, specialized equipment, which had to be located in centralized clearing centres. The investment in this equipment acted as a disincentive to moving to new methods of payment, especially as the equipment could only be used for clearing and therefore had very little resale value.

The law regarded the account as being domiciled at the branch, and the clearing system allowed this by using decentralized sorting codes. This complicated branch closures and rationalizations as accounts needed new sort codes (and sometimes new account numbers). The need to route cheques through a clearing centre and then distribute cheques to branches imposed a minimum clearing cycle, which became an increasing source of customer dissatisfaction.

Different technology was used for bank giro credits, requiring increased investment in technology and further locking financial services organizations into the existing clearing system. The technologies were combined into a single reader/sorter device but at the cost of further investment in single-purpose equipment.

Therefore the automation of the clearing system delayed the move away from cheques into other forms of payment. The high investment in equipment created an exit cost that organizations wishing to move away from cheque clearing would be required to write off.

7.2   Process centres

Most financial services organizations now centralize their back-office functions into process centres. These operate as a *factory* or *production line* environment. The main features of a process centre are:

- *Specialization*. Each operator specializes in a small number of work types. This allows them to develop expertise in these processes.

- *Measurement*. Each operator's productivity and quality are measured. This provides a basis for identifying problems and training needs.

Financial services organizations benefit from using process centres in three ways. First, by taking back-office processing out of the branches they are able to release more space for customers. Second, productivity is higher in process centres than in the branch environment. Third, error rates are lower in process centres than in branches, reducing the amount of rework.

The improvements in both productivity and quality are largely the result of specialization. Operators in process centres will typically handle less than half a dozen work types, against the many different types of work that branch staff may be called on to handle in a day. This also means that training can be more focused. Process centre staff also get used to common problems – they may see the same problem several times a day, as compared with once every two or three weeks for branch staff, and will have a better understanding of how to resolve such problems.

Process centres do not necessarily rely on the heavy use of IT. We can describe two separate approaches, low automation and high automation.

Low automation

The low automation approach uses technology similar or identical to that used in branches.

As work items are received, they are sorted by work type and put into batches, each of which represents a certain amount of work (for example, one hour). All the batches for one work type are sent to a team specializing in that work type, where they are distributed by the team leader.

The operators will work through the batches they have been given, and their productivity is measured on the number of batches they process. A sample of batches – typically 5–10% of an operator's work – is pulled out for random quality checking.

High automation

The high automation approach uses document image processing and workflow technology (these are discussed in Chapter 10).

As work items are received, they are automatically scanned. The system recognizes the work type from a bar code or from identification information on the form and puts it in a 'queue' for that work type. If the system cannot identify the item it puts it into a general queue.

The work item may be indexed at this stage. It is sent to an indexing queue, and the customer and transaction type (if not identified automatically) are entered. This will link the image to the customer so that it can be called up if there is a query in future.

The system allocates work items to operators automatically. Each operator has a *profile* showing the work types in which the operator is trained. When new work is requested by an operator, the system will allocate the next suitable work item. Each operator will usually be allocated items of a single work type.

The system may use optical character recognition (OCR) technology to attempt to interpret some of the data on the work item. Alternatively, the operator will see a split screen with an image of the work item and a data entry form, and will enter the details.

The system will select a sample of work items for checking. Again, this will usually be 5–10% of the operator's work. The system will record the number of items processed and also the error rate.

Comparison of approaches

Both approaches produce significant savings over other forms of work organization, and there is no conclusive evidence as to which is the most effective. The high automation approach incurs significantly higher costs but has the potential to produce greater savings. The high automation approach also offers additional benefits such as saving filing and archive costs, as electronic images are stored instead of paper.

7.3   Call centres

The growth in the number of people employed in call centres was one of the most obvious features of the 1990s. Why has this taken place and how effective has this been in cutting costs?

We shall be discussing the technology which is used in call centres in Chapter 11. We can identify two types of call centre:

- Call centres dealing predominantly with inbound calls. These include helplines and call centres dealing with customer enquiries. An automated call distributor (ACD) is used to route calls through to the next free agent.

- Call centres dealing predominantly with outbound calls. These include telemarketing and debt recovery call centres. A Powerdialler or similar system is used to place calls automatically. When the telephone is answered the call is routed to the next free agent.

Inbound calls

A call centre dealing with inbound calls takes telephone calls away from the branch environment. This can directly improve productivity by removing work interruptions, and agents may handle calls more efficiently because they are specialists in customer interaction who have been selected on the basis of their skills and have received appropriate training.

Call centres use *scripting* to ensure that the agent complies with any legal requirements and to deliver a consistent message to customers. Calls may be recorded to provide further legal protection in the event of a dispute.

Call centres may result in the identification of additional demand. In the branch environment, calls may be left unanswered at busy times or the delay in answering may be so long that the caller hangs up. This is less likely to happen in call centres, which improves customer service but may result in the call centre processing additional work. Anticipated cost benefits may not be achieved, but there may be quality benefits instead.

Outbound calls

A call centre dealing with outbound calls also takes calls away from the branch environment, taking staff out of branches. This saves branch costs but results in the loss of a 'pair of hands', reducing branches' flexibility in coping with busy times.

Such call centres usually set very aggressive targets for average call length, and produce substantial cost savings. However, customers are often unhappy with these calls, and the agents' need to manage call lengths can make them seem impolite.

These call centres are able to operate much longer hours than a branch, and will be able to contact customers who cannot be telephoned during the normal working day.

Impact on staff

Call centres have been described as the battery farms of the electronic age, and they can be high-pressure environments. During quiet periods staff may be expected to process infill work on behalf of process centres, and social interaction may be limited. Call centre staff also deal with a higher proportion of complaints than branch staff, and tend to see the worst of the organization, reducing task significance (see Chapter 2).

Call centres are often associated with high staff turnover, but this depends greatly on local labour markets. The tendency for clusters of call centres to open in the same area increases staff turnover and salary levels, although it does allow organizations to benefit from recruiting more experienced staff.

7.4 Electronic processing

Processing paper imposes considerable costs on financial services organizations. Paper is heavy to move, bulky to store, and has safety implications (for example increased fire risk). Therefore financial services organizations are increasingly attempting to process work electronically.

One example of this is the replacement of cheques with payments through the Bankers Automated Clearing System (BACS). Financial services organizations' promotion of direct debits is one example of this. Others include the development of bill payment systems (through direct banking channels) and electronic cheques (e-cheques). E-cash products such as Mondex reduce costs even further by allowing the direct transfer of value between customers without the involvement of the banking system.

Another example is the exchange of images by financial services organizations rather than physical cheques. This would reduce costs by allowing the physical cheques to be retained at the collecting organization without compromising the validation process. This has been used by Royal Bank of Scotland and CoreStates Bank for international cheques, and it has been proposed that this will be used for cheque clearing in the UK.

A further example is electronic data interchange (EDI). The technology used for EDI is discussed in Chapter 11. EDI is the exchange of commercial documents over electronic links. Early EDI systems operated independently of the financial services organizations, and did not allow payment to be made electronically. Fully integrated systems are now available that allow both the commercial and the financial element of the transactions to be completed. This allows automated reconciliation of these elements, allowing customers significant cost savings. The delivery of EDI over the Internet is likely to be standard practice in the near future.

7.5 Business process re-engineering

Given the limitations of automating existing processes as a source of competitive advantage, the alternative is business process re-engineering (BPR).

BPR is defined as 'the fundamental thinking, rethinking and radical redesign of business processes to achieve dramatic improvements in critical contemporary measures of performance, such as cost, quality, service and speed'. The important words are 'fundamental' and 'radical'.

Most change is evolutionary. Automation is an example of evolutionary change as it takes existing processes and allows them to be completed faster. Approaches to evolutionary change include total quality management and continuous improvement.

There is a limit to the improvement that evolutionary change can achieve, and revolutionary change is needed to make further improvements. BPR allows change of this type.

There are a number of different BPR lifecycles, one of which is as follows:

- Identify the core business processes.

- Map and cost these processes.

- Conduct detailed analysis of customer requirements – identify what the customer wants.

- Prioritise the core processes for BPR.

- Radically redesign the process by simplifying and rationalizing.

- Manage the change to ensure benefits are achieved.

- Establish ongoing measurement systems to ensure continuous improvement.

One of the distinctive features of BPR is its ability to improve a number of factors simultaneously. For example, TSB re-engineered its mortgage process and both produced a 25% cost saving and reduced the mortgage processing time from over 30 days to less than 7 days. Other approaches tend to focus on reducing costs or improving service, rather than looking at both.

8

HIGHEST PERCEIVED QUALITY

Introduction

With financial services increasingly seen as a commodity product, improving perceived quality is rarely seen as a driver for investment in information technology. However, customers increasingly expect higher quality, and quality is one of the factors they look at when comparing competitive offerings. What does quality mean in this context?

We have already discussed the idea of quality as 'fitness for purpose' in Chapter 5. Therefore one measure of quality is how well products and services fit with the needs of the customer.

A more traditional view of quality considers the service offered. Does the financial services organization handle customer requests promptly and without mistakes? If problems do occur, how does the financial services organization deal with complaints? On this view, quality is the elimination of errors. This is sometimes called 'right first time' or 'zero defects'.

This is an important area for financial services organizations. Government estimates suggest that *quality costs* account for up to 25% of the total costs for firms in the UK. This includes the costs of preventing quality failures (for example, market research and quality checking), and also the costs of those failures, such as:

- The cost of rework. This is sometimes expressed as 'we never have time to do it right but we always have time to do it again'.

- The cost of waste and scrap, both of materials and of finished products. For financial services organizations this will include any interest costs associated with correcting errors.

- The cost of handling complaints and, where necessary, of compensating customers.

These costs do *not* include the costs of poor publicity and the cost of attrition – customers moving to a different financial services provider because of dissatisfaction with the quality of service received.

8.1 Identifying and anticipating customer needs

We can improve quality by improving our ability to match our products to our customers' requirements through:

- Propensity scoring;
- Profiling;
- Tailoring.

We have already discussed propensity scoring. This matches products to customers on the basis of past experience.

Obviously we cannot use this approach for new products. Instead we can draw up a profile of what we would expect the typical customer to look like and use the customer database to reach these customers using techniques such as direct mail or statement inserts. The profile will be based mainly on the marketing concept for the product but we can also look at the profile of customers who have purchased similar products in the past.

We can develop an understanding of our customers' needs and attempt to offer them the product they want when they want it. This goes beyond propensity scoring in that it looks at the customer relationship as a whole rather than the demand for individual products. We can tailor our standard products to suit the customer better. This approach to marketing is sometimes called the 'segment of one' in that it places each individual customer in a unique market segment.

8.2   Improving service quality

The definition of quality costs suggests some areas in which information is critical. Other ways in which we can improve quality include:

- Improving quality checking;
- Validation and verification of transactions to reduce errors;
- Identification of reasons for attrition;
- Identification of customer satisfaction.

Quality checking

Information is also important to support the quality-checking process. Statistical process control techniques use statistical methods of data analysis to identify whether variations in error rates fall within normal limits. Upper and lower limits are defined using statistical techniques to take account of any natural variation in error rates. This allows investigation to focus on error rates that fall outside these limits.

This investigation will search for common and specific causes. *Common causes* are problems with the process whereas *specific causes* are problems with the way individuals carry out the process. Common causes must be addressed through improved process design whereas specific causes can be addressed through training.

Validation and verification

Technology is used to reduce the number of errors by validating and verifying data entered into the computer.

Validation checks that the data is in a form that can be accepted. For example we might validate a date of marriage by checking that it is a valid date (not 31 June, for example), by checking that it is after the date of birth, and by checking that it is not after the processing date.

Verification checks that data is correct against the information provided. For example we might verify the date of marriage by checking it against a copy of the wedding certificate.

Attrition

The use of scoring techniques to identify the propensity for attrition allows us to identify customers at risk. It also allows us to identify *why* these customers are considering changing their arrangements.

The process of building a propensity for attrition model provides a considerable amount of information. The model analyses the relationship between events in the account history and the customer's decision to close the account or allow it to become dormant. This will include events such as returning cheques and refusing credit, providing the financial services organization with a quantified measure of the impact of such events on the attrition rate. This can be analysed in greater detail using techniques such as interviews and focus groups.

Customer satisfaction

Customer satisfaction is a critical measure of service quality. We can collect information about customer satisfaction in three ways:

- Through customer satisfaction surveys;
- Through mystery shopper surveys;
- By monitoring compliments and complaints.

Customer satisfaction surveys can be used to look at the service as a whole or at specific aspects of it. A number of techniques are used including selected focus groups, open evenings at branch premises, and mailings to a sample of customers. As call centres become more important, call back surveys can be conducted. The customer is telephoned shortly after the completion of the transaction to determine the level of satisfaction.

Customer databases allow customer groups to be selected according to a wide range of characteristics. They also allow customer mailings.

Mystery shopper surveys indicate whether employees are providing a good level of service to customers. The mystery shopper carries out a series of transactions, and scores the experience against a range of criteria, which might include politeness, knowledge and helpfulness. A variation on this used in call centres is for supervisors to listen in to calls and score staff on these criteria.

Call listening depends on the ACD and CTI technology used in call centres and discussed in Chapter 11.

Compliments and complaints provide direct feedback about aspects of the service with which the customer is happy or unhappy. Financial services organizations are increasingly concerned to monitor these in order to improve performance. Compliments may indicate things the organization is doing well, which should perhaps be adopted more widely. Complaints can indicate problems with the organization's processes or training that may need to be corrected.

Compliments and complaints received by telephone are increasingly logged and classified using software designed to support helpdesks. This allows the type of call to be recorded together with sufficient information to allow the compliments and complaints to analysed to identify the underlying causes. These systems also allow a closure code to be entered, which enables organizations to identify whether complaints are being dealt with in a timely and efficient fashion.

8.3   Marketing

Information is the lifeblood of marketing. A typical marketing database will include information about:

- Customers and prospects;
- Products;
- Market analysis;
- Campaigns;
- Direct mailings;
- Telemarketing;
- Sales management;
- Performance.

All existing customers are prospects for cross-selling; increasing product penetration (the number of products held by each customer) is one of the most important business drivers in the financial services industry, and has been a factor in the consolidation of the industry. Prospects also include former customers and those who have made enquiries about products.

Prospects may have had no previous contact with the organization. Most financial services organizations would regard major companies as prospects for corporate services and would maintain some information about key contacts within these companies. Retail prospects can be targeted through mailing lists based on matching their characteristics to the product being marketed.

Other information about customers and prospects includes geographic information such as ACORN codes and television region. ACORN is 'A Classification Of Residential Neighbourhoods', and links geographic information to demographic segmentation. Customers and prospects may also indicate that they do not wish to receive direct mail through the Mail

Order Preferences System (MOPS), and this must also be recorded.

Market analysis includes information about market segments. It includes market size and growth projections. A geographic information system (discussed in Chapter 12) provides information about the geographic dispersion of the market.

Campaign information includes information about the target audience and objectives of the campaign, together with the results of market tests and the campaign itself. It also includes campaign planning and control information such as schedules, budgets and progress reports.

Direct mailing information records all mailings and the mailing history for each customer or prospect.

Telemarketing information includes call lists, scripts and telemarketing history. Telemarketing can use either powerdialling or predictive dialling:

- Powerdialling automatically places a large number of calls, using the numbers in the call list. If the call is answered the system attempts to route it to a free agent. This is often used in the US – if no agents are free the system will play a recorded message saying 'please hold' – but is less suited for the UK where the playing of recorded messages on an outbound call would be classed as a nuisance call.

- Predictive dialling places calls when it predicts an agent will be free. This ensures that there will usually be an agent free if the call is answered.

Both powerdialling and predictive dialling use computer telephony integration (CTI), discussed in Chapter 11. When the call is connected the agent will also see the details of the person answering on the screen.

Sales management information includes the information necessary to administer the sales process, including territories, quotas, leads, contact history and diary information. It also includes sales planning information.

Performance information analyses revenues and costs by product, market segment, sales channel, campaign and individual employee.

Marketing plan

The marketing plan summarizes the organization's marketing activities and their relation to the overall strategic plan. The marketing plan will typically include the following:

- An audit of the organization's marketing capabilities;

- An audit of other capabilities such as production, distribution, finance and personnel;

- Objectives and strategies, linked to the organization's corporate objectives;

- Plans, linked to the corporate plan.

The marketing audit covers the marketing environment, marketing activities and the marketing system.

The marketing environment includes the business environment, the market environment and the competitive environment. The business environment is usually considered in terms of the acronym LPEST:

- *Legal.* The legal environment in which the organization operates.

- *Political.* The political environment.

- *Economic.* Factors such as interest rates, exchange rates and the general health of the economy.

- *Social or sociological.* Changes in social attitudes affecting customers and employees.

- *Technological.* Technological developments affecting the organization.

Other factors that are sometimes included in this analysis include the environment (in the ecological sense) and values.

The market environment considers:

- *Products.* What products are purchased. How they are used. The characteristics of the main products.

- *Prices.* The general level of prices and the price range.

- *Distribution and channels.* The principle channels of distribution, their characteristics and geographical coverage.

- *Communication.* The principle methods for communication, including advertising and public relations.

The competitive environment considers:

- *Industry structure.* Organizations operating in the market and their market standing and market share. Capacity utilization – whether the market is oversupplied. How open the market is to new entrants. Industry consolidation – mergers, acquisitions and diversification.

- *Industry finances.* Costs, profitability and investment. Sources of finance.

The review of the organization's marketing activities considers issues such as:

- Sales, market share and profit margins, all analysed by customer and by product;

- Marketing organization and processes;

- Marketing mix – price, product characteristics, place (distribution) and promotion (advertising);

- Other marketing capabilities such as market research, product development, point of sale advertising and after sales support.

The review of the organization's marketing systems considers how marketing objectives are set and the systems in place to support them, including responsibilities, information systems, planning and control.

Techniques such as SWOT analysis (strengths, weaknesses, opportunities and threats) can be used to assess the feasibility of the marketing objectives, and these are then converted into marketing plans.

9

EXAMPLES AND CASES

9.1   Merrill Lynch's Cash Management Account

Merrill Lynch's Cash Management Account allowed personal customers to see their overall financial position with Merrill Lynch, consolidating their assets, liabilities and securities holdings. This idea has been adopted by other financial services organizations, for example the Virgin One account, but at the time of its introduction it was unique.

Other features included the ability to set up sub-accounts for specific purposes such as retirement or education and the ability to sweep surplus funds into higher-yielding accounts such as money market accounts.

The Cash Management Account is often given as an example of using IT for competitive advantage in academic studies.

9.2   ATMs

Automated teller machines (ATMs) were originally introduced by the high-street banks as a response to competition from the building societies, who offered longer opening hours and Saturday opening. ATMs allowed the banks to offer encashment facilities outside normal banking hours at a lower cost than they would have incurred by extending branch opening hours. Therefore it is an example of attempting to secure competitive advantage through lowest delivered cost.

The first ATMs accepted a pre-paid plastic card. Customers purchased the card in advance and could use it to request cash when needed. They did not offer any facilities other than encashment.

In spite of their limitations, these early ATMs were popular. However, the services provided were not sufficient for the bank introducing them to gain significant competitive advantage over its banking rivals.

The next innovation was the introduction of the magnetic strip card. Customers did not have to purchase the card in advance and could draw funds up to a daily limit. These ATMs were not permanently on-line and again offered only encashment facilities.

This was clearly an improvement and rapidly replaced the plastic card ATMs. Two points are worth noting:

- Banks that had introduced ATMs based on plastic cards were faced with the need to replace them with the magnetic strip system. Attempting to secure competitive advantage through technology incurs the risk of technological obsolescence.

- Replacing pre-paid cards with magnetic strip cards transferred the risk from the customers to the banks, as these systems were not on-line and balances could not be checked. Therefore these cards were only issued to good customers – an early example of service segmentation.

The greater convenience offered by the magnetic strip card was a source of competitive advantage. However, competitors were able to use the same technology so any competitive benefit was short term. This illustrates the difficulty of obtaining sustainable competitive advantage through technology.

The next innovation was to offer additional services – balance enquiries, mini-statements, cheque book ordering – through ATMs. This took some of this work out of the branches, further reducing costs, as well as offering service improvements to customers – higher perceived quality.

Again, banks that had invested heavily in ATMs offering only encashment facilities were left with obsolete equipment. The nature of the change was less serious, and these banks were able to continue using their existing ATMs at the cost of a lower perceived quality of service than their competitors.

The next innovation was the development of ATM networks – both domestic (MINT, Four Banks and Link) and international (Visa, MasterCard and others). The potential source of competitive advantage here is higher perceived quality by providing customers with encashment facilities at more locations.

These networks had an unforeseen consequence in that they allowed banks to enter new markets without the need to build an extensive branch network. They lowered the cost of entry to the retail mass markets. An example of this is Robert Fleming, which was able to expand from its traditional merchant banking and private banking activities and enter selected mass market segments, providing encashment facilities through the Visa ATM network.

The final innovation we shall discuss is the development of automated branches and in-store branches. There is a difference in competitive drivers – automated branches primarily lower costs whereas in-store branches primarily improve quality by allowing customers to combine shopping with access to banking services – but the ATM is a key enabling technology and is required to provide encashment facilities.

The Bank of Scotland provides an example of the role of ATMs as a source of competitive advantage. The bank had adopted the early model ATM with its Scotcash machines but these had not been particularly successful. Therefore it was very reluctant to invest in more advanced ATM systems and decided that the business case was insufficient to justify the investment.

Its main competitor, the Royal Bank of Scotland, increased its number of ATMs tenfold between 1977 and 1980. It established its branded Cashline service as the generic term for

ATMs in Scotland (rather as Cashpoint is used as a generic term for ATMs in England) and started to gain market share.

Bank of Scotland management responded by reviewing the business case and launching a major programme of investment in ATMs. By 1984 they had eliminated the lead achieved by the Royal Bank of Scotland. At this point, ATMs ceased to be a source of competitive advantage, and the Bank of Scotland and the Royal Bank of Scotland were able to agree terms for ATM reciprocity shortly afterwards.

This illustrates both the ability to gain competitive advantage and its transitory nature. It is also worth making the point that the Royal Bank of Scotland did gain market share by introducing ATMs, and these customers would not have returned to the Bank of Scotland simply because the latter also offered ATMs. Although the competitive advantage gained through technology was transient this translated into a sustainable advantage through higher market share.

9.3   HOBS

The Bank of Scotland's experiences with the development of its ATM network were of value in the development of its home and office banking system (HOBS).

HOBS was a collaborative development with the Nottingham Building Society, and was based on the use of the Prestel network, allowing customers to interact with the system using a telephone and television. The Nottingham Building Society was the first to introduce its service – Homelink – in 1982, and the Bank of Scotland introduced HOBS in 1985. Most other major banks introduced similar services at about this time.

Most financial services organizations regarded these systems as a failure. Prestel, although a world leader at the time, was too expensive for the mass market and never achieved critical mass. The UK government's attitude at the time is in sharp contrast to that of France, where the government heavily promoted its competing Minitel service, distributing free terminals to France Telecom customers. Minitel is and continues to be widely used for a range of electronic services including home banking.

The Bank of Scotland showed far greater commitment to home banking than its competitors, most of which withdrew from the market after brief trials. HOBS allowed the bank to expand in England without the cost of setting up a network, and 60% of the customers attracted to the product were English. It positioned the bank as an innovator and allowed it to build niche positions in industries such as North Sea oil. It provided the bank with a useful market share as alternative approaches to home and office banking such as the Internet became more prominent, and HOBS is now available over the Internet.

9.4   First Direct

First Direct is a subsidiary of HSBC, and the UK's market leader in telephone banking.

UK financial services organizations made a number of attempts at introducing home banking systems in the 1980s, based either on Prestel (as in HOBS) or on telephone banking. None of these was particularly successful until the then Midland Bank introduced First Direct.

The competitive rationale for telephone banking is the ability to achieve lowest delivered cost through:

- *Low premises costs*. Call centres are located in out-of-town sites, which are much cheaper than the cost of branches' high-street sites.

- *Low staff costs*. Financial services organizations were able to recruit new staff for call centres, without the benefits packages offered to other staff. They were also able to operate with lower management:staff ratios. As the number of call centres has grown, salary and benefits packages have improved, and this cost advantage is now less pronounced.

- *Paperless processing*. Removing paper from transaction processing reduced handling and storage costs.

- *More intensive use of assets*. First Direct used the branch network for some items. By using the network more intensively the fixed costs associated with it could be spread over more transactions. This has the effect of lowering the transaction cost.

The cost of delivering a transaction through a call centre is typically half of the cost of delivering the same transaction through a branch.

First Direct was more successful than its competitors. To understand why, it is important to consider the characteristics of First Direct:

- It used human operators, rather than technologies such as speech recognition or interactive voice response (IVR – the use of touch tone telephones to enter instructions). This is relatively high cost but allows customers to make a wider range of requests and is popular with customers. Most of First Direct's competitors adopted one of the automated technologies, which are discussed in Chapter 11.

- It was a full service bank, while many of its competitors offered a very limited range of services. This was a result of using human operators rather than speech recognition or IVR.

- It was positioned as a separate bank. This meant that it avoided the 'baggage' associated with the Midland Bank name and also made it easier to recruit customers from other banks.

- It offered a 24 hour a day, 365 day a year service.

What First Direct achieved was to change the basis of competition. Instead of looking for competitive advantage purely through lowest delivered cost, First Direct offered a perceived quality of service higher than that of its competitors.

9.5   Direct Line

Direct Line can be thought of as the insurance industry's equivalent of First Direct. The method of operation is similar, with insurance services being delivered over the telephone and with the benefit of low premises and staff costs.

Direct Line was the first organization to deliver insurance services in this way and therefore benefited as the first mover. It has been extremely successful and widely copied by a range of financial services organizations.

9.6   Process centres

Process centres such as Lloyds TSB's customer service centres and HSBC's district service centres provide regional locations in which branch back office processing can be centralized.

The competitive rationale for introducing process centres is to achieve lowest delivered cost. The cost advantages of process centres are:

● *More efficient use of technology*. Having a limited number of process centres allows the use of technology such as document image processing and workflow, which could not be cost justified in a branch environment.

● *Lower premises costs*. Most process centres are located in out-of-town sites, which incur lower premises costs than high-street sites. This frees space in high-street branches, which can be used to provide increased customer space or which can be realized by relocating the branch into smaller premises.

● *Lower staff costs*. Process centre staff have no contact with customers and need only be trained in a limited range of tasks rather than in the full range of branch work. This allows staff to be employed at a lower grade, reducing staff costs. In addition, there are fewer security issues with process centres than with branches, which encourages the use of agency staff, who do not necessarily receive the full range of banking benefits.

● *Greater flexibility*. Some process centres operate an evening shift, which allows more intensive use of technology. It also increases flexibility, as the size of the evening shift can be reduced to reflect seasonal variations in workload.

Process centres have generally been effective in reducing costs. There has been an additional benefit in improving quality (highest perceived quality). This has occurred because process centre operators specialize in a small number of transactions. Therefore they are used to seeing this type of work and are more likely to be familiar with unusual situations than branch staff who may only see a transaction of this type once every few days or even weeks. Branches are also more vulnerable to holiday periods – process centres will have enough experienced staff to cover holidays whereas branches may find that the branch expert on a particular transaction is away when an item is received.

9.7   Egg

Egg is the direct banking operation of the Prudential insurance company and succeeded in capturing £3 billion of deposits in its first six months of operation. Egg, like First Direct, was developed by Mike Harris, and there are obvious similarities between the two.

The first similarity is the decision to position Egg as distinct from the Prudential, while ensuring that potential Egg customers were aware that the resources of the Prudential were behind it. With First Direct this was a factor in recruiting customers from the Midland's competitors. This may be less important for Egg than for First Direct but is useful in allowing Egg to start with very little baggage in the form of customers' preconceptions of what they would expect a 'Prudential Bank' to look like.

The second is the emphasis on using human operators. The quality of contact – the banking experience – and the ability to tailor the service offered to individuals' different needs is an important differentiator between Egg and its competitors.

The third is the focus on direct channels. Egg updates the First Direct concept in focusing on Internet banking and e-commerce, although it aims to support all direct banking channels – telephone, post, digital television and kiosk. One reason for the choice of name is said to be the initial letter 'e' and its associations with e-commerce and e-cash.

This backfired when Egg was launched. The intention was to launch only through telephone and post, and Egg's Internet address was not explicitly advertised. More potential customers than expected realized that it would probably be www.egg.com, and the initial Internet demand was well in excess of the capacity of the systems to cope.

One potential benefit of the focus on the Internet is the ability to collect marketing information based on Internet transactions. This will allow Egg to build up comprehensive profiles of its customers and to develop 'lifestyle products' designed to meet their needs.

Much of Egg's initial success was due to the very high deposit rates offered, which were above Egg's lending rates for the first few months. Therefore its ability to sustain its initial rate of growth has yet to be established. However, like First Direct it continues to pass on the benefits of its low cost base through attractive interest rates.

10

THE ELECTRONIC OFFICE

Introduction

We use the term *electronic office* to describe a computer or a network running software that can be used in an office environment by clerical staff with little additional training. The software is designed to replace traditional office activities such as typing (word processors), analysing accounts (spreadsheets) and filing (document image processing and databases).

Most electronic offices now run on a personal computer (PC) or on workstations linked through a local area network (LAN). Some electronic offices run on minicomputers, and an electronic office can also run on a mainframe computer, although this is now rare. Electronic office software can also run over the Internet or an intranet, and this will be considered in Chapter 14.

We can classify the software used in the electronic office into system software and application software. *System software* is the software used to run the computer, such as the operating system. Software such as word processors is *application software*.

10.1 Computer hardware

The *hardware* element of a computer system is the physical box. We can think of computer hardware as having four main components:

- The processor, which carries out calculations on behalf of the computer;

- Input devices, which are used to put information into the computer;

- Storage devices, which store information either on a short-term or a long-term basis;

- Output devices, which are used to get information out of the computer.

We can show the relationship between these as:

Figure 10.1

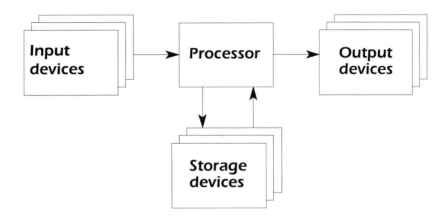

The three main types of computer are:

● Mainframe computers;

● Minicomputers;

● Microcomputers – usually described as PCs or workstations.

We shall describe mainframe computers in more detail in Chapter 11. Their main characteristics are:

● They cannot operate in a normal office environment. They need a dust-free environment with better air conditioning than is available within an office.

● They require special training to operate.

● They are very powerful, and can meet the computing needs of a large number of users at the same time.

Minicomputers were introduced to meet the needs of smaller organizations or of large organizations in small offices. Unlike mainframe computers they can operate in a normal office environment provided the air conditioning is adequate but they still require special training to operate. Minicomputers can typically meet the computing needs of perhaps 100 users, although their size can vary quite widely.

Although they are still quite common, minicomputers are less important than they were. Applications that were run on minicomputers can now often run on networked PCs at lower cost. This is particularly true of electronic office applications.

PCs are small computers designed to be used by one person at a time in a home or office environment. They are also called *workstations* and we shall generally use the term 'workstation' for a PC that is connected to a network.

You may also come across laptop and palmtop computers. These are small, portable PCs.

● Laptops are now common. They are usually a bit longer and wider than a pad of A4 paper and will fit comfortably in a briefcase. Laptop computers use the same hardware and software as other PCs and can be connected to networks.

● Palmtops are much smaller. They are of various sizes and capabilities, ranging from 'electronic organizers' through to fully functional PCs.

A PC looks like:

Figure 10.2

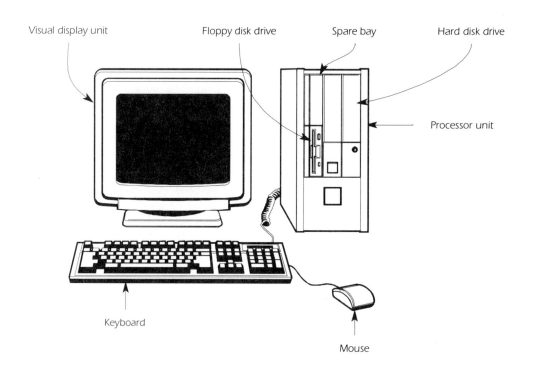

Visual display unit   Floppy disk drive   Spare bay   Hard disk drive

Processor unit

Keyboard

Mouse

The processor unit includes the processor and the storage devices. An important feature of PCs is that additional components can be added quite easily. The PC shown in the diagram above has a spare 'bay', which can for example be used to add further storage devices.

PCs originally only had one processor but now usually have a maths co-processor, which speeds up mathematical calculations.

Input devices

The main input devices for PCs are the keyboard and the mouse. Other common input devices include scanners, touch screens, 'pens' and speech recognition.

The *keyboard* looks very similar to a typewriter and uses a similar arrangement of keys. One difference between a computer keyboard and a typewriter is that the computer keyboard has program function keys (usually labelled F1-F12), either on the left side or at the top. These can be used by computer programs to allow the computer user to give instructions to the computer – for example, if the user does not know what to do next he or she can often ask the computer for help by pressing F1.

The *mouse* is a hand-held device that is attached to a microcomputer. It has a plastic ball embedded in its lower surface and two or three buttons on the top. As the mouse is moved round the desk top, the ball rolls in its socket and the computer detects that this movement is taking place. The computer translates the movement of the mouse into the movement of a pointer (the *cursor*) on the computer screen.

This is the most common type of mouse, but there are alternatives. The most important is the trackball, in which the ball is embedded on the top. Instead of the user moving the device round the desk, he or she rotates the ball directly.

The mouse is usually attached to the computer by a wire. There are wireless mice, which signal their position and button presses using infrared (similar to a television remote control). Some trackball mice, especially on laptop computers, are built into the keyboard.

A *scanner* works in a similar way to a photocopier. A document is placed or fed into the scanner and a bright light shines on it. Reflections from the document are detected by sensors, which calculate whether each part of the document was light or dark. Colour scanners use three passes using red, blue and green filters. Whereas a photocopier transfers the image onto another piece of paper, a scanner passes the image to the computer.

Touch screens work by people pressing the computer screen, either with their fingers or with a pointing device (sometimes called a *stylus*). They can work in several ways. For example:

- Older approaches were to place a pressure-sensitive or heat-sensitive pad in front of the screen. This would react to the pressure or heat of a finger.

- An alternative is to put a network of infrared rays in front of the screen. This has the advantage that there is no need actually to touch the screen and this prevents it from getting dirty.

The image shown on the screen will have 'buttons' for the user to press, and these will change depending on what action the user is expected to take. For example, touch screens are often used in foreign exchange dealing systems where the buttons on one screen might indicate the currency and the buttons on another screen might indicate the counterparty.

Pen computers also use touch screen technology. Instead of only pushing buttons, the pen may also be used to enter handwriting and drawings. The pen is an important input device for palmtop computers as these do not have a full-size keyboard. Some palmtop computers can be 'trained' to recognize a user's handwriting. An alternative is to show an image of the keyboard on the screen for users to touch the keys they require.

You may come across an older technology called the *light pen*. These are used mainly with mainframe computer systems and allow the computer to detect the part of the screen at which the light pen is being pointed. We shall not consider these further in this book.

Speech recognition systems use a microphone to accept spoken instructions. These systems usually need to be trained to recognize the user's individual voice characteristics. Speech recognition systems require considerable computing power but are becoming more reliable as PCs become more powerful.

Output devices

The main output devices for PCs are the screen and the printer.

The most common type of *computer screen* is a cathode ray tube, similar to the tube used in a television set. These cannot be used on portable computers because they are too large and use too much power, so different technologies such as liquid crystals have been developed for these.

The quality of the image you see on the screen depends on the number of picture elements (or *pixels*) on it and the number of colours it allows. The total number of pixels is called the *resolution* and is shown as the number of pixels across the width of the screen by the number of pixels across the height of the screen. Colour screens must have a minimum of three colours (red, green and blue) but give better colour quality if more colours are used – some screens allow up to 16.7 *million* different shades. Some screens allow you to choose either a higher resolution or more colours.

To use a high-resolution screen, the computer needs to have a suitable graphics adapter card. Most modern PCs currently have a super video graphics array (SVGA) card. A SVGA screen typically has a resolution of 1024 by 768 pixels, allowing 256 colours. A video graphics array (VGA) screen may still be found on some PCs and has a resolution of 640 by 480 pixels, allowing 16 colours.

The most common type of *printer* is the laser printer. This works in a similar way to a photocopier. An electric charge is placed on the paper and powdered ink (called *toner*) sticks to the charged areas. This is then sealed to the paper using heated rollers.

A common alternative is the inkjet printer. This has tiny jets, which squirt ink at the paper. Inkjet printers are increasingly common for personal use, as colour inkjet printers are much cheaper than colour laser printers.

Two other types of printer you may come across are line printers and plotters. Line printers are usually attached to mainframe computers and we shall not consider them any further in this book. Plotters use pens to draw the image required and are best used for diagrams that do not have solid areas of colour. We shall not consider plotters further in this book.

Storage devices

We can classify storage as 'primary' and 'secondary'. *Primary storage* is the computer's memory – computer programs have to be loaded into primary storage before they can run. Memory can be further broken down into random access memory (RAM) and read-only memory (ROM).

RAM is the computer's main working memory. Any computer program that is to be run needs first to be loaded into RAM, from which instructions are transferred into the processor for execution. In modern computers, RAM is also found on the graphics adapter card. This *video RAM* allows the computer to produce high-quality screen images without slowing down the computer's main processor (also called the central processing unit or CPU).

The main problem with RAM is that it is *volatile*. This means that information recorded in RAM is lost if the computer is switched off. It is possible to use a battery to maintain power to a small amount of RAM even after the computer has been switched off. A type of memory called complementary metal-oxide semiconductor (CMOS), which needs very little power, is used. The information held in CMOS is needed when the computer is switched on but cannot be stored in ROM because it can be changed. This includes any passwords required to access the computer, the date and time, and information about the computer's configuration – what input, output and storage devices are attached to it. If the battery fails for any reason, the computer will instruct the operator to run a special program called Setup to enter this information.

The volatility of RAM explains is why *ROM* is so important. Data held in ROM is non-volatile. When the computer is first switched on, the computer runs a small program (called the *bootstrap* program) stored in ROM. This program's job is to load the operating system (the program that has overall control of the computer's activities) from magnetic disk into RAM.

Because ROM is non-volatile, the data it holds usually needs to be set up when the ROM is made. However, the data in some types of ROM can be changed using special equipment. These types are called programmable read-only memory (PROM), erasable programmable read-only memory (EPROM), and electronically erasable programmable read-only memory (EEPROM).

The most important forms of *secondary storage* are magnetic disk, magnetic tape and optical disk. A special type of RAM called flash memory is also used for secondary storage, especially for portable PCs.

Magnetic disks are disks of metal or plastic rotating round a central spindle. The disks have a surface coating that can hold a magnetic charge. Magnetic disk storage is a lot cheaper than RAM and is also non-volatile. However, reading data held on disk is much slower than reading data held in RAM, and computer programs must be loaded into RAM before they can be executed. Magnetic disk can be fixed (called 'hard disk' or 'Winchester disk' in relation to PCs) or removable (microcomputer 'floppy disks' are removable).

Hard disks are housed in a sealed unit to prevent dust getting in and damaging the disk surfaces. The unit usually includes more than one disk. Hard disks are usually fixed in the computer (fixed hard disks) although the unit can sometimes be removed (removable hard disks).

Floppy disks consist of a single disk housed in a plastic sleeve to protect against dust and scratches. Both recording surfaces are usually used. Floppy are now usually of 3½ inch diameter although the older 5¼ inch diameter floppy disks may still be found.

Magnetic tape is plastic tape with a surface coating that will hold a magnetic charge. PCs use half inch magnetic tape mounted in cartridges, similar in appearance to the cassettes used in video camcorders. Digital audio tape (DAT) is sometimes used.

Optical disks are metal or plastic disks that can be read by a laser. The surface of the disk is treated to provide a contrast between the information held and the blank disk surface, and the laser is used to identify this contrast. The same technology is used in audio CDs. The most important types are CD-ROM, CD-RW and CD-R.

CD-ROM is an abbreviation for compact disc-read-only memory. It could strictly be regarded as an input device rather than a storage device as CD-ROMs cannot be changed once they have been created. CD-ROM uses tiny 'pits' on the surface of the disk to provide the contrast.

CD-RW is an abbreviation for compact disc-rewritable. Unlike CD-ROM, the information on CD-RW can be changed. Various approaches can be used, for example magneto-optical technology in which a magnetic field is used to provide the contrast when information is recorded.

CD-R is an abbreviation for compact disc-recordable. Information can be written to CD-R but it cannot then be changed. One form of this is CD-WORM (compact disc-write once read many, which has a surface film of a different colour from the disk itself. Information is recorded by burning a hole in the surface film to reveal the underlying disk surface and provide a colour contrast.

Flash memory is a type of RAM that is not volatile. This is most often found on laptop and palmtop computers, as flash memory cards are smaller and need less power than a floppy disk drive.

Flash memory is the size of a credit card and is an example of a PC card. These are sometimes called PCMCIA cards – this stands for the PC Memory Card International Association, an organization formed to promote their use. PC cards were developed for portable computers (although some desktop computers also accept them) and can be used for a wide range of PC add-ons such as modems and even hard disks.

Multimedia computers

Multimedia computers can store and output video, sound and high-quality photographic images as well as text and diagrams. This has become possible because of a number of developments in hardware and software:

- Improved storage, especially the development of CD-ROM. Multimedia sound and images use very large amounts of storage, and would not have been possible without these developments.

- Higher-resolution screens and faster and better graphics adapter cards. An important development here has been video RAM, allowing the graphics adapter card to format the image without using the processor's resources.

- Development of graphical user interfaces, without which it would be very difficult to use multimedia effectively.

Multimedia has many uses. It is used in presentations. It allows a wide range of reference material to be stored, including material that needs to use sound. It is increasingly used with DTP programs, especially with photo CD editors and libraries. It is also used in training.

Voice mail is another example of multimedia. The computer receives telephone messages (using a modem) and stores them. If the caller is using a touch tone telephone it can also respond – for example, by faxing information. The messages are often stored as part of an e-mail system and can be replayed at a later date. The system will usually give additional information such as the length of the message.

10.2   Local area networks

We can arrange computers into *networks* of two or more computers connected by telecommunications links. There are two main types of network, wide area networks (WANs) and local area networks (LANs). The difference between WANs and LANs used to be quite clear – WANs were spread over a wide geographical area (perhaps hundreds of miles) whereas LANs were confined to a single building or part of a building; WANs used external telephone lines as part of the network whereas LANs did not.

The distinction between WANs and LANs is no longer clear. WANs now use digital lines and the packet switching technology used in LANs. LANs can be linked using bridges and routers to cover very large geographical areas. The technology behind the Internet – perhaps the ultimate wide area network – is more similar to that used by LANs than to traditional WANs.

We shall discuss WANs in Chapter 11. LANs were originally introduced to allow computer resources such as storage devices and printers to be shared, usually within a single department. They usually include the following:

- A file server, which stores files and computer programs for the LAN;

- A print server, attached to one or more printers;

- A number of microcomputer workstations;

- Sometimes, repeaters to extend the length of the LAN;

- Often, a gateway that connects the LAN to a WAN;

- Sometimes, bridges and routers that connect the LAN to other LANs.

File servers store the software that runs on the LAN, including the network operating system that controls the LAN. Software designed for use on a LAN is sold on the basis that only a certain number of people can use it at the same time, and the software usually has controls to count the number of users and ensure these limits are met.

File servers can also be used to store data created or used by users of the LAN. Data that needs to be shared – accessed by different LAN users – should always be stored on the file server.

Software and data stored on the file server can be more tightly controlled than software and data held on workstations. Physical access to the file server is usually controlled (for example by placing the file server in a locked room). Software upgrading – updating software whenever a new version comes out – is easier if it is stored on the LAN, as the upgrade needs only to be made in one place. Backups – copying software and data to another storage medium in case of fire or other damage – are easier if the software and data are stored on the LAN, again because this only needs to be done in one place.

Print servers are usually workstations attached to one or more printers. Data for printing is *spooled* – copied to disk – and a print request is sent to the print server. This schedules the printing with requests received from other workstations and prints it when a printer becomes available. The order in which print requests will be dealt with may be changed, or print requests may be removed from the schedule. Some printers can be attached directly to the LAN.

Workstations allow users to access the LAN. They can themselves store software and data, and they can even be connected directly to a printer (this is useful where one LAN user needs to use an unusual type of printer – for example a colour printer or a plotter).

Repeaters are used to extend the maximum length of a LAN. An important limitation on the length of a LAN is that the signal gets fainter as it travels over longer distances. The repeater boosts the signal, in effect acting as an amplifier.

The difference between gateways, bridges and routers is very technical and of little importance for an understanding of the subject. Their main functions are as follows:

- Gateways, also called communications servers, are most commonly used to connect LANs to WANs. They can also be used to connect a LAN to a different type of LAN.

- Bridges are the main method of connecting LANs of the same type to each other. Bridges allow all the resources on the LANs to be shared – for example users of one LAN can access software or data stored on another – under the control of the network operating system.

- Routers allow a LAN to be connected to a LAN of a different type or, in some cases, to a WAN. Routers are also used to connect the networks which make up the Internet.

A LAN can be arranged in three different ways – as a bus LAN, as a ring LAN or as a star LAN. These are called *topologies*. The first two are the most important, and we shall not consider star LANs in this book.

A *bus LAN* uses a continuous communications cable to which the servers and workstations are attached. This type of LAN is sometimes called an Ethernet LAN (after one of the most important early suppliers) or a carrier sense multiple access with collision detect (CSMA/

CD – after the way in which the LAN works) LAN.

Each device 'listens' to the LAN at all times (this is carrier sense). If a device wants to send a message, it will wait until the LAN is quiet and then try to send its message. If another device wants to send a message at the same time (multiple access), the device will identify this (collision detect) and *both* messages will be ignored (this stops them getting mixed up).

Instead, the two servers or workstations will wait for a short period and try again. A system of random numbers determines how long the devices wait (this is to stop them trying to send at the same time again) and they will listen to the LAN to make sure it is quiet before trying again.

Bus LANs are cheap to set up, and repeaters can be used, allowing very large LANs. Their main disadvantage is that their performance deteriorates badly when the LAN gets busy – more messages mean more collisions.

A bus LAN looks like this:

Figure 10.3: Bus LAN

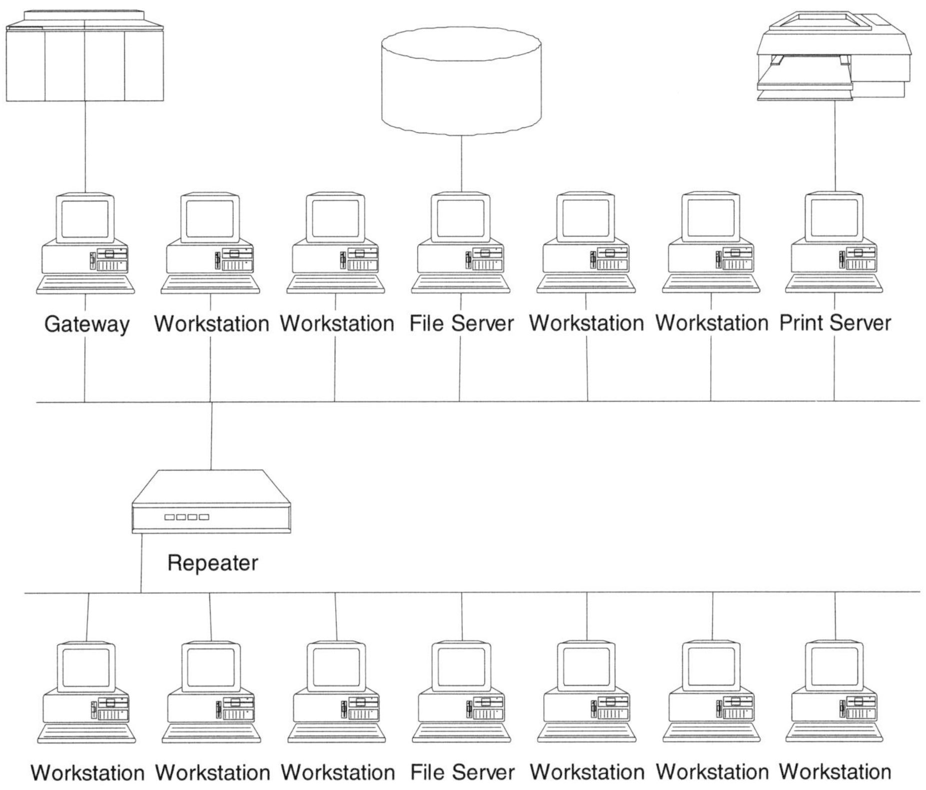

Gateway   Workstation   Workstation   File Server   Workstation   Workstation   Print Server

Repeater

Workstation   Workstation   Workstation   File Server   Workstation   Workstation   Workstation

In a *ring LAN,* the servers and workstations are arranged as a continuous ring. They are usually attached through a multistation access unit or MAU. The main purpose of the MAU is to prevent the ring from being broken in the event that the workstation or server is not switched on or does not work – if an MAU is not used and this happens, the LAN will not work.

The most common form of ring LAN is the token ring. A special message called the *token* is passed round the ring. When a server or workstation receives the token, it must first check whether the token is marked as 'busy'. If not, the device can send a message (by marking the token as busy and attaching the address and message). If the token is busy, the device cannot send a message but must check to see if the message the token is carrying is addressed to it.

The token will then pass round the ring until it reaches the destination device, which will take the message. The token will still be marked as busy and will pass round the ring until it returns to the server or workstation that sent the message. Only then will the device remove the address and message, and mark the token as free.

The performance of a ring LAN depends on the number of messages sent. Unlike the bus LAN, the deterioration in performance is proportional to the increase in the number of messages. The main limitation of ring LANs is the maximum distance between workstations (100 metres) which makes the topology unsuitable for large LANs.

A ring LAN looks like this:

Figure 10.4: Ring LAN

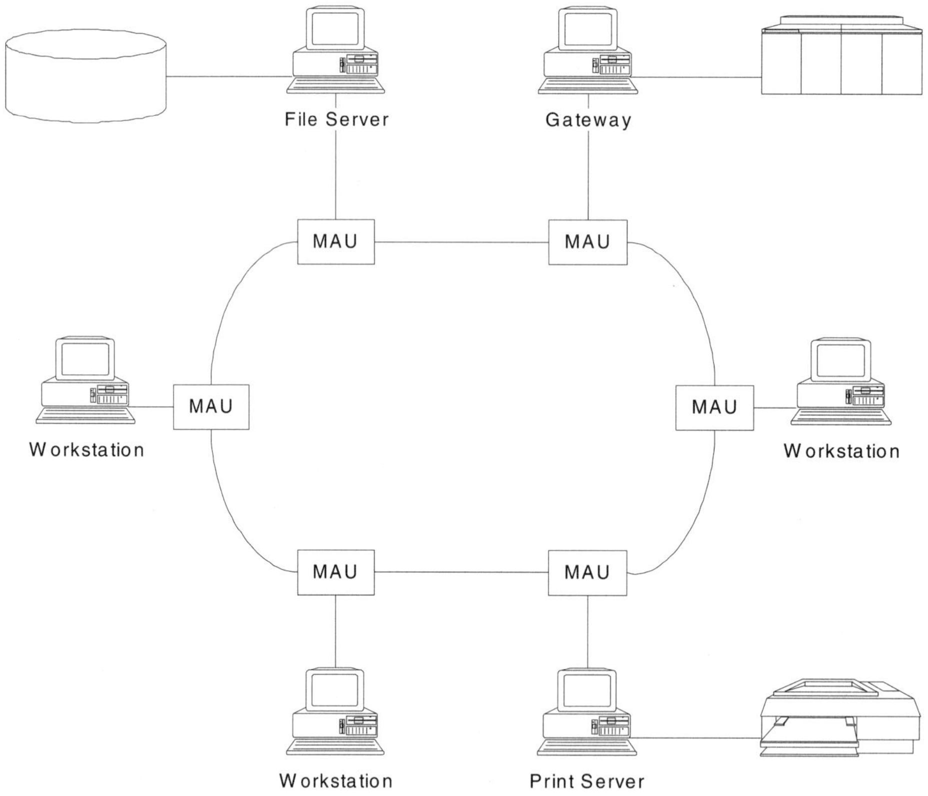

Files

Computers hold data on magnetic disk, magnetic tape and optical disk as files.

On a typical PC, most files will either be software or files created by software – for example word processor or spreadsheet files. There may also be a few data files, although these are much more common on minicomputers or mainframes.

The word 'file' sometimes causes a bit of confusion. If you are used to manual filing systems you might think of a file as something that holds all the information we have about a customer – 'Mr Smith's file' will hold a record of all our dealings with Mr Smith over the years.

Computers do *not* use the word in this way. Think instead of a card index file, possibly holding customer addresses for a mailing campaign. Within this file there will be a record card for Mr. Smith.

A data file is used to hold a *type* of data – for example the customer file or the account file. A file is made up of a number of records, each of which represents an *occurrence* of that type of data – for example an individual customer or account.

Records are made up of pieces of data called *fields*. A customer record will usually contain fields called Customer Name, Date of Birth, Sex, etc., which are pieces of information about the individual customer.

Directories

Even a small PC can store hundreds or thousands of files on its hard disk, and networks of PCs can hold many more. How can we find a particular file on magnetic disk?

The obvious answer is to give the file a name, and this is our starting point. It is still common to see file names on PCs in the form TEXTFILE.TXT, where the eight characters before the full stop identify the file and the three characters after it (called the *extension*) usually identify the type of file. An extension of .TXT is usually used to identify a file containing text only, such as letters, numbers and punctuation marks.

The limitation on the number of characters in the file name is a restriction imposed by the DOS operating system that is used on most older PCs. More modern operating systems such as Windows 95 do not have this limitation.

On its own, naming files is not enough. We would still have hundreds or thousands of file names to look at, and it is also possible that several different files could have the same name. We need some way of uniquely identifying files, and we also need some way to organize them.

We can say on which magnetic disk files are stored by identifying the drive. A stand-alone (not networked) PC will typically have one floppy disk drive and one hard disk drive. Each of these is allocated a letter – usually 'A' for the floppy disk drive and 'C' for the hard disk drive. We can identify our file as A:TEXTFILE.TXT if is stored on the floppy disk drive or as C:TEXTFILE.TXT if is stored on the hard disk drive (note the use of the colon to separate the drive identifier from the file name).

This is particularly useful for networked microcomputers. We do not need to know what the file server's hard disk drive is called or even where the file server is. We can simply allocate a drive identifier to it (say 'F') and identify our file as F:TEXTFILE.TXT.

We are not restricted to a single drive identifier for a magnetic disk. We could choose to split the file server disk into two *logical disk drives* and allocate these the identifiers 'F' and 'G'. This is useful because we can place restrictions on one of these disk drives. For example, if we use drive 'F' to hold data and drive 'G' to hold programs, we can prevent any changes to the files on drive 'G'. This gives protection against computer viruses (see Chapter 4).

We are not restricted to data held on our microcomputer and file server. We can allocate a drive identifier to the hard disk of any microcomputer on the network and access this through any other microcomputer. The network operating system (discussed below) is responsible for managing this.

This still leaves us with the problem of organizing files. We do this by setting up directories. For example we can set up a directory called MYDIRECT on the file server. If we store our file in this, we can identify it as F:\MYDIRECT\TEXTFILE.TXT. Note the '\' before both the directory name and the file name. This can also be used if we do not store the file in a directory – we could use F:\TEXTFILE.TXT instead of F:TEXTFILE.TXT for example.

We can set up several levels of directory. For example, we can set up a directory called BANKING within MYDIRECT and identify our file as F:\MYDIRECT\ BANKING\TEXTFILE.TXT. Directory names can have extensions although this facility is rarely used. The combination of drive and directory identifiers (i.e. F:\MYDIRECT\ BANKING in the example) is called the *path* of the file.

10.3 Computer software

The *software* is the element of the computer system that makes the computer carry out our instructions.

Most of the software that you will come across uses a graphical user interface (GUI), and we shall discuss what this means and why it is important.

The only system software we will discuss in this chapter is the operating system. However, two other types of system software are discussed elsewhere in this book – security software in Chapter 4 and browser software in Chapter 14.

Most of the software you will use is application software. In this chapter we shall discuss the standard software tools that form part of the electronic office but there are other types of application software including:

● Bespoke software developed specifically for the organization;

- Software developed for the financial services industry such as Kindle Bankmaster;

- More general software that can be used in a wide range of industries such as general ledger systems.

Graphical user interfaces

Graphical user interfaces have four main components:

- *Windows.* A window is an area of the computer screen. A GUI can have several windows on the screen at the same time, each of which may contain information about a different computer program. We can copy information between windows – for example, copying a table from a spreadsheet into a word processor.

- *Icons.* An icon is a picture that represents a computer program or some data. We can use the mouse to start the computer program from the icon (by moving the cursor to point at the program icon and clicking twice), or to move or copy the data (by moving the cursor to point at the icon, holding the mouse button down and 'dragging' the icon to where we want it).

- *Mouse.* We can move the mouse until the cursor is pointing to the right place on the screen. We can then press (or 'click') one of the buttons on the mouse to tell the computer to carry out an action. The mouse can be used for a number of reasons including:

  - To press a button on the screen instructing the computer to carry out an action;

  - To choose items from a list offered by the computer;

  - To position the cursor on an input form so the user can enter data.

- *Pull-down menus.* GUIs have a menu bar – a list of options – which is usually across the top of the computer screen. If we use the mouse to point at one of the options and click the left mouse button, a more detailed list of options will appear below the option chosen. This is a pull-down menu. We can use the mouse to select the option required.

GUIs are also sometimes called WIMPs after the initial letters of these four components.

GUIs were developed by Xerox at their Palo Alto Research Centre (PARC), and were first commercially used by Apple in their Lisa and Macintosh computers. They provide a very easy way for users to give instructions to the computer. The advantages of using GUIs rather than character-based user interfaces are:

- Without GUIs, users would need to learn a complicated language in order to tell the computer what to do.

- GUIs can be used for communicating with any computer program. This makes it quicker to train people because GUIs are so easy to use. It also makes it much easier to train people to use different computer programs because systems that use GUIs look very similar to the user.

Operating system

The operating system is the program that controls the computer. This is true even of devices that we may not think of as computers – for example, MasterCard have developed the MULTOS operating system for use on smart cards.

It is also true of networks, particularly LANs. PCs networked to form a LAN usually need an operating system, which usually runs on the file server, although some computer operating systems (such as Unix) can control networks without additional software.

LAN operating systems usually run 'on top of' the operating systems for the individual workstations – the LAN operating system is in overall control. This is not true of WANs controlled from mainframe computers, where the mainframe operating system stays in control. Although system software is still required to run the network, we call this a transaction processing (TP) monitor rather than a network operating system.

A computer with a single processor, for example a PC, can only carry out one task at a time. PCs are able to use *multitasking* to carry out several tasks apparently simultaneously. The operating system schedules work so that only one task is using the processor at any one time. Other tasks in the computer may be suspended or they may be using an input, output or storage device.

We shall not discuss how multitasking works in any great detail, except to say that it relies on three capabilities:

- *Priorities.* Each different task may be given a different priority. High-priority tasks are given more use of the processor than lower-priority tasks.

- *Interrupts.* Tasks cannot use the processor when they are using input, output or storage devices. When the operation on the device is complete, it sends an interrupt to tell the operating system that it has finished and the task can be restarted.

- *Timeslicing.* Each task is allocated an amount of time for which it can use the processor. When this time slot has been completed the task will return control to the operating system.

You may also come across the terms *multiprogramming* and *multiprocessing*. Multiprogramming means that the computer can run more than one program apparently at the same time. It is very similar to multitasking. Multiprocessing means that the computer has more than one processor and can run more than one task at the same time – it can run one task for each processor. Minicomputers and mainframes usually have a number of processors, each of which is capable of multi-tasking.

The features of the operating system include:

- *Scheduling tasks.* This includes setting priorities, handling interrupts, allocating time slots and deciding which task will next get use of the processor.

- *Managing input,* output and storage devices. Tasks can only access these devices through the operating system and, as we have seen, when they have finished the operation requested they will send an interrupt to return control to the operating system.

- *Memory management.* Allocating tasks sufficient RAM for their needs and also recovering RAM when it is no longer required. Also protecting the integrity of RAM – for example, stopping one task from trying to use RAM which is already in use by another task.

- *Error correction.* Dealing with any error conditions that may arise, either in software or in the hardware.

- *Communication with the operator.* Informing the operator of any situations that require operator intervention. Allowing the operator to enter commands, including changing task priorities and halting tasks. The operating system will usually keep the operator informed about what is happening to the tasks running on the computer – on a PC this often takes the form of a *status bar* at the bottom of the screen.

There may also be certain utilities that are not part of the operating system but which it controls. A common example on mainframe computers is a sort utility, which can be used to sort data files into the required order.

Word processors

Word processors have largely replaced typewriters in the office. A word processor consists of a workstation or PC with a printer (usually a laser printer) attached running a word processing program. Common examples of word processing programs are Microsoft Word for Windows and Lotus Ami Pro.

Whereas documents produced on a typewriter are output directly to paper, word processors hold the document being worked on in storage. Word processors hold documents mainly as files on magnetic disk, although small documents may be held in RAM while they are being worked on.

The features available in word processors include:

- *Features to do with files.* The ability to save documents as files and to load them when needed for changes or more work. The ability to save and load files in several ways – for example as plain text or in a form suitable for a different word processor. The ability to include other types of file in a document – for example pictures or spreadsheets.

- *Navigation features.* The ability to move through a document using the arrow keys and the page up, page down, home and end keys on the keyboard. The ability to include bookmarks and to go directly to any bookmark, page or section in the document. The ability to find particular words or phrases, or even particular formats. Bookmarks can also be used for purposes such as putting page references into a document.

- *Editing features.* The ability to select blocks of text and delete them, or to move or copy them within the same document or in another document. The ability to replace some or all occurrences of a particular word, phrase or format. The ability to mark changes to a document.

- *Formatting features.* The ability to show text in various sizes or fonts, or <u>underlined,</u> in **bold** or *italicised.* Paragraphs can also be shaded or outlined.

- *Layout features.* The ability to print a document with the long edge of the paper down the side (*portrait*) or across the top (*landscape*), and to create documents in newspaper-like columns. The ability to add headers and footers to pages. The ability to include tables of contents, tables of figures and indexes in documents.

- *'What you see is what you get' or WYSIWYG features.* The ability to see the document on the computer screen exactly as it will look when printed. Hence the ability to check the appearance of a document and make final adjustments before printing it.

- *Tools.* The ability to check documents for spelling or grammatical style. The ability to merge documents with other documents or with files, for example to produce letters from a list of addresses (*mailmerge*). The ability to include information about the document, for example the author, the page number or the number of words.

- *Interface features and macros.* The ability to set up forms for the input of data. The ability to run simple programs – these can be recorded to copy a series of actions or they can be written in a macro language. Macros can also be set up to run automatically when the document is opened or closed – this is a cause of security problems, and macro viruses are one of the most important sources of virus infection (see Chapter 4).

One of the main advantages of using a word processor is that it is very easy to correct mistakes. Instead of retyping the whole document or using correction fluid, the document can be reloaded from disk, corrected and reprinted. This allows word processors to be used by people who do not have particularly good typing skills.

Spreadsheets

A spreadsheet is a computer view of the accountant's 'analysis pad', allowing financial information to be shown as a series of columns so that it can be analysed by type of expense. Spreadsheets show data as tables and can also be used for simple databases. Spreadsheets were among the first computer programs to be developed for the microcomputer, and their use has spread far beyond accountancy.

Spreadsheets contain a number of *cells* into which we can enter data. Spreadsheets were originally two dimensional, with the cells arranged as rows and columns. They are now usually three dimensional and include a number of sheets. Microsoft Excel 97 allows 65,536 rows, 256 columns and 16 sheets – over 268 million cells.

The data that can be entered includes text, numeric data and formulae. Numeric data includes dates, times and percentages as well as integers and decimals. A wide range of formulae can be entered, ranging from simple arithmetic operators such as add through to complex financial, statistical and trigonometric formulae. Formulae can refer to cells in the spreadsheet, and the sheet name, row and column number are used as the address of the cell.

The features available in spreadsheets include:

● *File, navigation, editing and layout features* similar to those available in word processors. Some tools, such as the ability to check spelling, are available, as are the interface features and macro language.

Formatting features include the ability to change the width of all cells in a column or the height of all cells in a row. Numbers, dates and times can be shown in various formats including (for numbers) as currency amounts or fractions. Special effects such as shading or boxing can be used to highlight groups of cells.

● *Mathematical features*. The ability to carry out a wide range of mathematical operations, including financial features such as discounted cashflow calculations and statistical features such as calculating standard deviations.

● *Charting and graphing features*. The ability to show data as charts and graphs. Most of the common graph formats, including line graphs, bar charts, stepped bar charts and pie charts, may be used.

● *Goal seeking*. The ability to enter the answer required and allow the spreadsheet to calculate what values other variables must take. So if a return on investment of 20% is required, this can be entered into the formula and the spreadsheet will calculate the level of sales needed to achieve this.

● *Consolidation features*. The ability to consolidate data from different sources into a single spreadsheet. This can be used to consolidate financial information from different departments, products or markets to give an overall financial position.

● *Database features*. Spreadsheets can be used to provide simple databases. Common examples include holiday rotas and telephone lists.

Databases

A database is an organised collection of data controlled by a database management system.

There are a number of different types of database, of which the most important is the relational database. This is the only type we shall consider in this book. A relational database is made up of a number of tables, each of which stores a specific type of data – for example, there will be a customer table and an account table.

Each table consists of a number of records, each of which refers to one occurrence of that type of data. For example, the customer table will have one record for each customer. The records are made up of a number of different fields, each of which contains an item of information about that record. For example, John Smith's record on the customer table will include his name, address and date of birth. Records are also called rows and fields are also called columns.

You will notice that the terms used in describing a database are similar to those used in describing both data files and spreadsheets. The similarity in terminology between these data files and databases can be explained because early computer software used data files where now we would use a database – the same terms were carried forward to the more modern technology. The use of 'rows' and 'columns' is unique to relational databases, and both these and spreadsheets present data as a series of tables – we have already discussed the use of spreadsheets for simple databases.

To create a relationship between two tables in a relational database, we put a common item of data in both tables. This is called a *key*. Let us consider an example:

Customer Table

Customer No.	Customer Name	Date of Birth	Sex	Occupation
111111	Ann Barrow	12-Mar-45	Female	Manager
222222	Colin Davies	03-Apr-56	Male	Accountant

Account Table

Account No.	**Customer No.**	Account Type	Currency	Balance
12345678	**222222**	Current	Sterling	376·00
23456789	**111111**	Deposit	US Dollar	5,000·00
34567890	**222222**	Deposit	Sterling	528·00

Here we have two tables. There is a common item of data (Customer No.) in both tables, and this defines the relationship between them. Ann Barrow has Customer No. 222222, and we can use this to find her record on the Customer Table *and* the record of all her accounts on the Account Table.

Customer No. is called the *primary key* for the Customer Table. This means that only one record in the table can have a particular value of Customer No., which allows Customer No. to be used uniquely to identify this record.

Each of the customer's accounts has the same value of Customer No. – it is not unique for the Account Table. We use it if we want to get data from the Customer Table, for example if we want to show the balance of a particular account (from the Account Table) *and* the customer's name and address (from the Customer Table). We say that the Customer No. is a *foreign key* on the Account Table because it is used as a reference to another table.

The primary key for the Account Table will be Account No.

Database management systems

The database is kept in order by the Database Management System (DBMS). The DBMS provides a buffer between application programs and the data. Instead of reading the data directly, they ask the DBMS to get the data for them.

This means that the DBMS can store the data where and how it likes. It does not need to organise the data in a way that suits the applications programs but can organize and store it in the most efficient way. We can show this as a diagram:

Figure 10.5

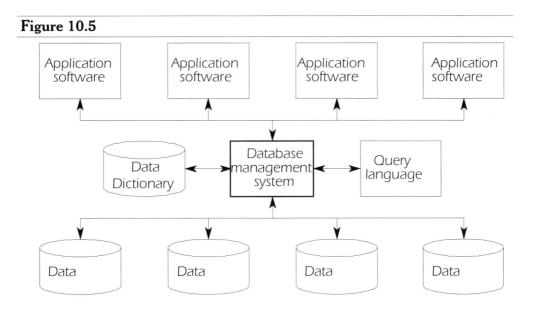

The DBMS also looks after the security and integrity of the data. If a program requests access to data, the DBMS checks that it is allowed this access. Some programs may only be allowed to read data (not to add or change it) or some data may be very confidential and only accessible to certain programs. The DBMS also keeps the database tidy, making sure that data that is not needed is removed.

The DBMS needs to store information about the database. This is held in the *data dictionary*. This is itself a database and is managed by the DBMS, but the data it holds is concerned with the databases (including itself!) managed by the DBMS.

A *query language* is a computer language designed to access data held in a database. Early query languages would only work with one specific DBMS but there is now a standard (Structured Query Language or SQL) that can be used with most relational databases.

Electronic office databases

There are considerable differences between databases designed for minicomputers or mainframe computers and the electronic office databases found on PCs. This is because minicomputer or mainframe databases are designed for large amounts of data and large numbers of users, whereas electronic office databases are usually designed for a single user and a relatively small amount of data. For example, electronic office databases do not have the same security and integrity features as minicomputer and mainframe computer databases.

Features specific to electronic office databases include:

- *File, navigation, editing, formatting and layout features* similar to those available in spreadsheets. Some tools, such as the ability to check spelling, are available, as are the interface features and macro language.

- *Direct manipulation of data.* Electronic office database management systems allow the user to manipulate the data directly rather than having to go through either a program or the query language.

- *Forms, query and macro languages.* Forms can be used to design a screen for the direct input of data. We have already discussed query and macro languages, which allow data to be accessed in a variety of ways.

- *Report writers*, allowing us to produce simple reports.

- *Utilities* allowing us to sort the data or to set filters to include only records that meet certain conditions.

- They are sold as 'shrink wrapped' packages, and installation is very simple. Minicomputer and mainframe databases must be tailored to the technical environment in which they will operate, and installation is a lengthy and complicated process.

- They have links to other electronic office products such as word processors and spreadsheets.

Electronic mail

Electronic mail (or *email*) uses computers to send messages to other computers over telecommunications links. Email can be sent over the Internet (discussed in Chapter 14) or through products such as Lotus cc:mail.

The features available on email include:

- File, navigation and editing features similar to but more limited than those available in word processors. File features include the ability to save messages to archive for long-term storage. Messages are entered into the email system as plain text, and the only formatting features generally available are control over the message font and colour. Some tools, such as the ability to check spelling, are available.

- *Attachments.* The ability to attach files (for example, word processor files or spreadsheets) to messages. The recipient can read the file using the software with which it was created or can usually look at or print it directly from the email system.

- *Address book and mailing list features.* The ability to store email addresses in an address book. The ability to set up mailing lists, allowing the same information to be sent to all recipients as a single message.

- *Bulletin board features.* The ability to publish information on a bulletin board, which can be read either by anyone with access to the email system or to a specified group.

- *Rules-processing features.* The ability to define rules that allow messages to be automatically filed or forwarded. The ability to nominate a 'delegate' to deal with someone's email while they are absent.

Email has advantages over both the telephone and letters. Unlike the telephone it leaves a permanent record, which can be filed (either electronically or after printing). It is faster than sending letters, and the person receiving it can read it into another computer program directly – a letter would have to be retyped or scanned, for example. It is generally cheaper to send than a facsimile (fax) message, although email systems can sometimes be used to send messages to a fax machine.

Computer software can be 'mail enabled'. This means that it will send messages by email under specified circumstances. This can operate over the Internet or through products such as cc:mail.

Schedulers and organizers

Schedulers and organizers are the electronic equivalent of time management systems such as Filofax.

The features available on schedulers and organizers include:

- *Electronic diary and planner features.* The ability to record appointments in an electronic diary, either as individual appointments or as regular repeating appointments. An electronic planner for recording holidays etc. which can also be linked to the electronic diary.

- *Group scheduling features.* The ability to link schedulers and organizers over a telecommunications network and to book meetings involving a number of people. The ability to look for a time when all participants are available.

- *Address book features.* The ability to record names, addresses and telephone numbers. The ability to telephone people automatically. Telephone calls can also be linked to the electronic diary.

- *Notepad and to do list features.* The ability to record notes and 'to do' items. To do items can also be linked to the electronic diary.

- *Security features.* The ability to limit access to the scheduler and organiser, either by creating an access list of those authorized or by marking individual items as confidential.

Workgroup computing

Workgroup computing allows people to work together in groups even if they are in different physical locations. It uses computer systems and telecommunications networks to allow people to communicate and to coordinate their work.

An example of a workgroup computing system is Lotus Notes. This is a text database, and differs from relational databases in that the information in the database is held as large blocks of text rather than in fields. Lotus Notes does have fields but these are used mainly for keys.

The features available in workgroup computing systems include:

- *File, navigation and editing features* similar to those available in word processors.

- *Database features.* The ability to define keys, which can be used to present the information in the database as a series of 'views' allowing users to see the data in the order most relevant to their needs. The ability to produce forms to enter data.

- *Audit trail features.* The ability to record who has proposed changes to documents and what has happened to them. An approach taken in products such as Lotus Notes is to record proposed changes as 'responses' to the original document and comments on these proposals as 'responses to responses'.

- *Knowledge management features such as search engines.* The ability of the workgroup computer system to act as a 'corporate memory' recording management experience. Knowledge management is discussed in Chapter 14.

- *Replication.* The ability to change copies of the database held on different computers and to reconcile these changes at a later stage. This allows workgroup computing systems to be used on portable computers and any changes to be added to a central database when the portable computer is next linked to a telecommunications network.

Many of the features of workgroup computing systems are now available using intranet software. Some features have also been incorporated into word processors, for example the ability to combine comments from different reviewers into a document.

Document image processing

Document image processing (DIP) uses a scanner to record the image of documents coming into the system. Instead of physically moving the document between different processes, its electronic image is transmitted over the computer network.

The features available on DIP systems include:

- *Data storage and retrieval features.* Documents are usually stored on a database held on an optical disk 'jukebox' attached to a mainframe computer. The document must be indexed to identify the customer, the date received and the type of document. Bar codes are sometimes used to identify the document type. The ability rapidly to retrieve any document on information such as customer, document type and date.

- *Concurrent working.* As the document is held as an image, several different people can work on it at the same time.

A DIP system might be as shown in the following diagram:

Figure 10.6

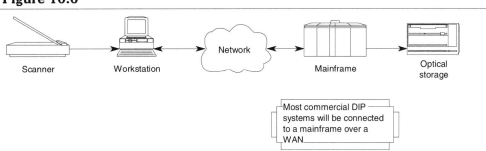

One advantage of DIP is that documents can be stored away from the office, saving valuable office space and reducing costs. Because the computer controls the workflow there is less chance of a document being lost or forgotten.

DIP can be used on its own or with an optical character recognition (OCR) system. OCR allows typed or printed characters to be interpreted. Some OCR systems can interpret handwriting, especially block capitals. OCR is sometimes used to interpret as much of the document as it can, with an operator verifying the OCR system's interpretation and entering any information the OCR system was unable to understand.

DIP can also be used as part of a workflow automation system.

Workflow automation

Most computer systems are designed to automate a single process (for example opening an account). The overall workflow of the organization – how the application is received, what checks are carried out, where documentation is filed – remains largely manual.

Workflow automation systems automate everything from the initial receipt of the document through to final archiving or disposal. Instead of the operator deciding what to do and using the computer to support individual processes, the computer controls the sequence of events.

Common examples include telemarketing and telephone banking systems. These rely on scripting to tell the agent exactly what action to take during the call. They also use the statistics produced by the system to monitor the agents' work. These systems are described in Chapter 11.

The features available in workflow automation systems include:

- *Identification and routing features.* The ability to identify the type of document and to send (route) it to an operator with the appropriate skills.

- *Queue management features.* The ability to monitor the number of items of each type in a 'queue' waiting to be processed. This allows work to be switched to different operators to ensure that priority items are completed and to avoid large backlogs of one type of work. Problems and errors are also handled using queues – if an operator is uncertain what to do or takes an action which causes an error the work item is routed to a supervisor for resolution.

- *Modelling features*. The ability to describe the transaction in terms of a process model. Some workflow automation systems allow the flow of work through the process model to be simulated, which allows inefficiencies and bottlenecks to be identified. These models are used in business process reengineering, as we discussed in Chapter 7.

Workflow automation is often used in conjunction with DIP. This might work as follows:

- Documents are marked with bar codes, similar to those used to identify goods in supermarkets. When the document is scanned the bar code is used to identify the document type.

- OCR is used to recognize as much of the information on the document as possible. This minimizes the amount of keying required of the operator.

- Workflow is used to route the document to an operator who will identify the document (if this has not been done automatically) and enter information that has not been recognised through OCR.

- The document may be processed by the same operator, but will often be routed to a different operator who is currently dealing with documents of that type.

A system combining workflow with DIP might be as shown in the following diagram:

Figure 10.7

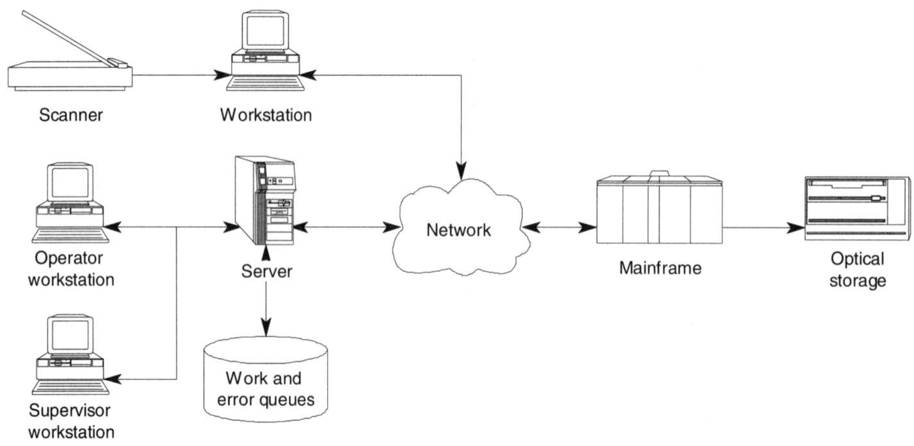

Desktop publishing

Desktop publishing (DTP) systems are used to produce very high quality printed material including both text and graphics. The text is usually taken from a word processing program, although DTP systems have some word processing capability. The graphics often include photographs entered using a scanner as well as diagrams produced using graphics software.

The features available on DTP systems include:

- *File, navigation and editing features* similar to those available in word processors.

- *Formatting and layout features.* DTP programs allow very good control over the layout of documents – text can be put in columns, columns can be reshaped or resized, text can 'flow' round pictures, etc. They also have good facilities for building tables of contents and indexes. *Style sheets* can be used to make sure that documents produced are similar in appearance.

  Documents can be shown precisely as they will appear on paper (WYSIWYG), and special computer screens the same size as A3 or A4 paper are often installed on workstations used for DTP. A wide range of different print fonts and sizes can be used. The spacing between individual letters can be changed ('kerning' or 'tracking') to make it seem more regular – without this letter pairs such as AW will appear to be more widely spaced than letter pairs such as HN.

- *Output features.* Some DTP systems can provide output as print-ready files, which can be used directly by commercial printing equipment.

Early DTP programs were intended to be used with a word processing program and had very limited word processing facilities. More modern DTP programs have most of the capabilities of a word processing program. Similarly, word processing programs now offer many of the same layout options as DTP programs – for example kerning and the ability to flow text round pictures.

One of the main reasons for this is developments in microcomputer hardware. Word processors were originally designed to be used on low-cost PCs. DTP programs were originally designed for more powerful and expensive workstations equipped with high-resolution screens. However, the development of low-cost, high-power microcomputers with high-resolution screens and large amounts of disk storage has allowed this convergence of word processors and DTP programs.

Graphics and presentation graphics software

Graphics software includes any type of computer software that can be used to create pictures. This includes simple drawing software such as Microsoft Paintbrush as well as software designed to be used in professional presentations such as Microsoft Powerpoint.

The features available in all graphics software include:

- *Drawing features.* The ability to draw using a mouse. Another input device that can be used is the digitizing pad or graphics tablet – these are usually used by graphics designers, who require great accuracy.

- *Palettes of standard shapes and line styles.* The ability to include standard shapes such as rectangles, triangles and circles in diagrams. The ability to include various styles of line, for example dotted line, double lines and thick lines, and to add various types of arrow to either or both ends of the lines.

- *Text features.* The ability to include text information in various fonts, sizes and styles.

- *Colour control features.* The ability to define outline and fill colours for shapes. The ability to add special effects such as shadow.

Some graphics software is designed for specific purposes. One example is organization diagramming software, which can be used to draw organization charts (*organigrams*). Another example is graphing and charting software, which can be used with spreadsheets to produce many more types of graph. There is also industry-specific graphics software such as computer-aided design (CAD) software used by architects and production engineers, and production engineers, and flowchart software used in the design of IT systems.

The additional features available in presentation graphics software include:

- *Templates.* The ability to define standard backgrounds, headers and footers for presentations.

- *Handouts and notes.* The ability to produce handouts and speakers' notes to accompany presentations.

- *Presentation features.* The ability to present a series of slides, applying effects such as fades between slides. This can be achieved using a cathode ray tube projector (often called a 'Barco' after one of the most important makes) or a *projection tablet* (which fits onto an overhead projector).

Two other types of software which fall under this general category are:

- *Photo CD editors*, that are designed to allow photographs captured on CD to be edited. This is a relatively new type of graphics application, which is of great commercial importance. It allows photographs to be retouched and colours to be changed. Colour pictures can be converted to black and white, while various techniques can be used to ensure the clearest possible picture.

- *Clip art libraries and photo CD libraries.* These contain images produced by graphic artists or professional photographers. The images can be incorporated into a graphics package and changed (sometimes) or added to. Many graphics packages already have their own clip art libraries but these are also sold separately. One feature that is sometimes found is the ability to show the images on the screen as a reduced size *thumbnail*, making it easier to choose the image required.

11

DATA PROCESSING

11.1 Transaction processing

Many applications process transactions. A transaction is a logical piece of work such as an account opening or a cheque encashment. Applications hold data in master files or databases. Transactions entered into the computer are used to update the master files.

We can classify applications that process transaction as batch, remote batch, or demand. Batch and remote batch processing applications both involve a delay between the transaction being recorded and the master files being updated. Demand processing includes on-line processing, real-time processing, client/server and Internet technology applications, all of which involve the master files being updated when the transaction is entered into the computer.

The approach to transaction processing has changed as IT has evolved:

Figure 11.1

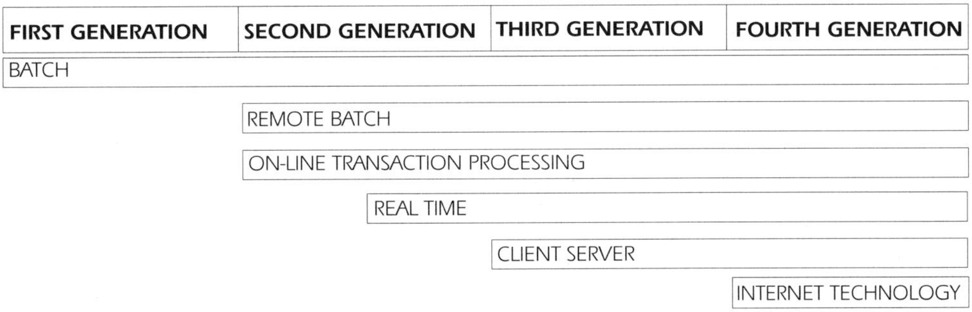

FIRST GENERATION	SECOND GENERATION	THIRD GENERATION	FOURTH GENERATION
BATCH			
	REMOTE BATCH		
	ON-LINE TRANSACTION PROCESSING		
		REAL TIME	
		CLIENT SERVER	
			INTERNET TECHNOLOGY

Batch processing

In batch processing, transactions are collected into batches of similar items. For example, a batch might contain all cheques presented over the counter. These are entered into the computer, where they are recorded on a transaction file, which is used to update the master files at a later time – often overnight.

Many of the financial organizations' older systems rely heavily on batch processing. This is particularly true of the high-street banks, whose main accounting systems use batch processing. On-line data entry and remote batch processing are increasingly replacing batch voucher processing, with the important exception of the clearing system.

Financial organizations use batch systems for three reasons:

- Batch processing uses IT resources very efficiently, especially where very large numbers of transactions are involved.

- Many financial processes naturally take place outside the normal working day (e.g. interest calculation, charges calculation, statements, standing orders) and would not benefit from the higher costs associated with on-line or real-time processing.

- Other financial processes were designed round the use of batch processing. A good example of this is clearing, where the traditional three-day clearing cycle was based on the physical delivery of cheques outside working hours. As a result, the financial organizations have a considerable investment in batch systems to maintain.

The simplest form of batch processing works as follows:

- Forms and documents that need processing are collected during the day.

- At the end of the working day, the forms and documents are sorted by type. Each separate type of form or document will form one or more separate batches. If there are a large number of forms or documents of a specific type, this may be split into a number of batches each containing (typically) between 20 and 100 forms or documents.

- A batch header slip will be completed. This may contain a batch number (which allows the batch to be identified), a batch type (indicating the type of form or document), a count of the number of items in the batch, and a batch total (the total of the amounts on the forms or documents in the batch).

- The batch will be entered into the computer. The batch entry system will also check the batch header information (item count and batch total). The items in the batch will be written to a transaction file, which may also include a batch header record (containing the batch header information) and a batch trailer record to tell the system when it has finished processing a batch.

- The transaction file will be used to update a master file. This may be a sequential file, for example a file of accounts sorted in account number order, in which event the update process will involve the following steps:

  - The transaction file will be sorted into the same order as the master file.

  - The transaction file will then be matched against the master file, with the changes recorded on the transaction file being applied to the master file records that have the same key.

  - A new copy of the master file will be created, based on the original master file and the changes from the transaction file.

  - Input and error reports are produced, allowing the results of the update to be checked.

We can show the batch update process as a diagram:

Figure 11.2: Batch update process

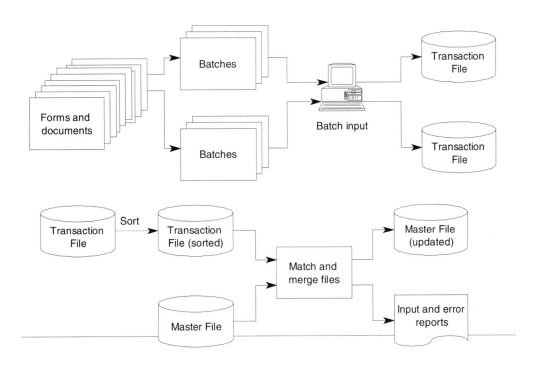

This approach to batch processing is still quite common. It is particularly effective where there is a high *hit rate* – a high proportion of records on the master file will be changed by the transaction file.

Where the hit rate is low, this may be inefficient. In this event, we could store the master file either as a different type of file or as a database, allowing us to go directly to the record we want to change. Instead of creating a new master file, we will make the changes directly to the master file we are using. We could enter batches in exactly the same way as described above, or we could use remote batch.

Remote batch processing

Remote batch processing differs in that transactions are entered into the computer immediately they are received. However, when they have been entered they are still placed on a transaction file. The master files can be updated at the end of the day or, as is becoming increasingly common, as a background task during the day when sufficient computer resources are availble.

Remote batch systems do not include the batch checking (record counts, batch totals) described above, and may work as follows:

● Forms and documents that need processing can be entered when they are received or at any convenient point during the day. The data entry system will carry out some validation because there is no batch checking.

● When the transaction is entered it will be placed on a *queue* – in effect a temporary transaction file. Transactions in the queue will be processed in the order in which they are entered.

● When the transaction reaches the front of the queue *and* the computer has sufficient spare resources to process it, the record(s) to be changed will be read and updated. Note that remote batch processing as a background task is only effective where the master file records can be accessed directly – usually through a database.

Alternatively, the processing can be carried out at the end of the day, in which event the master file can be sequential or allow direct access.

Remote batch processing is replacing the older approach as more forms and documents are entered directly into the computer by front-office staff.

On-line transaction processing

On-line processing applications also involve the transactions' being entered into the computer immediately they are received. However, the transaction immediately updates the master file.

On-line processing works as follows:

● As forms and documents are completed, they are entered into the system.

● Each item entered will have a transaction code. The system will use this to decide which program will need to process it.

● The program will validate and process the item and update the master file, which again is usually stored as a database.

Real-time processing

Real-time processing applications are a special type of on-line processing application. The important difference is that an application only involves real-time processing if *the event which causes* the transaction is almost simultaneous with its being entered into the computer and the database being updated.

Consider a dealing system as an example. If the dealer enters the details into the system while carrying out the deal, and the payment instructions and account updates are produced immediately, this is a real-time system. If the dealer completes a dealing slip and the details are entered by the back office, this is either an on-line processing system (if payment instructions and account updates are produced immediately) or a remote batch system (if account updates are processed later – for example overnight).

Real-time systems work in much the same way as on-line systems. As the originating event is taking place at the same time as the real-time transaction, it is important that the system performance is acceptable and that the user is not kept waiting for a response that requires a database.

If forms are used they will be completed on the computer screen. Some real-time transactions, such as ATM withdrawals, do not require forms.

In practice there is often little difference between on-line transaction processing systems and real-time systems. Even though the data is not updated simultaneously with the event causing the transaction, the update usually happens seconds or minutes later. This is sometimes called *pseudo-real-time*.

Client/server and Internet technology

We touched on client/server and Internet technology in Chapter 1, and we shall be giving more detailed consideration of client/server in Chapter 16 and of the Internet in Chapter 14. Both are forms of demand processing.

11.2   Data centres and networks

In Chapter 1 we discussed how the mainframe computer located in a data centre was the driving force behind the first generation of information technology. Although the 'death of the mainframe' has been predicted at regular intervals since the start of the third generation in the mid-1980s, data centres are still alive and well. Why have these information technology dinosaurs survived?

We can identify a number of factors:

● Mainframe computers offer better data security (discussed in Chapter 4) than many of the alternatives. Data centres offer strict control over environmental conditions, reducing the risk of hardware failure. Techniques such as checkpointing and logging were originally developed for mainframe computers and are most effective in this environment.

Client/server and web environments are not insecure in terms of data. Techniques such as mirroring and striping are used to protect sensitive data where rapid recovery is a requirement and can be used for business-critical systems such as dealing systems. However, mainframe computers are generally preferred where the requirement is secure processing of very large amounts of data.

● By locating mainframe computers in data centres we have more central control over data. With two or three data centres accessible by a small number of staff it is easy to apply physical security measures such as security badges and airlocks, and to ensure that sensitive data is not removed from the building without authorization. The data centre can be designed to be secure against a wide range of possible disasters (the 'Jumbo jet landing on the roof' scenario) and the computers can be protected against environmental damage by installing backup generators and protecting the computer rooms against dust, humidity and static electricity.

- Mainframe computers are more efficient for some types of processing. A surprisingly large number of computer systems continue to work in a similar way to the batch processing systems of the first generation. Unless there is a requirement for information to be up to date, large volumes of transactions with a high hit rate are most efficiently processed on a mainframe computer running in batch mode.

- Many systems from the first and second generation are still in service in the late 1990s! Financial services organizations invested considerable resources into the development of these old (legacy) systems and there was no commercial incentive to replace these. The 'millennium bug' problem of the change of year from 1999 to 2000 has provided an incentive to replace some of these systems, but many are little changed.

  These legacy systems were designed to run on mainframe computers. Although there have been occasional attempts to move some legacy systems to minicomputers or servers (called downsizing or rightsizing) these have rarely been effective, and most of these systems still require mainframes.

However, it is clear that the roles of the mainframe and the data centre are now very different from the first and second generation. The third generation saw the transfer of responsibility for processing from the mainframe to servers and workstations located in branches. The fourth generation has continued this trend, and mainframes are increasingly seen as 'data servers' providing a robust source of data to the network.

Wide area networks

Financial services organizations use wide area networks (WANs) to connect workstations in their branches and offices to their data centres. We can look at the network as a funnel down which data is concentrated towards the data centres:

Figure 11.3

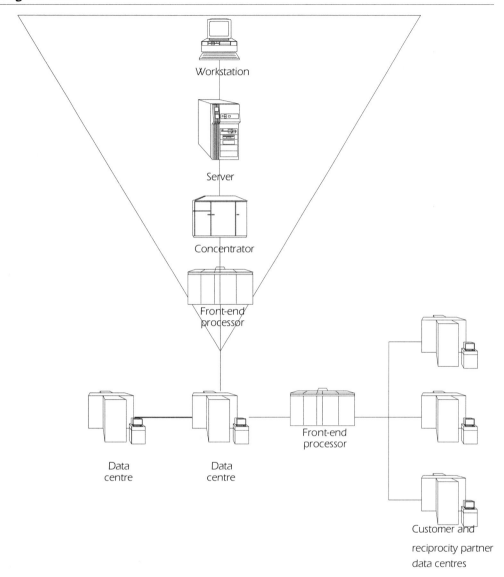

Workstation

Server

Concentrator

Front-end processor

Data centre

Data centre

Front-end processor

Data centre

Data centre

Customer and reciprocity partner data centres

Workstations

A workstation is any device through which the user can interact with the system. In many financial services organizations this will now be a PC connected to the network, although it may also be a terminal computer or another device such as network computers (discussed in Chapter 14).

Workstations are generally robust, and there are sufficient workstations in most branches or offices to provide contingency in the event of one failing.

Workstations are generally linked to each other and to a server to form a local area network (LAN). We discussed LANs in Chapter 10.

Servers

We use the word 'server' here as an abbreviation for file server. We shall discuss the idea of client/server in Chapter 16, and we discussed the other types of server that may be found in Chapter 10.

A file server is a more powerful computer that controls the LAN. A fast PC with sufficient memory and disk storage can be used as a server. Programs and data are stored on the server and backups are taken from it.

Servers can be mirrored to provide contingency. Two servers are used, each controlling half of the network, and all data is copied between them. If one server fails the other will take over the entire network. This is only used where it is essential that the network continues to operate without interruption.

It is possible to design the system to allow users to work *off line*. Data can be entered through the workstation and used to update the database at a later stage (effectively operating as remote batch). As real-time and pseudo-real-time applications become more important this has become less common.

The server is linked, directly or through a *gateway*, to the financial services organization's wide area network. The type of connection will depend on the amount of information to be sent:

- Where very large amounts of data are to be sent (as with a process centre) or where speed is very important (as with a call centre) a high-speed digital line will be used.

- Large amounts of data (as with a large branch) will be sent over a digital line leased from the telecommunications supplier.

- Smaller amounts may be sent over a leased analogue line or a public digital network such as ISDN (integrated services digital network).

- Public analogue networks (PSTNs or public switched telephone networks) are used where data will be sent only occasionally. Branches and offices may use PSTNs for contingency in the event of failure of their main links.

Concentrators

Concentrators collect messages sent from a number of servers and send them to the data centre over high speed links. There may be several levels of regional concentrator between the server and the data centre.

This allows cheaper telecommunications links to be used for branches and offices that do not need to send large amounts of data. The concentrator allows the most efficient use to be made of high-speed links into the data centre.

Connections from concentrators to data centres will almost always be digital. Some larger branches and offices may also have digital links but many branches and offices are likely to use analogue links for the foreseeable future.

The main network, whether it is digital or analogue, will use telephone lines leased from the telecommunications supplier. Contingency arrangements should allow every branch or office at least two routes into two different data centres. These will often use dial-up lines, by which the branch simply dials into the PSTN using a modem and low-speed analogue line to connect to a packet switched network. The data centres, regional concentrators and possibly some branches may have direct links to a packet switched network.

Front-end processors

Data coming into the data centre may pass through a front-end processor before it is passed to the mainframe. This provides an extra level of security by validating the data received and rejecting anything that may cause problems for the mainframe. It also improves performance, both by rejecting invalid data (reducing the mainframe's workload) and by prioritizing data received.

Firewalls, discussed in Chapter 15, offer many of the functions of a front-end processor.

Data centres

There is usually a minimum of two data centres. High-speed links allow the rapid transfer of data between them, and there is sufficient spare processing capacity to allow the network to continue operating even if one data centre fails (although there may be a reduced level of service).

The data centre contains the mainframe computer. We shall not discuss mainframe computers in any detail but their main features include the following:

● They are much more powerful than PCs and can deal with many hundreds of users at the same time.

● They are very robust and fail very rarely – data centres are air conditioned and dust free to prevent failure due to environmental factors.

● They have a number of processors and are capable of multiprocessing as well as multi-tasking.

The trend is towards 'dark computer rooms' in which the mainframe computers run without operator intervention, following a work schedule. Robots are used for physical tasks such as changing tapes and disks.

Customer access and external networks

Customers (office banking), external information services and external networks (for example ATM networks, EFTPOS and EDI) will be connected to the data centres. A front-end processor will usually be used to handle any differences in standards and, especially for office banking, to provide additional security features such as authentication and encryption. Firewalls will usually be used to prevent hacking.

Data communications

Computers and telephone lines carry information in different ways. Computers carry information digitally – as if it were a series of 0s and 1s. This can be compared to a digital clock, where the numbers only change every minute or second. Signals in the computer are made up of two different frequencies, and might look like this:

Figure 11.4

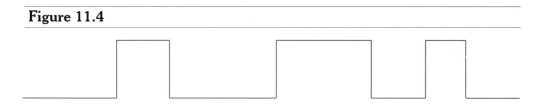

Most telephone lines use analogue transmission – carrying information as a continuously varying signal. This can be compared with an analogue clock face, where the hands seem to go round continuously. Signals sent over analogue telephone lines are of a range of frequencies that vary continuously (the *carrier*) with the information being carried as a small distortion to the carrier. The carrier wave might look like this:

Figure 11.5

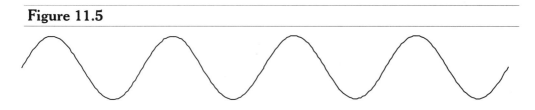

Therefore if we want to send information over the public switched telephone network (PSTN) we need to convert it from digital to analogue form before transmission, and back into digital form on receipt. To do this we need a piece of equipment called a *modem* (short for modulator-demodulator). The modem converts (or modulates) a digital signal from a computer into an analogue signal, which can be sent over a telephone line. At the other end, a second modem demodulates the analogue signal back into digital form for the computer.

The alternative is to send the information in digital form. LANs use digital transmission and do not need a modem. Instead of using the PSTN to send information over a WAN, we can use a digital telephone line instead. BT offers a national network of digital lines called ISDN (Integrated Services Digital Network). This has a number of advantages:

● A modem is not needed.

● The lines can carry more information.

- Messages can be corrected automatically and so are more likely to be received correctly.

Digital lines are more expensive than analogue lines, but their use is becoming increasingly common, especially where large amounts of data need to be transferred at high speed.

Another data communications device that might be included in a WAN is a multiplexer. A multiplexer is a device that allows several terminals to share the same telephone line. We could, for example, connect five terminals to the multiplexer. The multiplexer would then be connected to one modem, and messages from all five terminals would be sent over a single telephone line. There would be one modem at the other end, and the messages would go to another multiplexer. This would separate (demultiplex) the messages into five sets of messages – one from each terminal – for processing by the mainframe computer. Using a multiplexer allows us to reduce the number and cost of telephone lines we need, but the mainframe computer still needs to be able to handle one connection for each terminal.

Packet switched networks

Instead of relying on a permanent link between the terminal and the mainframe computer, the message can 'switch' across a number of telephone exchanges. The link is set up only when the message is sent. The information is sent as packets, and this is called a *packet switched network*.

Compare this with making a long-distance phone call. When we dial, the exchange to which the phone is connected will take the call. It will use the dialling code to find the right exchange for the person we are trying to call, and it will set up the connection. It may have to go through intermediate exchanges to do this, especially if we are phoning abroad.

Packet switching works in exactly the same way. The message is broken up into packets, the first of which contains address information (equivalent to the dialling code and number). When the first packet is sent, the exchange will work out how to get the message to its destination and may set up a *virtual circuit* between the sending computer and the receiving computer, which will stay open until the last packet has been sent. An alternative is the 'connectionless' approach by which the PSE may set up a different route for each packet.

Packet switching is used for data communications for the Internet.

11.3   Front-office systems

Front-office systems use IT to support staff dealing directly with customers. The most important types of front-office system are counter terminals in branches and dealer support systems.

Counter terminals

Counter terminals are similar to the type of terminal used to support telephone banking. They allow the teller to answer questions about the customer's accounts and carry out routine transactions such as cheque book ordering. Building society counter terminals also have passbook printers for customers with passbook accounts. Counter terminals can provide sales prompts and warnings. The teller may also be able to enter transactions. An example of this occurs when cashing 'house cheques' for customers – cheques cashed at the issuing branch – the teller can enter the details and update the account balance immediately.

Dealer support systems

Dealer support systems provide information for dealers in the foreign exchange, securities and money markets. They can take exchange rate and security price information from outside organizations such as Reuters. Most systems rely on the dealer to enter the details of the transaction (often using touch-sensitive screens) and will automatically update the financial services organization's position.

Dealer support systems also make payments through the organization's payment systems, and create the accounting entries needed to keep the organization's books up to date.

11.4   Back-office systems

Back-office operations are increasingly carried out in process centres, releasing expensive branch space for customers. Many traditional back-office operations such as account opening are now carried out either by front-office staff or in call centres. The most important back-office systems are standing order/direct debit systems and client/account maintenance.

Standing orders and direct debits

Standing order systems create a payment to another account. The account may be with another financial services organization, in which event payment is made through the Bankers Automated Clearing System (BACS – discussed below) or it may be made through a transfer between accounts.

Most systems set up the next payment on a *diary*. This has a frequency code, and when the payment is made the system will calculate the next payment date and set up another payment on the diary.

If the payee account has changed, closed or does not exist, the payee bank will attempt to identify the account intended. If it can, it will advise the paying bank, which will need to change its records. If it cannot it will return the payment.

Direct debit systems authorize third parties to transfer funds out of an account. Once the direct debit has been set up the system will wait for claims against it and, if they are valid, will make a payment to the payee account. This may be made through BACS or as an internal transfer if both accounts are with the same financial services organization. If the claim is not valid the claimant will be advised.

If a claim is received for an account that has changed, closed or does not exist the claimant will be advised. If a claim is made in error the direct debit indemnity scheme allows the financial services organization to recover the payment from the claimant.

Standing order and direct debit systems were traditionally batch systems, but these are being replaced by remote batch or on-line systems. As payments are made or claims received overnight there is no reason why these systems need to be on-line or real time.

Client and account maintenance

Client and account maintenance includes events such as name and address changes and registering deaths. These systems are usually on-line.

11.5 Payment systems

Automated teller machines

Automated teller machines (ATMs) are widely used for basic services such as cash withdrawals and balance enquiries. Customer activated terminals (CATs) are similar to ATMs but provide additional facilities.

An ATM includes a reader for a magnetic strip card, a computer screen and a keypad, which the customer can use to give instructions to the ATM. ATMs in some countries (such as France and Japan) will read smart cards as well as magnetic strip cards. The ATM is connected to the financial services organization through telecommunications links.

When a customer wants to use an ATM to withdraw cash, he or she will put a magnetic strip card in the reader. The computer in the ATM will check that the card is valid and will ask the customer to enter a personal identification number (PIN) to prove that it is his or her card. The computer will check the PIN against information held on the card and against information held on the financial services organization's computer. It will also check the account balance and any withdrawals made the same day. If everything is in order the ATM will issue the cash and will update both the magnetic strip on the card and the financial services organization's computer.

Most bank ATMs are on-line processing systems. The transaction is recorded on the bank's mainframe computer but the account balance is not updated until the end of the day. Many building societies and a few banks have real-time systems, where the account balance is updated immediately. Remote batch systems – where the ATM carries out its checking against the information held on the magnetic strip and stores transactions itself to load to the mainframe computer at the end of the day – are no longer used in the UK because of the risk of fraud.

All of the major banks and building societies use ATMs to offer cash withdrawal, balance enquiries and facilities such as ordering statements and cheque books. Although they have their own ATM networks, they have built links between these, and there are now three combined networks:

- MINT (Midland, National Westminster, Lloyds TSB);
- Four Banks (Barclays, Lloyds TSB, Royal Bank of Scotland, Bank of Scotland);
- Link.

The Link network originally included the building societies and former building societies, together with some smaller banks. The high-street banks have now joined the network, which may eventually become the sole UK ATM network.

Bank and building society customers can use the ATMs of other organizations in the same network. The banks and building societies monitor withdrawals made by their partners' customers and make *reciprocity charges* if more use is made of their machines by their partners' customers than the other way round. To date the banks generally have not passed these charges on to their customers, although Link rules permit this and it may become more prevalent.

Most financial organizations' ATMs are also linked to either the Visa or the MasterCard network, providing an international ATM network. Other international networks include Cirrus and Europay. ATMs are also linked within the HSBC group, providing a global network.

One innovative application of technology to ATMs is its use to image cheques. The cheque image is printed on the receipt to provide proof of deposit. This has been developed by the Citizens Federal Bank of Dayton in the US.

Electronic funds transfer at point of sale

Electronic funds transfer at point of sale (EFTPOS) systems use magnetic strip cards, and both debit cards and credit cards can be processed. Smart card systems such as the Mondex 'electronic wallet' work in a slightly different way, and will be considered later in this Chapter.

EFTPOS is a bit more complicated than ATMs, with up to six different parties involved – the customer, the customer's bank, the card issuer, the retailer, the merchant acquirer (who processes the transaction for the retailer), and the network that links these together.

The retailer needs a magnetic card reader attached to a point of sale terminal. When the customer offers his or her card for payment it is swiped through the reader to read the information recorded on the magnetic strip. The computer in the point of sale terminal first checks that the card is valid. It may also check a local hot card file, which records cards reported lost or stolen. This will be held on the point of sale terminal's computer and updated on a daily basis.

The retailer will have a *floor limit* and transactions up to that limit do not need further authorization. If the transaction is above that limit the point of sale terminal will send a message to the computer controlling the network. This will check that the card is not recorded on its own hot file (which is updated as cards are reported lost or stolen), and will send a message to the card issuer to check the balance or limit.

The card issuer may be the customer's bank or building society or an organization such as MasterCard or Visa. If the transaction is in order, the card issuer will 'earmark' the amount of the transaction to prevent the customer drawing out funds that would make him or her overdrawn or overlimit, and will send an authorization message back through the network to the retailer. If the computer controlling the network or the card issuer's computer rejects the transaction, a rejection message will be sent instead.

If the transaction is valid, the point of sale terminal will print out a slip for the customer to sign to authorize the card issuer to debit his or her account. The retailer keeps these slips in case the customer disputes the transaction.

If payment was made by credit card, the retailer gets paid immediately. Debit card transactions were originally settled three days later (the same as a cheque) but they are now often settled earlier – next day settlement is usual for very large retailers. Settlement is made between the retailer's bank and the customer's bank or building society using the Bankers Automated Clearing System (BACS), which credits the retailer's account and debits the customer's account.

Electronic cash – Mondex

The Mondex system was developed by National Westminster Bank in conjunction with British Telecom and works in a slightly different way. The Mondex card is an integrated smart card containing a processor and three different types of memory – random access memory (RAM), read-only memory (ROM) and electronically erasable programmable read-only memory (EEPROM).

ROM cannot be changed, and holds the card's operating system. Mondex has developed an operating system called MultOS specifically for smart cards. EEPROM can be changed, and is used for storage of variable information. It holds security information such as the PIN, electronic money ('e-cash') and the computer programs that provide the Mondex service. The operating system and any other programs must be loaded into RAM before they can run. Java, discussed in Chapter 14, can be used to develop programs for smart cards.

The Mondex card is a *stored value* card, and needs to be loaded with money before it can be used. The customer can load the card through an ATM or over the telephone – either a modified BT payphone or an adapted home phone. A Mondex card can only transfer value to another Mondex card. When the customer pays for goods, value is transferred from the customer's card to the retailer's card. The value on the customer's card is immediately reduced and the value on the retailer's card is increased.

E-cash is issued by loading Mondex 'bullion' cards held by the Mondex-issuing banks. Mondex International loads the bullion cards under the supervision of the Bank of England. When the customer loads his or her card, value is transferred from the bullion card to the customer's card, debiting the customer's account. The retailer 'banks' the takings by transferring value from the retailer card to the bullion card, crediting the retailer's account.

The Mondex card, unlike the rival VisaCash card, is *non-accounted*. This means that there is no central record of transactions made. The only record is on the card, where the customer can look at the last ten transactions carried out. This makes security very important as there would be no way of identifying whether e-cash on a Mondex card was forged.

Mondex security takes three forms:

- *Handshaking.* The two Mondex cards will 'talk' to each other to ensure that they are both valid Mondex cards before any value is transferred.

- *Encryption.* All messages to load cards or bank takings are encrypted to ensure that they cannot be read or altered during transmission

- *PIN.* Each Mondex card has a personal identification number (PIN) which can be used to lock it – preventing it being used for payment.

Mondex customers can unlock their cards at special unlocking points provided by the retailers. Note that there is no authorization process at the point of sale, and cards *cannot* be unlocked at the till. The customer will unlock the card using the device before going to the till. He or she will pay using the card and will use the unlocking device to lock the card again before leaving the premises. The customer will also be able to lock and unlock the card using a special wallet or an adapted telephone.

The Mondex card is multi-currency in that it can store values in up to five currencies. Each currency will have a separate issuer, and they can only be exchanged through a bank account. This is different from the position with credit or debit cards, where the customer can pay a bill in (say) US dollars, with his or her account being debited in (say) sterling.

Midland Bank are also taking part in the UK trial of Mondex. Mondex is now owned by MasterCard.

MasterCard, Visa and Europay have developed an accounted system (the Europay MasterCard Visa or EMV system), in which there will be a central record of transactions. MasterCard's involvement in this consortium preceded its take-over of Mondex, and EMV has become a standard to which Mondex partly complies.

Clearing House Automated Payment System

The Clearing House Automated Payment System (CHAPS) is a method of transferring payments electronically within the UK over telecommunications links. Financial services organizations taking part in the system must have a Tandem fault-tolerant computer connected to the CHAPS network. Fault tolerance is discussed in Chapter 4. CHAPS messages are sent over BT's packet switched etwork.

Payments sent over CHAPS are *cleared funds* – once the payment has been made it cannot be stopped. This is an important difference between a payment made over CHAPS and a cheque.

Settlement between financial services organizations for CHAPS payments is through real-time gross settlement, which requires CHAPS members to settle as each payment is made. They must deposit collateral with the Bank of England, against which the Bank will advance intra-day settlement funds. They are allowed to use their holdings of gilt-edged securities – held by the Bank of England in the Central Gilts Office – for this purpose.

Every time a CHAPS payment is made, funds will be transferred at the Bank of England from the CHAPS member making the payment to the CHAPS member receiving the payment. At the end of the day the members will have to redeem their collateral, transferring additional funds to the Bank of England if the total of payments made is greater than the total of receipts.

Figure 11.6

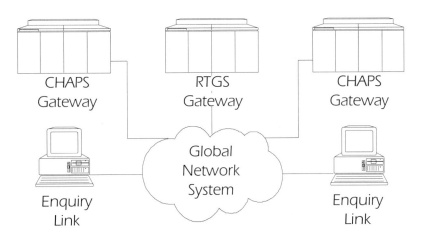

Bankers automated clearing system

The Bankers Automated Clearing System (BACS) allows organizations to clear credit items such as standing orders, direct debits and employee pay electronically. Non-financial organizations may become members of BACS but must be sponsored. Alternatively banks can submit items on behalf of their customers.

Items for clearing can be entered using magnetic tape or diskette. Alternatively BACSTEL can be used to allow items to be entered on-line.

Figure 11.7

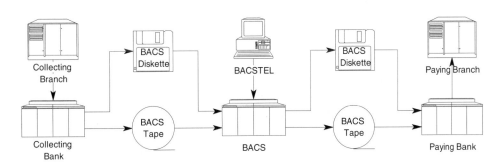

Society for Worldwide Interbank Financial Telecommunications

The Society for Worldwide Interbank Financial Telecommunications (SWIFT) is a method of transferring payments and other financial transactions electronically around the world.

SWIFT members have a SWIFT Interface Device – often the member's own mainframe computer – which is connected to a regional processing centre. BACS is the UK regional processing centre. This, in turn, is connected to one of the three regional operating centres located in Belgium, the Netherlands and the United States.

Members will send a message through the regional processing centre to the regional operating centre. It will then be passed to the regional processing centre for the member to which it is addressed, through one of the other regional operating centres if necessary.

Figure 11.8

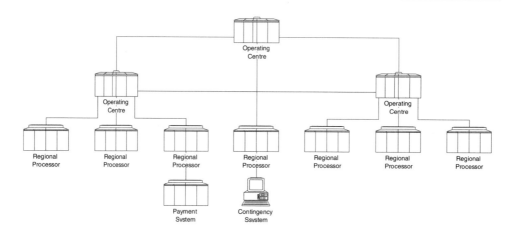

As well as payments, members can send transfers and trade finance transactions (such as letters of credit) over the SWIFT network. SWIFT also handles eurobond and euro-security transactions for the clearing houses CEDEL and Euro-clear.

Small payment systems

International payments may be too small to justify the costs of a SWIFT transaction, and small payment systems can be used to make these transfers.

Interbank file transfer

SWIFT can also be used to make small payments. Interbank file transfer (IFT) allows members to transfer files of small payments between different countries. There are plans to provide this service to customers through electronic data interchange (EDI).

Alternatives to IFT

IFT is not the only method for making international small payments. Some automated clearing houses (ACHs – the international equivalent of BACS) provide this facility. Ibos provides this facility for member banks. The European Giro banks have developed Eurogiro, and the European co-operative banks have developed TIPA-NET. The European savings banks are intending to develop a similar service. Visa also offer an international small payment service.

Electronic data interchange

Electronic data interchange (EDI) is the exchange of commercial documents by electronic means. It is a form of electronic mail but the messages must follow a standard called EDIFACT (Electronic Data Interchange for Finance, Administration, Commerce and Transport). This lays down the format of the message and various rules to do with how it is sent.

EDI covers commercial documents such as orders, invoices and despatch notes. It does *not* cover financial documents, and a payment cannot be sent over EDI. To get round this, financial services organizations have developed systems that allow the commercial documents to be sent over EDI and the payment to be sent over a payments system such as SWIFT or CHAPS. This allows the business customer to send all the paperwork electronically and automatically to match the financial and commercial parts of the transaction.

EDI is a potentially valuable market for financial services organizations. It allows them to make use of their existing telecommunications networks and links to payment systems. It provides opportunities for cross-selling and to earn fees from customers for using the system. It also gives them much more information about their customers' activities – a large order might be a warning that a customer would soon need working capital, for example. The service is also of great benefit to customers, who are able to process orders much faster and with less manual effort.

We can show how an EDI system provided by a financial services organization works as a diagram:

Figure 11.9: EDI system

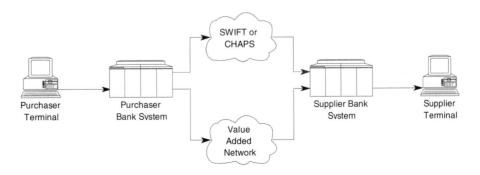

EDI can be used even if only the purchaser (for example) has access to it. The Royal Mail's EDIPOST service, used by all the high-street banks, allows messages received in EDIFACT format to be printed and delivered by post.

EDI is increasingly being delivered over the Internet. We have considered how linking EDI and electronic payment systems has benefited customers. The Internet allows suppliers to publish on-line catalogues, and customers can use intelligent agents (discussed in Chapter 14) to find the best price. Using the Internet for EDI allows more of the purchasing process to carried out electronically.

Clearing

The clearing system uses batch processing. Cheques are preprinted with sorting code, account number and cheque number using magnetic ink. When the cheque is presented for payment, the paying branch adds the amount, also using magnetic ink.

The cheques are usually sent to the organization's clearing department or to a specialist cheque-processing centre. The information recorded in magnetic ink is read by the collecting organization's computer and the cheques are sorted by sort code, using magnetic ink character recognition (MICR) reader-sorters.

MICR systems use an ink that can be magnetized for letters and numbers. These characters also have a special shape. An MICR reader magnetizes the ink and sensors detect the shape of the letter.

The cheques are split up by settlement organization – the organizations that are members of the Clearing House – and details recorded on magnetic tape. A report is produced for each settlement organization showing the amount of cheques collected. The settlement organizations exchange the magnetic tapes and the cheques and settle the difference between the amount collected and the amount owed through their accounts at the Bank of England.

To illustrate this, Lloyds TSB will collect Barclays Bank cheques through its branches and Barclays will collect Lloyds TSB cheques. They will sort these and split them. Say Lloyds TSB has £520 million of Barclays cheques and Barclays has £500 million of Lloyds TSB cheques. Lloyds TSB will give the cheques drawn on Barclays to Barclays and vice versa. Barclays will also pay Lloyds £20 million (the difference between £520 million owed by Barclays and £500 million owed by Lloyds).

The MICR reader/sorter is also used to split the cheques up by branch. Cheques collected by other banks or by other branches of the settlement bank will be sorted by the branch on which they are drawn. These were originally sent to that branch, but this has been replaced by *paying bank truncation* by which cheques remain in the paying bank's clearing centre.

Cheques may be returned by the paying organization, for example if there are insufficient funds on the account. The cheques are split into batches by collecting bank and returned. The amount of returns is deducted from the amount of cheques presented for payment. So in our example the £500 million collected by Barclays could represent £502 million collected less £2 million returns.

Credit clearing – the clearing of bank giro credits (BGCs) – works in much the same way. The main difference is that optical character recognition (OCR) is used instead of MICR. Cheques and BGCs can also be processed together using a magneto-optical character reader.

OCR readers read information in the same way as a photocopier or a scanner, by shining a bright light on the paper and detecting the reflections. OCR systems can detect a wide range of character shapes – some can even interpet handwriting – but the systems used for credit clearing are designed to look for the specific shapes used on BGCs.

OCR is cheaper than MICR because it does not need special ink. The disadvantage of OCR is that folds in the paper can make it difficult to read – this would be a problem if OCR was used for the cheque clearing as cheques may be folded when they are sent through the post.

11.6   Expert systems

Expert systems can take 'decisions' based on rules and on experience. There are three main types of expert system.

The most common are *knowledge-based systems*. An expert in a particular field describes the process he or she goes through to assess something. The steps are coded as *rules* and entered into a *knowledge base*. Someone with less expertise can consult the system, which will ask a series of questions. Depending on the responses to those questions, the expert system's *inferencing engine* will use the rules in the knowledge base to decide the most likely answer to the question. Some systems have a learning capability – they can adjust the rules depending on the results of their decisions.

A typical approach to building a knowledge-based system might be as follows:

● A human expert would define a set of rules, working with an IT expert systems specialist or possibly directly with the computer. These would be entered into the system's knowledge base.

● The system would be tested and the rules adjusted depending on the results. This process would be automatic if a self-learning program were used.

● A user would be able to consult the system, by answering questions or by supplying data. The inferencing engine will compare the information against the rules in the knowledge base and reach a conclusion. This may be a single statement or it may be a range of possibilities, each with a percentage probability (expert systems used for medical diagnosis often work this way).

● If the user does not understand or does not agree with the conclusion, he or she can ask the explanatory interface how it has been reached. This will show which rules were applied and how the conclusion was reached.

We can show this as a diagram:

Figure 11.10

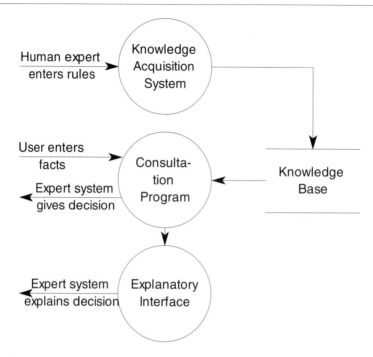

Neural networks are becoming increasingly important. These learn in much the same way as the human brain. They contain a large network of interconnected processors. Information fed into this chooses its own path through the network, based on rules that have been entered and on past experience. If a particular path has been successful under a set of circumstances, it is more likely that the same path will be chosen if the circumstances are similar. By running a large number of cases through the neural network, it learns and improves its rate of success.

Another relatively new approach is the *genetic algorithm*. These 'evolve', with the less successful in each generation becoming extinct while the more successful go through forced mutation to form the next generation. As with neural networks, feeding a large number of cases through the genetic algorithm allows it to learn and improve its rate of success. An important difference between neural networks and genetic algorithms is that the latter only require software and can be run on a standard PC.

Case-based reasoning is a different approach. This relies on a large library of similar cases with known results. Every problem that is presented is compared with the cases in the library and the most similar cases are identified. The result of the new case can be predicted on the basis of the results of similar past cases.

There are also computer languages designed to be used for expert systems development, such as Lisp and Prolog, but these are of little commercial importance and are mainly used in academic and research institutions.

Knowledge-based systems, without a self-learning capability, are the most common form of expert system used in financial services organizations. Their main advantage is that they give consistent answers, unlike the other systems, where the answer will be affected by what the system has learnt from recent experience.

The disadvantage of knowledge-based systems is that they assume that the rules stay the same. Although this is generally true in retail finance it is not the case for the wholesale markets, and neural networks and genetic algorithms are widely used in, for example, securities trading. Neural networks and genetic algorithms are also used in fraud detection.

Case-based reasoning is used to some extent in the credit assessment of small business customers. It allows customers to be ranked against other firms in the same line of business. This is more common in the United States, where information about industry segments is available through the bankers' trade association.

Credit scoring and behavioural scoring

Credit scoring systems attempt to predict how likely a borrower is to repay a loan from a combination of demographic information (age, occupation, residential status, etc.) and past account behaviour. They carry out the functions of expert systems, although they are not generally developed using expert systems technology.

Demographic scorecards give loan applicants a score depending on their answers to the questions on the application form. For example, a residential status of owner occupier might be worth 20 points whereas a status of tenant might be worth only 5.

Behavioural scorecards work in the same way but use account history information. For example, if the customer has not gone over limit at all in the last 18 months this might be worth 20 points, one or two limit excesses might be worth 5 points, and three or more limit excesses might be worth −10 points.

Credit scoring systems also include policy rules. These are conditions under which the loan will automatically be refused, for example if there are county court judgements outstanding against the applicant.

The scores for all the questions are added up and compared against a cut-off. If the total score is below this the loan will be refused. If the score is above the cut-off and all the policy rules are satisfied the loan will be granted.

Credit scoring systems often include links to external credit reference agencies, discussed in Chapter 1. These match applicants against records such as the electoral roll, county court judgements, and information drawn from applicants' credit history. This may include both black and white information.

Credit scoring systems have three main advantages for financial services organizations:

● They ensure that customers are treated in the same way throughout the branch network. By automating the system they avoid situations where the same loan application would be treated differently by different lenders.

- They allow lending decisions to be made by less experienced (and therefore cheaper) staff.

- The organization can adjust the cut-off score and policy rules depending on its overall strategy. If it is trying to build market share it can lower the cut-off score, accepting more business. If it is trying to cut loan losses it can raise the cut-off score. This is much easier than changing the behaviour of hundreds of individual lenders.

11.7   Direct banking systems

Telephone banking

The most important form of direct banking is telephone banking. Most banks and some building societies now offer telephone banking for personal customers. An effective telephone banking system relies heavily on the use of IT to get customer information as quickly as possible: delays that may be acceptable when the customer is standing at a branch counter are not acceptable on the telephone.

An automatic call distribution system (ACD) is used to route calls to free agents. The ACD also allows calls to be transferred between agents, and provides statistics such as the average length of call.

Computer telephony integration (CTI) allows an ACD to be linked to a computer system. When a telephone call is transferred to another agent the details on the screen are transferred as well. This saves time when transfers are made and also allows 'blind transfers' where a call can be transferred to an agent who is unaware of the caller's identity: this is useful for taking password changes over the telephone as the agent handling the change does not know the caller to whom it relates.

CTI can also be used with caller line identification (CLI). This allows the caller's telephone number to be identified, and the agent can be presented with a list of possible callers on the screen when he or she takes the call.

Some telephone banking systems use interactive voice response (IVR), which recognizes the 'tone' – the sound made by pressing a number on a touch-tone telephone. For customers without touch-tone telephones, we can get the same effect by giving them a tone-pad. This approach is taken by the Alliance and Leicester and Nationwide systems.

An alternative is to use a speech recognition unit. This recognizes a limited number of words and phrases, allowing the customer to give instructions directly to the computer. This is more complicated than a voice response system because the computer needs to recognize words spoken by people who may have colds or strong accents. This type of system is good for handling a relatively small number of standard transactions and enquiries. This approach is taken by the National Westminster Bank and Lloyds TSB systems.

The market leader in telephone banking is the Midland Bank subsidiary First Direct. First

Direct has chosen to use human operators instead of voice response or speech recognition. This is slightly more expensive but it makes the customer feel more comfortable, and allows First Direct to use the telephone contact to try to sell extra services to the customer. A similar approach can be used to sell other financial products such as insurance (e.g. Direct Line) and mortgages.

PC banking

Financial services organizations are increasingly allowing customers who have a PC with a modem to access financial services. These services are increasingly delivered through the Internet, and we shall discuss them in more detail in Chapter 17.

Alternative delivery channels

Smart phone

A recent development is the smart phone. This is a telephone that also has a keyboard – either a pull-out keyboard stored under the phone or a touch-sensitive screen that can show numbers (as in a normal telephone) or letters and numbers. In effect, the smart phone can be used as a simple terminal computer, which makes it suitable for home banking. There are some experiments under way in the United States, but nothing has been announced in the UK.

Interactive television

A variation on telephone banking is the use of interactive television. Cable television can not only carry signals from the broadcaster to the subscriber's television but can also carry signals back again. This connection can be used to make telephone calls, and also makes interactive services such as home shopping and banking possible.

The first major trial of interactive television banking took place in Cambridge in late 1995. The National Westminster Bank participated in this. Services offered included balance and transaction enquiries, travellers cheques, foreign currency, insurance quotes, and the ability to make an appointment with a financial advisor.

Kiosks

Multimedia kiosks allow financial services organizations to market their services to customers through direct channels. A kiosk will typically include the following:

- A multimedia presentation using video, sound and image to demonstrate the organization's products;

- A touch screen allowing the customer to request more information about products;

- A videophone link allowing the customer to speak to an advisor. The organization can also use the videophone to monitor what is happening near the kiosk for security purposes.

Kiosks can be used with ATMs to provide an unmanned 'virtual branch' offering most of the services of a full branch. The National Westminster Bank has trialled kiosks,offering loan quotes, travel facilities (currency and insurance), and information about savings products. The Nationwide Building Society has also trialled kiosks.

12

Management Information

Introduction

Management information is, not surprisingly, the information that managers need to do their jobs. So any discussion of management information should start with the question: what do managers do?

At about the beginning of the twentieth century Fayol defined the functions of management as planning, organizing, controlling, coordinating and commanding. Later theorists have changed commanding to motivating or leading. We shall break the role of a manager down into three main areas:

- Deciding and organizing;

- Planning and controlling;

- Communication (which includes coordinating and commanding/motivating/leading).

Different levels of manager need different types of information. We usually distinguish between:

- Strategic information, used by senior management;

- Tactical information, used by middle management;

- Operational information, used by first-line management and supervisors.

In this chapter we shall discuss these different types of information and the three management roles. The final part of the chapter discusses what systems and tools can be used by managers.

12.1   Types of information

We have introduced the idea of management information as being strategic, tactical or operational. We can summarize some of the differences between these:

	Strategic information	**Tactical information**	**Operational information**
Used by	Senior Managers	Middle Managers	First line Managers
Time horizon	1-10 years	3-18 months	Up to 1 month
Sources of data	External and strategic management information systems	Operational and tactical management information systems	Operational systems
Internal or external	Internal and external	Mainly internal	Entirely internal
Frequency of decision	Infrequent and at irregular intervals	Weekly, monthly, quarterly or yearly	Very frequent during the day
Basis for decisions	Facts, projections and judgements	Facts and projections	Facts
Type of decision	Unprogrammed – each decision is unique	Programmed – follows overall policies and precedents	Prescriptive – follows defined rules and procedures
Presentation	Summaries and trends	Summaries and supporting detail	Usually detailed
Examples	Market share and product profitability	Actual costs and revenues vs. budgets	Customer financial histories

12.2 Processes – deciding and organising

Decision making

The key stages in the decision making process are:

1) Define objectives.

2) Collect information.

3) Develop options.

4) Evaluate and decide.

5) Implement and monitor.

The *define objectives* stage is very important – if we do not know where we are going, how will we know when we get there? To put this in the context of information management, we need to express our objectives in terms that we can measure. We shall not consider this stage any further as the various techniques are outside the scope of this book.

The *collect information* stage involves taking information from various internal and external sources. Many of these have been discussed in Chapter 1, but internal information is often taken from a management information system (MIS), a data warehouse or a datamart.

MISs and datamarts are very similar, and the differences between them are due to changes in the technology used – this will be discussed later in this chapter.

The *develop options* stage involves identifying candidate solutions. We shall not consider this stage any further as the various techniques are outside the scope of this book.

The *evaluate and decide* stage usually involves building some form of model to allow the alternative solutions to be compared. Possible approaches include using a decision support system (DSS) or building a financial model or a simulation.

The *implement and monitor* stage involves putting the decision into effect and monitoring it to ensure that the original problem has been solved. The monitoring stage usually relies on some form of MIS to capture the data required for monitoring and evaluation. It is at this stage that the quantitative objectives set in the *define objectives* stage are assessed.

Organising

Organizing covers two main topics:

- Organizational structure, for example levels and spans of control;
- The allocation of resources between different functions.

The problems of *organizational structure* are predominantly those of communication, and we shall deal with these later in the chapter. It is perhaps worth emphasising that technology has reduced distance as a constraint on organizational structure – it is possible to design an organization such that groups that need to work together are physically a long way apart. This has been described as the 'death of distance' in a recent book.

Presentation graphics systems are often used to produce organizational diagrams ('organigrams'), although specialist software is also available to depict organizational structures. Managers use organigrams to ensure that staff are aware of reporting lines and areas of business responsibility. These are particularly useful for new entrants and for staff from other parts of the organization.

In addition to the formal organizational structure there will usually be an informal organization. Again, the problems of this are predominantly those of communication. While workgroup and workflow technology are often used to improve communication in the formal organization, the informal organization relies on less structured means of communication such as email, bulletin boards and intranets. This has sometimes been called the 'virtual water cooler' after its role in replacing informal conversations by the water cooler in American organizations.

The *allocation of resources* between functions is closely associated with planning, and will be considered under that heading.

12.3 Processes – planning and controlling

We can show the relationship between planning and controlling as a feedback diagram:

Figure 12.1

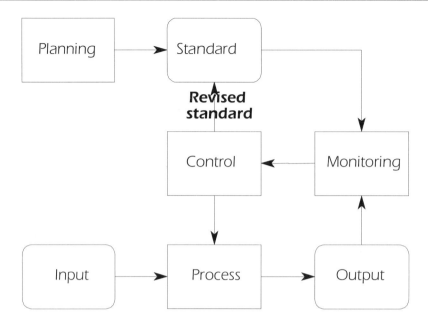

The *planning process* involves defining a standard to be met. This standard will usually be expressed in terms of time (do this by then), quantity (do so many of these), cost (do this within this budget), quality (do this to this standard), or a combination of two or more of these.

The *monitoring process* involves measuring the output from the process being controlled, comparing it against the standard, and identifying the reasons for any difference. The *control process* involves predicting the consequences of any difference and, if necessary, taking some action in response. This action will usually involve a change either to the process being controlled itself or to its inputs, although sometimes it is the standard that will be changed.

Planning

Managers produce many different types of plan. Two of the most important are financial plans such as budgets, and project plans. Budgets are such an important part of the manager's role that we shall be considering them separately below.

We discussed project planning in Chapter 5. To recap, this involves:

● Identifying all the activities needed to complete the project and estimating the amount of work required;

● Identifying any relationships between these activities;

● Identifying the resources available to carry them out and allocating these to the activities in the most efficient way.

We have also discussed the project management software available to managers to help them plan and control projects.

Another aid to planning is a geographic information system. This is discussed in later in this chapter and can be used in the planning of marketing campaigns or branch openings.

Monitoring and controlling

Monitoring and control are closely linked to planning, and it is not surprising that most budget systems and project management systems also allow budget and project monitoring and control. Some other types of monitoring and control systems are:

● *Exposure monitoring systems*. These show how exposed the organization is to various types of financial risk, and vary from simple limits systems through complex systems such as behavioural scoring to elaborate risk simulations. We have discussed behavioural scoring systems in Chapter 11 and approaches to risk management in Chapter 5.

Limits systems define acceptable limits for certain types of exposure. If the exposure goes above this limit, this is reported. Such systems often have 'warning' limits before the exception limit is reached. Limits are usually applied to lending (for example by customer, by industrial sector and by country) and to foreign currency exposure.

● *Time recording systems*. These are used to record how staff time is spent. This may be used to calculate costs or to ensure that staff are not spending too much or too little time on activities.

Systems such as workflow or automated call distribution systems can collect this information automatically but many systems require it to be entered manually. Manual methods of collecting this include:

   ● Manually completed timesheets. Individuals either keep a record of how much time they spend on the activities being monitored or keep a diary showing how they are using their time. This information is then entered into a database. Some project management systems will allow timesheet information to be entered and may well produce a *pro forma* timesheet showing what the individual is scheduled to be working on during the time-recording period (typically either one week or one month).

   ● Sampling uses a sample of activities to determine how time is spent. Sampling is typically carried out by organization and methods staff, and is used for purposes such as allocating costs between different office activities.

   ● Tagging attaches a form to the front of each document. Everyone receiving a tagged document will record the time they received it, the amount of time they spent working on it, and the time they passed it on. Tagging is typically used to identify the flow of documents about the office, often as a basis for redesigning the process (business process reengineering – discussed in Chapter 7) or to introduce workflow automation.

- *Early warning systems.* These attempt to predict what will happen in future by monitoring indicators. Credit scoring is a form of early warning system; they are also widely used in economic forecasting (for example, indices such as the Purchasing Managers' Index are 'leading indicators' for economic activity).

The benefit of using early warning systems is to identify future events early enough to take appropriate action.

12.4   Processes – communication

Communication is one of the most important management skills. The roles that managers perform are usually characterized as:

- Interpersonal: figurehead, leadership and liaison;

- Informational: monitoring, dissemination and spokesman;

- Decisional: negotiator, entrepreneur, troubleshooter and resource allocator.

Of these, the first seven require communication. The communication process involves the following steps:

- Develop the message. The message must be designed for the target audience and for the action that the sender wants the recipient to take.

- Select the appropriate medium. The medium will be affected by these factors and by the urgency of the message. For example, the appropriate medium for a message that the recipient will need to use as a source of reference in future must be permanent and easy to access – paper or email rather than telephone or a video.

- *Encode* – translate the message into a suitable form for the medium. Long and complex messages should usually be sent on paper. Some messages – for example changes to employment conditions – require a formal presentation, for which email may not be suitable.

- Send the message.

- Receive the message.

- *Decode* – interpret the message. The recipient will not necessarily interpret the message in the way intended. Differences in background, attitude and knowledge between the sender and the recipient increase the possibility of misinterpretation.

- Respond. Take action in response to the message.

In order to be effective, communication must:

- Gain the *attention* of the recipient;

- Ensure the recipient's *understanding*;

- Ensure the recipient's *acceptance*;

- Prompt the recipient to take some form of *action*.

Technology can be used to improve communication in a number of ways:

- It provides a much wider range of communications media. This is not always a blessing – junk electronic mail (also called spam) and other peoples' mobile telephones can be major sources of irritation – but it does allow us to choose media that better reflect the message we are trying to get across.

  The impact on the communication process allows a wider range of media for *selection* and therefore a wider range of formats for *encoding*. A particular benefit of technology is in providing methods for rapid communication such as fax, email and videoconferencing.

  The impact on communication effectiveness is more limited although some media allow the recipient to gain the *attention* of the recipient. An example might be marking email or voicemail messages as urgent.

- It allows high-quality presentation at a relatively low cost. This helps to gain the recipient's attention, and can help to promote understanding through the use of diagrams.

  The impact on the communication process is to support the *encoding* and *decoding* stages. Messages presented in a quality format are usually clearer and easier to understand, and the sender can use techniques such as bold or italicized text to draw the recipient's attention to the most important parts of the message.

  The impact on communication effectiveness is to gain the recipient's *attention* and to increase *acceptance* of the message. The use of graphics helps to gain attention – for example the use of animated graphics in banner advertisements on the Internet. Presenting messages in a professional format helps to establish the sender's credibility to the recipient.

- It allows the recipient to respond more quickly – for example the 'reply' and 'forward' functions of electronic mail systems.

  The impact on the communication process is to improve the speed and ease of the *respond* stage. Similarly, the impact on communication effectiveness is to prompt the recipient to take *action*. An example is the use of banner advertisements on the Internet. Although most people ignore these, the 'click through' rate tends to be higher than the response to a newspaper advertisement or mailshot would be.

Some systems to aid communication have been discussed in Chapter 10, including:

- Electronic mail (email) systems;

- Presentation systems;

- Workgroup computing systems.

Also important are executive information systems, discussed later in this chapter.

12.5   Systems

Management information systems

Management information systems (MISs) are databases that are designed to be used by managers to select and cross-reference data. An MIS consists of a relational database holding the data of interest and a user interface that allows managers to specify the data they want to extract.

There are usually differences between the information held in an MIS and that held in the corresponding operational database. Reasons for this include:

- *Need for history.* Managers need to monitor what is happening over a period of time – for example, monthly sales figures for the past 18 months. Operational systems usually need data for much shorter periods.

- *Operational systems* may include physical data related to transactions such as delivery instructions. This information is usually of little relevance to managers.

- *Scope.* Managers often need to compare data from a number of different operational systems and external data sources to get an overall picture.

Because of these differences, MISs are usually built up over time from data extracted from the operational database systems. Much of this data is in summary form.

Data held in an MIS is a copy of data taken from operational systems. This means that it will usually be out of date when the data is accessed. This is rarely important for management information but it does limit the uses to which it can be put. Data warehouses and datamarts (discussed below) also contain copies of operational data.

The data for an MIS is taken from the operational systems and external sources, as shown in the following diagram:

Figure 12.2: MIS data sources

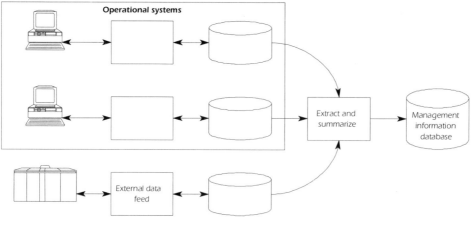

The features of an MIS include:

- Either a query language or a number of standard queries into which the manager can enter parameters.

  Canned queries are a feature of older MISs whose query language capabilities were often limited. A series of basic queries was set up into which managers could enter parameters such as date ranges, market segments and minimum and maximum amounts.

  Modern query languages are easier to use, and include functions such as *query by example*. This allows managers to show the system what information they require and allow the query language to work out how to get it.

- Interfaces to electronic office products such as spreadsheets. The simplest way to achieve this is to extract data from the MIS into a data file and import this into the electronic office product: and this approach is used in some older MISs. It is also possible to extract data from the MIS in the required form – for example as a spreadsheet file – or to create a link between the MIS and the electronic office product. Database connectivity, discussed in Chapter 13, can also be used, and this allows the electronic office product to request the data directly from the DBMS.

- Standard calculations such as cost and profitability calculations. The MIS allows executive management to compare information from across the organization, and standard calculations are needed to make sure the values being compared have the same meaning.

- Most MISs hold some data in summary form. An example might be transaction posting data, where the amount of data is very large but the individual postings are not needed as management information and monthly summaries can be used instead.

The ability of managers to enter queries is an example of *end-user computing*. Providing end-users with the tools to get the information they need directly, without having to go through the IT function, increases the benefit of IT to the organization. However, end-user computing is less efficient than producing a report to provide the same information, and the additional costs must be balanced against the benefits.

We introduced the idea of power users in Chapter 5. The problem with end-user computing is that it uses computer resources very heavily and often inefficiently. We can improve the efficiency by using a powerful computer language such as SQL, but these are not designed to be used without training. Power users have the training and knowledge to use these languages. This knowledge equips power users to act as a bridge between business users and systems developers, as they understand the problems of both sides.

Data warehouses

At its simplest, a data warehouse is a very large database that is used for the long-term storage of data likely to be of continuing value to the organization. As with any warehouse, the data is only of value if it can be accessed when it is needed, and the other aspect of a data warehouse is some form of query language.

Data warehouses have been made possible by two main developments:

● Improvements in the size, performance and cost of storage devices and relational databases.

An example is the development of tiered storage. This allows the most frequently used data to be stored on hard disk, less frequently used data to be stored on optical disk, and rarely used data to be stored on magnetic tape. The user does not need to know where the data is stored, and can use a single instruction to access the data irrespective of its physical location

We can show this as a diagram:

Figure 12.3: Tiered storage

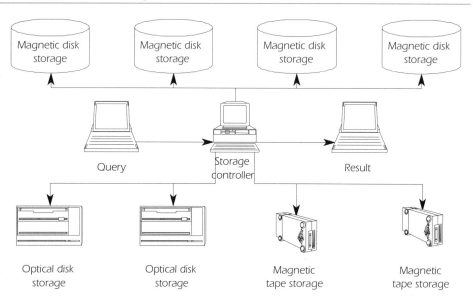

● Improvements in the technology available to access data. This includes developments in computer hardware and software.

An example is the database machine. This spreads the data over a number of different storage devices, each of which has its own processor. This allows very rapid access to data, as each processor will look for the data requested on its own storage device. In simple terms, if there are a hundred processors the database machine will find the data one hundred times quicker than a conventional computer.

We can show this as a diagram:

Figure 12.4: Database machine

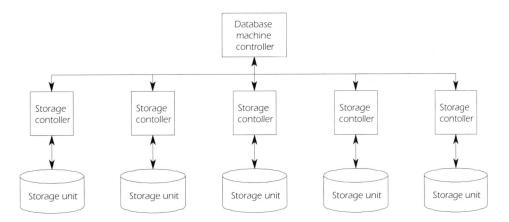

There are three things we can do with our data warehouse:

- We can run enquiries against the data. We can use a standard query language, but there are also a number of query languages designed to be used in a data warehouse environment. It is also possible to use software such as spreadsheets and electronic office databases and link these to the data warehouse using database connectivity tools – these will be discussed in Chapter 13.

- We can extract some of the data into one or more datamarts. These are discussed in the next section.

- We can analyse the data. This is discussed below under on-line analytical processing.

Datamarts

A datamart differs from a data warehouse in that it includes only the data relevant to a specific function – often a single department or line of business. The advantage of a datamart is that it is much easier for the business users to find the information they need as, by definition, the datamart contains only the data relevant to them, and can be organized in the way that best suits their needs. The users can retrieve this information using a query language or database connectivity.

Traditional MISs are increasingly being replaced by data warehouses and datamarts and it is useful to understand the differences between them.

The traditional approach to management information took a series of data extracts from the operational system databases and loaded this into the corresponding MISs:

Figure 12.5

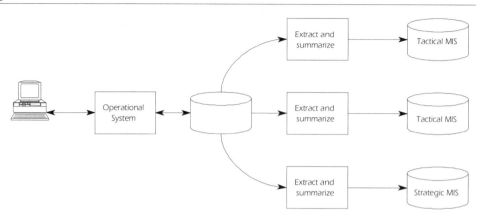

The problem with this was that the data could be inconsistent between the various MISs. Different managers with access to different information could take different and even contradictory decisions.

If a data warehouse is used, all data is first loaded into the data warehouse. Extracts are then carried out against the data warehouse to load the individual datamarts:

Figure 12.6

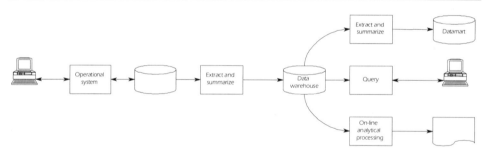

The data warehouse presents a 'single image of business reality', and helps to ensure consistency between the various sources of management information. Datamarts are designed round the needs of their business users, presenting the data needed in the format needed.

Decision support systems

Decision support systems (DSSs) allow managers to predict the results of selecting a specific option, usually in terms of financial criteria such as profit, return on assets or net present value. They are general-purpose products, and the user must build a model for each of the options.

We have already discussed spreadsheets, and these are one form of decision support system (DSS). Spreadsheets allow two or three dimensions of model. Most other DSSs are similar to spreadsheets but allow more dimensions.

For example, a financial model will typically show income and expense items as rows, and periods – months or years – as columns. Using a spreadsheet, this could be consolidated by setting up separate sheets for departments *or* products *or* markets. A multidimensional DSS would allow a single model to be set up covering all of these.

Decision support systems are most often used to build financial models. For example, managers can enter information about the cash flow they would expect to get from an investment in order:

- To calculate financial measures of the value of the investment such as internal rate of return or net present value;

- For 'what if' analysis, by changing the value of some of the variables (e.g. interest rate). This allows the manager to look at how such changes would affect the value of the investment.

The 'what if' analysis is likely to show that the value of the investment will be particularly affected by small changes in a one or two variables. This is called *sensitivity analysis*, because it identifies the factors to which the investment is particularly sensitive, indicating the variables to which the manager needs to pay close attention.

If the manager has to earn a particular rate of return on the investment, 'goal seeking' can be used to find the worst values of the variables that will still meet this rate of return.

Although decision support systems and spreadsheets include some statistical analysis functions, specialist statistical analysis software is also available. Managers can use this where more detailed analysis is needed to make decisions. For example, a manager might use this type of software to identify how much of the variation in sales is due to seasonal factors, and whether the underlying trend is improving or deteriorating.

On-line analytical processing

On-line analytical processing (OLAP) is a development of DSSs. Like a DSS, an OLAP system holds data in a multidimensional form. The features of an OLAP system include:

- *Usability.* Speed – an OLAP system should respond to an on-line query in less than 20 seconds. 'Intuitiveness' – business users should be able to make queries by taking simple, obvious actions. Flexible presentation – the ability to present the results of a query in a number of different formats to suit the user's needs.

- *Database and 'reach through' features.* Reach through is the ability of the OLAP system to identify when it does not have the data required to answer a query and to retrieve missing data from a data warehouse or from the operational systems. This is related to transparency – the business user does not need to know where the data is physically stored. Other database features include data security and integrity.

- *Analysis features.* The ability to produce standard reports based on parameters (this is similar to the idea of canned queries described for MISs). The ability to 'slice and dice' data – looking at different subsets of the data, similar to the idea of 'views' discussed under workgroup computing in Chapter 10. This is usually supported by 'drill down', which is discussed later in this Chapter. The ability to support goal seeking and 'what if' analysis.

- *Multidimensional features.* Rotation – the ability to switch easily from one view of the data into a different view. For example, the ability to switch between a product and a market view of revenues. Auto-consolidation – the ability to consolidate data automatically in a hierarchy. For example, the ability to consolidate data from branch level to area level, and from area level to regional level, without significant effort.

Simulation systems

A simulation system contains a computer *model* of part of the real world. By changing some of the variables in the model we can see what might happen if those variables really were to change.

Let us consider some examples:

- HM Treasury has a model of how the economy is expected to behave (the Treasury Economic Model). Assumptions on variables such as tax and interest rates can be changed to see the predicted effect on inflation, the balance of payments and unemployment. Many financial organizations and academic institutions have their own models, covering the economy fully or in part.

- We discussed how process models can be used as part of a workflow automation system in Chapter 10. These models can also be 'animated' to simulate the workflow through the system. This allows us to identify the amount of work that should be processed, any bottlenecks in the system, and any areas where more resources may be needed.

- Prototypes, discussed in Chapter 5, are models of how computer systems will work. If we use a prototype we can understand how people will want to use the system and what situations may arise for which the system will need to cater.

Budgets

Budgeting as a topic is covered in accounting texts. In this book we are concerned with budgets in the context of information management.

A budget is a model of the financial position of an organization or part of an organization (e.g. a branch or department). If the budget is held in a spreadsheet or DSS it is possible to change variables such as levels of sales or costs to see the effect on net earnings.

Budgets are typically held in spreadsheet format. Although most organizations hold the master copy of their budgets in an accounting system database, departmental budgets may well originally be entered in spreadsheets and spreadsheets, are often used to give the final budget figures to the departments. We can show this as a diagram:

Figure 12.7

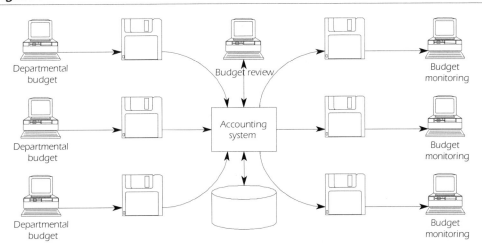

Budget monitoring requires actual costs and income to be taken from the accounting system (and possibly other systems). This requires links between the budgetary control system and other systems as shown in the diagram:

Figure 12.8

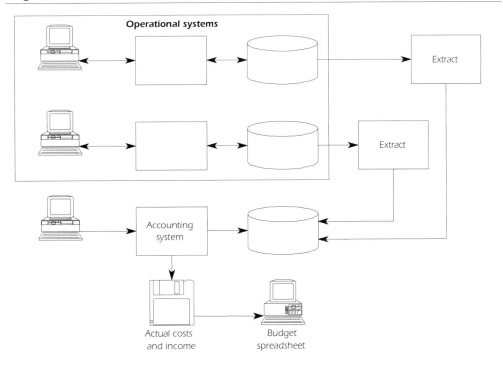

Budgetary control requires that the effects of any variances from the budget are projected to give a forecast of the impact on costs, revenues and profits. A decision can then be made as to whether corrective action is needed or whether the variance can be ignored.

Geographic information systems

A geographic information system (GIS) is a type of database that also has information about location. Typically this will include map references, and the system will be able to show this information on a map, either on the screen or printed.

A GIS may be used to hold marketing information, and systems of this type are widely used by financial organizations to select branch and ATM locations.

For example, managers planning a new branch will be concerned with a number of factors including:

- 'Footfall' – the number of people walking past the door;

- Distance from other branches;

- Distance from ATMs;

- Location of competitors' outlets;

- Location and type of potential business customers;

- Location and demograhic characteristics of potential personal customers;

- Other special factors such as transport links.

A GIS can provide all of this information and present it as a series of easily understandable maps.

Executive information systems

Executive information systems (EISs) provide a way of presenting information to senior management. An EIS works in much the same way as an MIS except that it is usually less powerful at retrieving information but better at presenting it.

The main features of an EIS are:

- It presents information in a way that is very easy to understand. It can highlight figures that are particularly good or bad (green is usually used for above target, yellow for below target and red for well below target). It allows information to be shown as either a chart or a table and to be switched between these presentations in a very simple way.

- It can 'drill down'. For example, if a region is shown as well below target the manager can see how the area figures contributed to that. If one of the areas is well below target he or she can go down to the individual branches.

For example, an EIS system and its links to its data sources might look like this:

Figure 12.9: EIS system

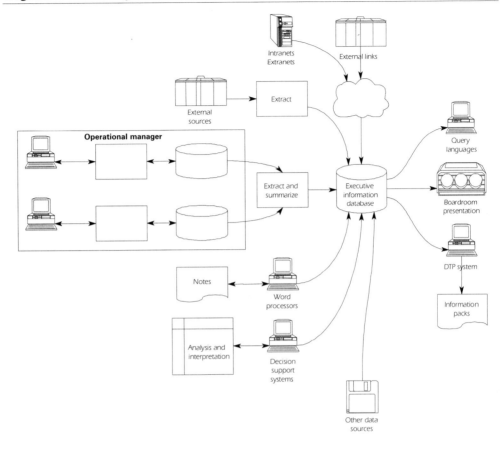

13

SYSTEMS INTEGRATION

Introduction

Systems integration is the ability to put different systems together so that they behave as if they are a single system. By a 'system' we mean any combination of hardware and software.

Why is this so important? There are a number of contributing factors, some of which we have already discussed:

- The need to integrate structured and unstructured data;

- Technological convergence;

- The need to support new delivery channels;

- The move to open standards and the use of special-purpose hardware and software;

- The need to take an overall view of the customer relationship.

Structured and unstructured data

In Chapter 1 we discussed how unstructured data has become increasingly important as IT has progressed through the generations. It should not be assumed from this that structured data is no longer relevant; financial services organizations continue to hold their most valuable data in a structured form in their central databases.

The problem is how to pull together structured and unstructured data to get an overall picture. Third-generation databases – especially relational databases – were able to store unstructured data as blobs but were not able to understand it. Fourth-generation software such as browsers can store and understand unstructured information but these are less efficient and robust with large databases of structured data.

Technological convergence

Technological convergence, discussed in Chapter 2, creates a need to pull together technology based on many different disciplines. Consider how we can access the Internet:

- We can use a PC. This derives from the computer industry.

- We can use a television and set-top box. This derives from the television industry and, in particular, from cable and satellite television.

● We can use some mobile telephones. This derives from the telephone industry and, in particular, from mobile telephones.

Because the history of these devices is different there is no reason why the underlying engineering designs and assumptions should be the same. If we assume that these are the same, we may well find that the technology will not work in the way we intend.

This has prompted much of the recent merger activity between telecommunications companies from a telephony background and those from a data communications background. The different engineering designs produce different strengths and weaknesses. Telephony companies usually offer higher levels of reliability whereas data communications companies and technologies such as packet switching use the network more efficiently. These technologies need to be brought together to produce a hybrid technology with the strengths of both.

New delivery channels

Financial services organizations want to offer their customers a range of delivery channels. One way of doing this would be to develop a different system for each channel, but this would be very expensive, and it would be difficult for the organizations to ensure that each system behaved in the same way. So the preferred alternative is to have a single *back-end* system to process the transactions and one *front-end* system for each delivery channel.

We can show this as a diagram:

Figure 13.1

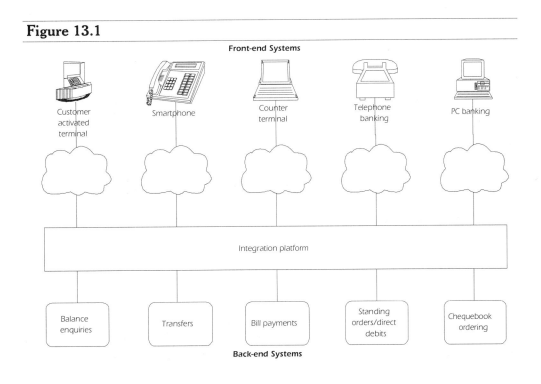

Front-end Systems

Customer activated terminal — Smartphone — Counter terminal — Telephone banking — PC banking

Integration platform

Balance enquiries — Transfers — Bill payments — Standing orders/direct debits — Chequebook ordering

Back-end Systems

Again, there is a need to bring together different technologies. A single back-end system must be able to meet the very different requirements of a PC banking system, a telephone banking system, and a branch counter terminal system. We can use a common integration platform to translate messages between the various formats required and route them to the appropriate back-end system.

Open standards

We discussed open standards in Chapter 6. One effect of open standards is to make it more attractive for vendors to develop special-purpose hardware and software.

Let us consider an example. Financial services organizations verify signatures on documents such as cheques. There would be obvious advantages in replacing signature cards by signature images stored on a database (for example, this could allow customers to draw funds from another branch without prior arrangement).

An individual financial services organization may be concerned about the difficulties of this. We have discussed the difficulty of managing both structured (customer) and unstructured (the signature) data together. We also need special equipment to capture the image of the signature. We may be concerned about obsolescence – if we develop a system that stores images, will one of our competitors develop a system to compare the stored image with the image on the cheque?

We can buy a system for capturing and storing signature images from an external vendor. Because this uses open standards, we shall be able to link it in to our own systems. Although there is some risk of obsolescence, the vendor will face competitive pressure to improve the system to match what is available in the market.

Overall customer view

Data can be spread over various computer systems in an organization. Even where systems are held on the same computer, they may well use different and possibly incompatible databases. This can happen for a number of reasons:

- Financial services organizations may outsource or use packages for activities not considered as strategic. For example, credit scoring was originally introduced to allow loan applications to be considered during Saturday opening – this was not considered to be a strategic application at the time. Therefore many financial services organizations outsourced these to credit reference agencies, who used different hardware and software from that used by the organization itself.

- Many financial services organizations allow individual business units considerable freedom to develop their own systems or to use packages. These may develop systems that use different hardware and software to that used elsewhere in the group.

- Mergers can result in groups' acquiring a variety of different hardware and software. In some cases the problems anticipated in putting the hardware and software together are of such magnitude that the merger does not take place. More commonly, the group tries to select the best option for each of its major business units (this is called 'best of breed'), which can result in its having different hardware and software for these business units.

13.1   Integration problems

These do not present a problem until the organization has to bring the information from these various systems together to give management an overall view of the business. Possible problem areas include:

- Matching data from different systems;
- Concurrency;
- Data integrity;
- The technical issue of how to move the data from one system to another.

One of the problems we face is how to match information from the systems. How do we know whether John Smith in one system is the same as John Smith (or J Smith or John A Smith) in another? If we cannot match the data held about the same customer in different systems we cannot get an overall view of the customer's relationship with us.

Another problem is concurrency. What do we do if the data on the systems is at different dates? We could get a totally misleading position of the customer's position. This could also be a problem if transactions are being processed. If we look at the customer's position after the balance on the credit card has been taken from the current account but before it has been applied to the credit card account this will be seriously misleading.

Another problem is data integrity. Assume that John Smith has a current account and a mortgage account with us and that they are recorded on different systems. If he closes his mortgage account we may remove all information about him from the mortgage account system. But we shall have lost this information and, if he subsequently applies for a loan, we will base the credit assessment purely on his current account. If there were missed repayments on the mortgage account we shall not be aware of this and we may grant the loan.

Technical problems arise because different hardware and software holds data in different ways. If data is created on one system, a different system may not even recognize that it is data, or may recognize it as data but be unable to interpret it. This may arise because the software that runs the computers (the operating system) is different, or because the software that stores the data (for example a database) is different. Even if the software is the same, different versions of the software may give problems – software can usually read data created by earlier versions but often cannot read data created using later versions.

13.2   Integration technology

We have a number of approaches to the technical problem of moving data, including:

- Standards and protocols;
- Bridging;
- Database connectivity.

Standards and protocols

Standards and protocols are rules agreed within the information and communications technology that allow systems to communicate.

'Standards' is a word used in computing to mean different things. Here we are concerned with the meaning of defining standard ways in which hardware, software and telecommunications devices can communicate with each other. These include standard formats and standard ways of doing things.

An example of a standard format is Data Interchange Format (DIF). Before the development of database connectivity, microcomputer databases were able to exchange data by creating DIF files which were of a standard format and could be read by other microcomputer databases.

An example of a standard way of doing things is data correction by automatic repeat request (ARQ). The sending device understands that it must wait for an ACK before sending the next block of data, and that it must re-send the previous block if it receives an NAK instead. This is discussed in Chapter 4.

Bridging

Bridging typically involves copying the data required out of the system on which it is held, transferring this to the computer on which the system needing it is located (using telecommunication links or methods such as a magnetic tape or floppy disk), and then copying it into the computer system that needs it.

This approach is quite common but has great disadvantages. There is no guarantee that the data held in the two systems will be concurrent or that it will be possible to match information between them. Where a number of systems are involved the links between them can become very complex, with a serious risk that a problem with one of the links can cause a number of the organization's systems to fail.

Database connectivity

Database connectivity allows us to read data stored in different databases.

For example, say we are working on a workstation attached to a mainframe computer. Both the workstation and the mainframe computer may have databases. Database connectivity would allow us to access data held either in the workstation database or in the mainframe computer database.

There are a number of ways of achieving some form of database connectivity.

Structured query language

Structured Query Language (SQL) is a computer language used for database access. In principle this gives us database connectivity, as a single SQL command should access data in the same way irrespective of the database on which it is stored. In practice this is not always possible because of the problem of accessing different databases (because of database access security systems) and because of differences between the versions of SQL used by different database suppliers.

Open database connectivity

The Open Database Connectivity (ODBC) standard provides a higher level of connectivity. It uses ODBC *drivers*, which convert data between the database's own format and the ODBC standard format.

For example, say we are using a Microsoft Access database on a workstation and we want to access data held in a DB2 database held on the mainframe computer. We shall ask for the data from within the Access database, and the ODBC driver will format this as a request. This will be sent to the mainframe computer, where the DB2 ODBC driver will use the DB2 DBMS to retrieve the data for us.

The DB2 ODBC driver will convert it into a suitable format, and it will be sent back to the workstation. Here the Access ODBC driver will convert it into a format that the Access DBMS can understand. The Access DBMS can then add it to the Access database.

The process can be shown as a diagram:

Figure 13.2

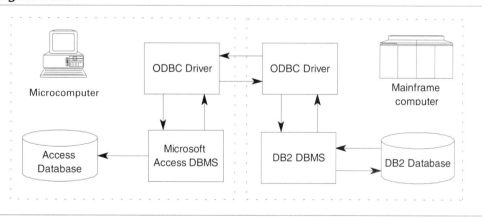

An alternative to ODBC is the Integrated Database Application Programming Interface (IDAPI), which works in much the same way.

Object linking and embedding

In Chapter 1 we discussed how we could hold data as blobs, allowing a database to store it but not to understand it. Object linking and embedding (OLE) is an approach used in PC software that overcomes the problems this can cause.

OLE stores the data together with information about the software used to create it. When we open a 'compound document' that contains OLE information, we can see what the object will look like. If we want to edit the object, the OLE link will start the software that created and can change the object.

Dynamic data exchange (DDE) allows information to be shared between programs. The advantage of DDE over OLE is that DDE allows us to change the data in one program and see it immediately change in the other.

One example is where we use DDE to link a letter to a spreadsheet. The spreadsheet might contain a calculation, for example a loan repayment. By changing the interest rate in the spreadsheet we can *automatically* change the repayment amount in the letter. We could extend the link further by storing the interest rate on a database and linking the spreadsheet to the database. A change to the interest rate will automatically change the spreadsheet, which will automatically change the letter.

This extends the idea of connectivity from data to other types of information such as image. These are called *objects*. Object technology is outside the scope of this book, but an object includes data and a number of actions that the object can take. The data can only be changed through one of these actions.

For example, consider an image linked through OLE to a word processor document. What actions can we take? We have the usual word processor capabilities of copying, moving or deleting the object, but these do not really change it. The actions OLE offers us are the ability to view the object or to change it by going into the software that created it.

There are similarities between using object technology and using a database management system: for example, data stored in a database can only be changed using one of the actions allowed by the DBMS. The difference is that objects are *encapsulated* – the data and the actions are tied together. This is not true of a DBMS, where the data and the DBMS programs are separate.

Browsers and viewers

A more limited form of connectivity is provided by browsers and viewers. Even where these only allow us to view information, this is often all we need. Many browsers will also allow us to print it. If we need to change it we may be able to save it to hard disk, where we can use other programs to change it.

Knowledge management

We shall discuss knowledge management in Chapter 14. Two applications of database connectivity are considered in this chapter:

● *Data mining.* Data mining applications analyse data to look for relationships between items – for example, whether one item of data can be used to forecast another. Data mining applications require database connectivity to ensure the pool of data they examine is as large as possible.

● *Intelligent agents*. Intelligent agents search for information – usually on the Internet, but also on the Internet.

Management information

When we discussed management information (Chapter 12) we identified the need to take data from operational systems into management information systems, data warehouses and executive information systems.

This is an application of database connectivity, and these systems use the methods we have described in this chapter to access the data they require.

14

THE INTERNET

Introduction

The Internet is the most important development in information technology of the last decade. What is the Internet, and why is it so important?

The Internet is the name given to a worldwide network of computer networks. The term 'Internet' refers to the physical computers – the hardware – and the telecommunications links. In order to use the Internet we need to access the software, of which the best known is the *World Wide Web* (WWW or the Web), which allows the Internet to carry text, pictures, audio and video.

The term *information super highway* refers to the process of integrating computer networks into a worldwide network that makes best use of technology such as fibre optic data-communications links. The German term *Infobahn* is sometimes also used. The Internet is the position that has currently been reached in this process.

The direct ancestor of the Internet was ARPANET, developed by the US Government Department of Defense's Advanced Research Projects Agency in the 1960s. The main features of both ARPANET and the Internet were:

- It did not need a central controlling computer. The Internet is an example of a peer-to-peer network in which computers send messages addressed directly to each other without going through a central computer. One reason for this was to allow the network to function even in the event of a nuclear attack – the network did not contain a 'single point of failure' the destruction of which would close down the entire network.

- It sent information over the telecommunications network using packet switching, developed in the UK. Packet switching has been discussed in Chapter 11; it allows much more information to be sent over a telecommunications network than other methods.

- It allowed computers to instruct other computers in the network to carry out actions. This is called interoperability, and was developed at Bell Laboratories in the US. This was the ancestor of client/server (discussed in Chapter 15), and computers attached to the Internet are able to request services that they would be unable to carry out themselves.

Much of the early initiative for the development of the Internet came from universities and colleges, and academic networks such as NFSNET in the US and Janet (Joint Academic

Network) in the UK were important components of it. The involvement of research organizations such as NASA greatly expanded the amount of information available through the Internet. The US government, in particular, played an important role in encouraging the use of the Internet by subsidizing telecommunications costs.

The World Wide Web was developed by Tim Berners-Lee at the European nuclear research agency CERN. Scientists had the problem of cross-referencing large amounts of information, which could include diagrams and photographs as well as text. The response was to develop the hypertext mark-up language – HTML, discussed below – which is the basis of the Web.

In recent years, commercial information providers have become increasingly involved in offering services on the Internet. This may result in a greater proportion of Internet services being charged for – a move away from the principle of free access to data.

14.1   How it works

There are a number of common elements that define Internet technology. These include:

● The TCP/IP communications protocol;

● Web browsers;

● Hypertext mark-up language;

TCP/IP

TCP/IP stands for Transmission Control Protocol/Internet Protocol, and is the set of rules (protocol) used by the Internet. TCP/IP is needed to allow different computers to communicate with each other.

One feature of TCP/IP is the IP address. This is a number of the form 234.56.78.012, which provides a unique address for each computer on the network.

Fortunately we do not need to remember the IP address to use the Internet! The form of address that we shall use is the Uniform Resource Locator (URL), which will usually be of the form http://www.cib.org.uk. The 'http' prefix stands for the hypertext transfer protocol – the set of rules for the use of hypertext links. We discuss hypertext below. The 'www' refers to the World Wide Web. 'cib' is the reference to The Chartered Institute of Bankers, and the suffixes 'org' and 'uk' show that the Chartered Institute of Bankers is an organization based in the UK.

All IP addresses and URLs must be unique and must be registered. A central database is used to translate URLs into IP addresses.

Web browsers

Most software is designed to use data of one specific type. For example, a word processor will read and change files either created using that word processor or imported into that word processor format. Browsers can understand a range of different types of data and can be used to look at files of different types. Browsers are becoming increasingly important, and much recent software is able to view files in a number of different formats.

Browsers are a very effective way to access data stored on the Web. Web browsers use the links provided by HTML both to move between different places on the Web (navigation) and to access files of different types (for example, pictures, video and audio), which are then interpreted using the browser technology.

Most people access the Internet through a web browser. The two most important web browsers are Netscape Navigator and Microsoft's Internet Explorer. Web browsers also have standard buttons allowing access to common functions such as email and locations such as the Internet service provider's home page and the main search engines.

Hypertext mark-up language

We have already said that hypertext mark-up language (HTML) was developed by Tim Berners-Lee, and is the basis of the Web. What is HTML?

The word 'hypertext' means that the information can include links. We can click on a link to go from one page of information to a different page (which may well be on a different computer – possibly in another country). Or we can use the link to load more information onto the page – perhaps a picture or a video clip.

Apart from its ability to include links, HTML is similar to normal text. The new generation of word processors are able to produce HTML documents directly, allowing word processed documentation to be put on an intranet with little or no formal IT involvement, and Microsoft's Office 2000 products will store all data as HTML and XML (extended mark-up language) files.

14.2   Internet service providers

To access the Internet a subscriber will need to register with an Internet service provider (ISP). The ISP will offer one or more telephone numbers (also known as points of presence) through which we can connect to the Internet. ISPs usually offer at least one local number, and are increasingly offering connection through a single 0345 (local rate) number.

Many of the older ISPs are relatively small organizations, but multinational corporations such as Microsoft and British Telecom are now acting as ISPs. The introduction of free Internet access, initially by Dixons' Freeserve, has changed the economics of Internet service provision, and it is likely that the trend towards larger organizations acting as ISPs will continue.

Most subscribers still use modems to connect with the Internet over analogue telephone lines. However, connecting over digital lines such as ISDN or fibre optic cable is also possible.

14.3 Accessing the Internet

Internet devices

Most people access the Internet through a PC with a modem. The PC's hard disk stores the web browser and the other software (word processor, spreadsheet, database, etc.) that we might want to use. We also copy information from the Internet onto the PC's hard disk.

This has a number of disadvantages. There are a lot of things that can go wrong with a PC. The PC is a complicated and expensive piece of equipment. The software loaded on the PC soon gets out of date, and it is expensive and time consuming to upgrade to the latest version. Research by consultants Forrester Research shows that the annual support cost of a typical PC is $2,680 on top of the original purchase price in the range $2,000-$3,000.

The alternative is to access the Internet using simpler – and cheaper – devices. These are called *thin clients* because most of the work is carried out on the Internet servers. So instead of having a word processor installed on a PC we might access a word processor located on a server through the Internet. We would not have to buy the word processor, and we would always be using the latest version. The PC is called a *thick client* by comparison.

PC banking provides another example of thick client and thin client. We can deliver PC banking in two main ways:

- We can provide customers with the software to load on their PCs;

- We can provide customers with access through the Internet.

The first is a thick client approach. Before the PC banking system can be used, the customer must load the software onto his or her PC, where it takes up hard disk space. If we want to change the software we have to send this out to the customer, who then has to reinstall it.

The second is the thin client approach. The client gets access to the software when it is needed. Little or no information is stored on the customer's hard disk, and the customer always accesses the most up-to-date version of the banking system.

The only software that would need to be stored on a thin client would be the operating system and browser, with all other software – including such standard software as electronic office products – accessed through the Internet. Even the operating system and browser might exist only as 'bootstraps' offering the most basic of facilities, with the remainder of the software loaded from the Internet.

The first serious attempt at a commercial thin client device was the network computer (or NC). This had a powerful processor but no hard disk storage. Annual support costs for the NC would be about $800 on top of the initial purchase price in the range $700-$1,000. A commercial response to this was the Net PC, a low-power, low-cost PC designed to access the Internet but with a lower total cost of ownership than a fully functional PC. Annual support costs would be $1,480 on top of an initial purchase price in the range $1,200-$2,000.

Neither the NC nor the Net PC were particularly successful, although the NC was used by organizations such as insurer General Accident (now part of CGU) and the Association of British Insurers (ABI) to replace terminal computers.

A new generation of thin client devices is emerging as a result of the convergence of computing with telephony and consumer electronics. Important thin client devices are:

- *TV set-top boxes*. These allow a television set to be used as an Internet access device.

- *Smart phones*. These can work in a number of ways, including using a touch-sensitive screen as a keyboard or having a fold-out keyboard. Some mobile telephones such as the Nokia 9000 have a built in keyboard and can be used to access the Internet.

- *Windows-based terminals*. These are successors to the Net PC. They include the Java virtual machine but run under Microsoft's Windows operating system. (Java is discussed later in this chapter.)

The relative advantages and disadvantages of the approaches depend on cost and convenience. For example the advantages of thick clients include:

- Telecommunications costs are lower as the device can be used on a stand-alone basis, being connected to the Internet as required.

- Similarly the device can be used if the telephone network is not available or Internet performance is unacceptably slow.

- The user has more control over data, which can be stored locally.

The advantages of thin clients include:

- The total cost of ownership is lower as a less complicated device with less software is needed.

- The latest versions of programs and data are always available.

To date, thin clients have made little progress in the market place. There are a number of reasons for this including the large number of PCs already in use, customer concerns about the performance of the Internet and the additional facilities available to PC users such as CD-ROMs.

It might be expected that thin clients would be successful in the corporate market. The lower cost of ownership is obviously attractive, and the inability to store data or programs long term has security benefits – there is no possibility of out-of-date information being stored, and there is less likelihood of virus infection. So far this has not happened, with organizations continuing to use a mix of fully functional PCs and terminal computers. The growth in the use of Internet technology for internal networks – the intranet – may change this.

Push technology

We use browsers to request information, but we can also ask for information to be sent to us. This is called *push technology* and was originally developed by Pointcast although it is now a standard feature in browsers.

Push technology allows us to say what information we want and when we want it – usually when telephone charges are low and the Internet is relatively quiet. This will be sent to our computer at the specified time.

The effectiveness of push technology depends on its ability to customize the information it delivers to meet the needs of the user. This requires it to categorize and filter:

● Categorization is the ability to look for types of information that may be of interest.

● Filtering is the ability to exclude items from the category if they are not of interest.

These feature are also found in search engines. They are discussed at the end of this chapter under knowledge management.

One problem with push technology is that that it can use telecommunications resources – bandwidth – very heavily. Because it requires no effort to get the information, users are less selective about what they ask for. There are technical solutions to this problem (*caching* – moving the data through additional servers to distribute the workload), but these incur additional costs. This may be a factor that explains the limited take up of push technology within organizations despite its obvious potential for distributing information.

Do not confuse push technology with mail enabling, although there are some similarities. Mail enabling allows an email message to be sent in response to an event. Push technologies send data rather than messages and this is sent at a specified time rather than in response to an event. Email messages are delivered to a server while push technology delivers the data directly to the PC.

Search engines

One of the main problems with the Internet is that it contains so much information. Links between sites provide one way of getting around the Internet but are of little use for finding anything new.

One approach is to build an index. This was taken by Yahoo! and yahoo.com is the most popular site on the Internet. Information is classified into about 20 main categories, and each category is further broken down into a number of subcategories. These may be further broken down. Therefore we should be able to find any piece of information by following it through its categories and subcategories.

This works well for most routine enquiries. But sometimes there is not a category that matches what we are looking for. Alternatively, it may fall into two or three categories. Although we could use the index to find what we are looking for we may have to try several different categories, which is time consuming and can be frustrating. Search engines allow a search for a word or words within an item of information. Yahoo! combines a search engine with an index, allowing us to search the entire Web or to search only within a category or subcategory.

Even using a search engine, there may still be a very large number of items found. Some search engines can group similar items together – they will show one of the items with the option to look at the similar items. This is a knowledge management technique and is discussed later in this chapter.

The most popular index and search engine sites now offer additional services such as email. These are called *portals* to show that they offer a wider range of services. For example, Yahoo! offers services such as a currency calculator and a global weather service.

Java

Java is a programming language developed by Sun Microsystems and is designed to work on any computer. The computer's software must be modified to include what is called a Java *virtual machine* which translates the Java language into the language used by the computer.

Java is important for the Internet because the Java virtual machine is included in the Web browser software. A page of information containing a Java program (or *applet*) can cause something to happen on our computer when we read it. This is usually used for special effects such as animating advertising banners – although it can also be used to spread computer viruses.

Java has all the power of other programming languages. It is an interpreted language, which means that instead of being compiled into object code/machine code before it is run it is loaded as source code and interpreted on an instruction-by-instruction basis at run time. This makes Java applets machine independent – they can run on any machine.

The interpretation is carried out initially by the browser. The browser virtual machine converts the Java applet to machine code. Not all browsers have this facility at present, but newer versions of the most important browsers all include the Java virtual machine.

Because Java is a programming language, the workstation can interact dynamically with the computer being accessed. An example is probably the best way to illustrate this:

- Information may be held as a page of HTML. This information will not change on the computer storing it until it is replaced with another formatted page of HTML.

- Information may be held on a database. The information will change on the computer storing it as the contents of the database change but it will change on the workstation only when the user requests a new set of information.

- Information may be held as a database accessible through a Java program. An applet written in Java may be brought down to the workstation, which will periodically check to see whether the information in the database has changed. If so, it will automatically bring down the most up-to-date information to the workstation. This is called *dynamic updating*.

Java can also be used to provide additional capabilities on the browser. One use is to provide animation for images (although Java is not needed for this). Java can even be used to write the browser: the HotJava browser is written in Java and can modify itself from the Internet so that you always have the latest version.

Java was developed by Sun Microsystems. Although Microsoft supports Java, it also has an alternative product called ActiveX, which provides the same functions.

One disadvantage of both Java and ActiveX is that they can be used to write viruses. The Chaos Computer Club of Germany demonstrated a virus that could have used ActiveX to transfer funds fraudulently out of on-line bank accounts linked to the personal financial management product Quicken (this virus was never used and was intended purely to illustrate potential risks).

Java is being used for other purposes – for example it is a standard language for developing software for smart cards.

Intelligent agents

Intelligent agents are a development of search engines. A search engine is passive – we have to ask it a question before it will provide the information we need. It does not tell us when the information changes, and we may need to access the search engine again in order to identify any new sites relating to our topic of interest.

Intelligent agents are dynamic. They know the topics in which we are interested, and can carry out periodic searches to identify more up-to-date information and even new sites. Intelligent agent technology is still quite new but it has immense potential to ensure that users of the Internet have access to the latest information.

They can also understand the information. For example, an intelligent agent can be used to identify the lowest price from suppliers of a product. It is this ability that distinguishes intelligent agents from push technology.

14.4   Electronic commerce

Electronic commerce (e-commerce) is the use of the Internet for business.

The Internet is a very attractive market place for retailers. Internet users are usually young and wealthy, and the rate of growth of the Internet is phenomenal – 71% growth between 1996 and 1997 and predicted to triple to 268 million computers by 2001.

E-commerce is well established in the US, France and Germany. Experiments such as the multinational e-Christmas initiative showed a lot more people interested in looking than in buying outside these countries. The major constraint on the growth of e-commerce is the risk of fraud, and these are the countries that have developed local solutions to this problem. The use of the Secure Sockets Layer in the US is discussed in Chapter 15, as are the proposed transnational solutions SET and Cafe.

The most visible sector of the e-commerce market is retailing, with companies such as Amazon.com able to command very high stock market ratings even before becoming profitable. The advantages to the retailer include:

- They are able to work with very low operating costs as they do not need city centre premises.

- Once they secure name recognition they are able to carry advertising banners for customers browsing the site.

- Customers enter the transaction details themselves, reducing the retailer's costs.

- They can communicate with their customers at a very low cost through email.

The main problem with using the Internet is security, and this is discussed in Chapter 15. The most common current method of payment is a credit or debit card processed on a 'card not present' basis. There are concerns with this, the most important of which is the risk of credit card numbers being intercepted and used fraudulently.

Another problem is that the Internet does not have a mechanism for making very small payments of a few pence. This might be useful for accessing an electronic newspaper, where the customer could buy copies of articles at (for example) 5p each. These are called *micropayments*.

Obviously it would not be economic to use credit cards for micropayments – the charges would exceed the revenue. E-cash systems such as Mondex or VisaCash (discussed in Chapter 11) could be used, but few Internet devices have smart card readers. The most common approach to this type of transaction is to charge an annual subscription, but this is a disincentive to customers – why should we be prepared to pay an annual subscription of (say) £10.00 when we may only want a few dozen articles? There is general agreement that the development of an effective mechanism for micropayments would be an important stimulus for e-commerce.

Business-to-business e-commerce is often forgotten but is growing much faster than Internet commerce with consumers. This was discussed under the general topic of EDI in Chapter 11.

14.5   Knowledge management

We defined knowledge in Chapter 1. Knowledge management has been defined as 'codifying the knowledge your company creates and disseminating it to the people who need it – when they need it'. The key words are *codifying* and *disseminating*:

- Codifying includes both capturing and categorizing information.

- Disseminating includes both accessing information that is relevant and delivering it to the people who need it when they need it.

Categorization is perhaps the most important and the most difficult of these processes. We have discussed how knowledge is information that can be applied to a valued purpose. We need to categorise all the information we capture in a way that allows us to identify its relevance to the various purposes we may have for information dissemination. Therefore we first need to develop a system of classification – sometimes called an *ontology* – that meets the needs of the business.

The categorization process can be carried out manually, often by attaching keywords to each piece of information. This is time consuming, and will need to be reviewed whenever new keywords are added. There are a number of approaches to automatic categorization:

- The simplest is to automatically search for all occurrences of important words in information. These can then be used to build an index. This can be made slightly more sophisticated by also looking for synonyms – for example we might want to categorise both 'loan' and 'advance' under loan.

  There are some disadvantages to this. For example, the word 'credit' could refer to a loan or to a payment received.

- A variation on this is to look at the 'keyword in context'. The index is based on keywords but the words immediately surrounding the keyword are also shown. This is useful for identifying how the keyword is used.

- More advanced approaches attempts to identify similar pieces of information based on other words. For example, information containing the word 'credit' might be categorized differently depending on whether it also includes the word 'card' or the word 'account'. Search engines such as Excite use this approach.

Determining what information is relevant depends on our ability to express our needs in a way that matches the way the information classified. We have discussed a number of ways to do this in Chapter 12, including 'canned queries' and query by example. An approach that is attracting an increasing amount of attention is natural language queries, in which the query is expressed as if it were a piece of spoken English, and the 'assistants' supplied with the latest versions of office automation products and some Internet search engines such as Askjeeves make use of this.

Internet technology – an intranet – is usually used to make the results available to those who need it. This is an obvious application of push technology.

Some of the most important applications of knowledge management techniques are:

- Best practice databases;

- Summarization and abstraction;

- Knowledge discovery.

Best practice databases record the organization's experience of the best way to do things. Some studies have suggested that 20-30% of organizations' total costs are a result of 'reinventing the wheel' – solving problems that the organization has already solved. Best practice databases such as Ford's 'Things Gone Right Things Gone Wrong' act as the organization's memory and help to avoid these costs.

A new application for knowledge management is in *summarization and abstraction*. This allows text information to be automatically summarised without losing any important information. This helps to reduce information overload (discussed in Chapter 1).

Knowledge discovery is the 'non-trivial extraction of implicit, previously unknown and potentially useful information from data'. Knowledge discovery examines data to look for:

- *Correlations*. These may be events that usually happen together or items of data that are often found together. A trivial example of the latter might be if households that have two cars are more likely to take foreign holidays – this might be useful in suggesting that holiday insurance could be advertised in car magazines.

- *Forecasts*. These are events that form a predictable sequence. An obvious example is that a rise in interest rates precedes a rise in bad debts. Note that the use of data mining to identify forecasts does not require any causal relationship between the events, and data mining is perhaps most useful where it identifies relationships that do not have any obvious relationship but which do seem to be valid.

- *Classifications*. These are different ways of classifying data items. For example, it may be possible to classify groups of customers who will behave in a certain way from data held about them.

Building a scorecard as part of a credit scoring system (discussed in Chapter 11) is a form of knowledge discovery. However, 'data mining' tools are much wider in application:

- Scorecard development analyses the correlation between variables and a specific outcome (for example failure to repay the loan). Data mining tools look for any statistically significant correlation.

- Scorecard development looks for a set number of predictive variables. Data mining will consider any correlation however few (or many) variables are involved.

- Credit systems generally look for causality, and relationships that cannot be explained in terms of cause and effect are often disregarded. Data mining ignores causality.

- Scorecard development is a lengthy process with careful testing of statistical relationships. Data mining is an automated process.

Therefore data mining will identify a potentially large number of relationships that may be of value, but these need to be used with care.

15

INTERNET SECURITY

Introduction

It has been said that the problem with the Internet is 'security, security and security'. Why is this, and how can we overcome it?

The problem is that the Internet is an open network. Anyone can connect to the Internet, and the standards and protocols are widely published.

Another effect of the open nature of the Internet is that it can be (and is) used by criminals, terrorists and those opposed to their governments. Recent examples of the use of the Internet to bypass government control over communications have occurred in Mexico and Malaysia. As a result, governments have regarded encryption technology as a weapon of war. They have been reluctant to allow its export, and have attempted to secure control over encryption keys.

15.1   Encryption

We discussed encryption in Chapter 4. Both symmetric and asymmetric encryption are used to protect electronic transactions.

One security device that uses asymmetric encryption is the *digital signature*. With asymmetric encryption the message is usually encoded using the recipient's public key, with the recipient using the private key to decode it on receipt. A digital signature works the other way round – the sender uses the *private* key to encrypt the message. The recipient will use the *public* key to decode it, proving the identity of the sender. We call this the *signature key pair* to distinguish it from the encryption key pair.

Another security device is a *digital envelope*. This combines symmetric and asymmetric encryption. The system generates a random symmetric key, which is encrypted using the recipient's public key and sent to the recipient. The message is encoded using the symmetric key before being sent with the encoded key in the digital envelope. This provides an additional level of security.

15.2   Digital certificates

A particular problem with carrying out a transaction electronically is how to identify the parties.

This is similar in some ways to the problem of 'card not present' credit card transactions. Cardholders receive a measure of protection in these transactions through indemnities, rules on delivering goods to the cardholder's registered address, and expert systems that can identify attempted fraud. These measures are not generally available for electronic transactions.

This problem has been addressed through *digital certificates*.

A digital certificate is an electronic identity document issued by a certification authority and corresponding to a physical identity document such as a driver's licence or passport used to identify the parties in a physical transaction. A digital certificate may contain information such as:

● Identification information (for example name and address) for the certificate holder;

● The certificate holder's public key;

● Information about the certificate (for example serial number and validity dates);

● Identification information about the certification authority who issues the certificate;

● The certification authority's digital signature. This allows the parties to the transaction to authenticate the digital certificate.

The certification authority must be a 'trusted third party' in which all parties to the transaction have confidence. There may be a 'certification hierarchy' by which a certification authority of undoubted probity can certify others to issue digital certificates. Financial services organizations could act as certification authorities.

The integrity of the certificate-issuing process must be clear. Certification authorities must only issue certificates to parties of whose identities they are certain, and must have systems for tracking certificates in issue.

Digital certificates are generally issued as software at present. This creates a potential security weakness, and the security of the digital certificate can be compromized if the keys are known. In future it is likely that smart cards will be used to store digital certificates, providing additional security.

15.3   Secure electronic transaction standard

The Secure Electronic Transaction standard (SET) was developed by Visa and MasterCard as a method of protecting financial transactions over the Internet. It makes use of encryption and digital certificates. As SET is restricted purely to financial transactions it is not subject to the US government restrictions on the export of encryption technology. SET also allows brand differentiation between the Visa and MasterCard payment networks.

SET meets five major business requirements:

- It ensures the integrity of the data.

- It protects the confidentiality of payment and other information forming part of the transaction.

- It provides authentication of the cardholder's identity and status as a legitimate user of a payment card account.

- It provides authentication of a merchant's identity and ability to accept payment card transactions through an acquiring financial institution.

- It creates a set of rules that is independent of the security mechanisms used.

Integrity is ensured through a *message digest*. This operates on the same principle as the checksum we described in Chapter 4. The message digest is encrypted using the signature key, allowing any recipient to make sure that the message has not been altered.

Confidentiality is preserved through encryption. We may want different parts of the transaction to be accessed by different parties – for example we may want a financial services organization to have access to the payment details and the counterparty to have access to the commercial details. SET allows a *dual signature* by which different parts of a message can be kept confidential. There is one dual signature that covers both parts of the message. This includes the message digests, allowing the parties to have confidence that the messages have not been altered.

Digital certificates are used to authenticate the identity of all parties to the transaction. As well as the purchaser and merchant, these will include the payment gateway and the acquirer. The certification hierarchy is used to verify these certificates.

Although the account number is needed to validate the cardholder's certificate, the account number is not held on the certificate and cannot be calculated from it.

An alternative approach, which also uses both public key encryption and digital signatures, is the Secure Sockets Layer (SSL) developed by Netscape. One advantage of SSL is that the SSL client is included as standard in Netscape's Navigator browser so customers do not need any additional software. SSL is widely used in the US for e-commerce.

Another alternative is the Conditional Access for Europe (Cafe) standard promoted by the EC. Like SET, this is designed for financial transactions and offers the benefits of privacy to the parties to the transaction as well as providing security.

15.4 Firewalls

A firewall includes software and sometimes hardware, and protects the organization from viruses and other forms of malicious action. If the firewall does not have its own hardware it is installed on a router. There are two types of firewall:

- *Filtering firewalls*. A filtering firewall allows only specified types of data through. For example, a filtering firewall can be set to allow Internet access for email only.

- *Proxies*. A proxy is more sophisticated. Instead of allowing data through, the proxy 'pretends' to be the organization's systems to anyone trying to access them externally and pretends to be the external network (for example the Internet) to anyone trying to access it from inside the organization.

  This allows the proxy to examine the data much more thoroughly than with a filter firewall, and proxies are better at detecting and eliminating attacks such as viruses.

In practice most firewalls combine both approaches.

Firewalls also provide other services including:

- Providing an audit trail of all data passing through the firewall;

- Providing an alarm about apparent attempted security breaches;

- Supporting network address translation (NAT). NAT allows us to use different addresses within and outside the organization. This is very important if we want people to be able to send email over the Internet to people within the organization – it hides the real address and also allows us to register a single IP address rather than one for each server.

- Some firewalls allow authentication of security devices such as smart cards.

- Some firewalls can operate a virtual private network (VPN). A VPN uses public links, but messages are wrapped in a digital envelope to provide a very high level of security.

15.5   Handshakes

Handshaking allows two computing devices to recognize each other. This involves an exchange of information between the devices before any sensitive information is sent. The concept is similar to that of a digital certificate but it identifies devices rather than individuals.

This was used in ATM networks operating on a remote batch basis to ensure that the ATM was connected to the financial services organization's mainframe before sending details of any ATM transactions.

It is also used in the Mondex system. Mondex only allows e-cash to be transferred between Mondex cards, and the cards go through a handshaking routine before any transfer. This could also be used in transferring e-cash across the Internet.

15.6   Cookies

A cookie is a small text file stored on the PC's hard disk. When we access a Web page it may update the cookie file.

Cookies are used to store identification information about the PC. This is similar in principle to handshaking but is for convenience rather than security. It can be helpful as the Web site will not need to ask again for information it already has. Cookies are particularly useful for holding registration information as the Web site will know that the user is already registered the next time it is accessed.

Cookies are text files and cannot carry viruses. A cookie can only be accessed by the Web site that created it and cannot be used to trawl for information about what sites the PC has accessed. Current versions of browsers allow users to request a warning before cookies are created or to refuse to accept all cookies.

16

INTRANETS, EXTRANETS AND AFFINITY NETWORKS

Introduction

Internet technology is not only used for the public Internet but is now often used for communication inside financial services organizations. In this chapter we discuss how this technology can be used within the organization (an intranet), to communicate with customers (an extranet), or between groups with a common interest (affinity networks). We shall start with an outline of how financial services organizations currently use client/server technology.

16.1   Client/Server

We introduced the idea of client/server in Chapter 1. Client/server allows a distribution of work where a *client* can request a *server* to carry out a task on its behalf. The client and server are usually computers – for example a terminal or workstation as a client requesting information from a mainframe computer as the server. The client and server can also be software – for example an application program requesting data from a database management system as discussed in Chapter 10.

If we go back to the idea of the client and server as computers we can identify four forms of work sharing:

Figure 16.1

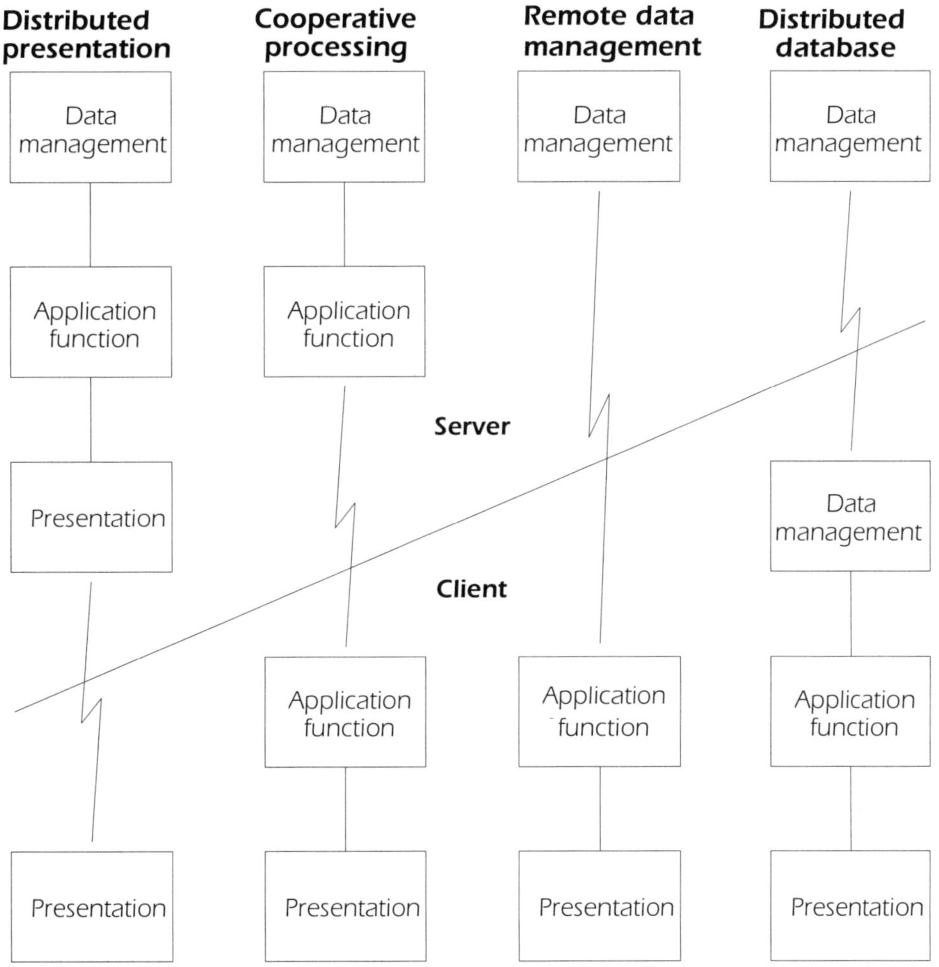

We would not usually regard distributed presentation as client/server in any real sense. Almost all of the work is carried out by the server, with the client taking only a minor role. The other three forms of work sharing are forms of client/server:

● *Cooperative processing* splits the application processing between the client and server. This makes use of the client's processing power without risking the integrity of data due to the weaker data protection offered by a workstation. This approach was very common in the early stages of the third generation.

● *Remote data management* uses the server purely as a source of data, with all processing carried out on the client. This approach is similar to the use of data warehouses, datamarts or the Internet as sources of reference information.

● *Distributed database* shares management of the data between the client and the server.

To achieve a distributed data environment, we must be able to manage a database spread across different computers. The main concerns with this approach are to do with data protection. If the data held on the clients is not carefully controlled this may give rise to problems with the Data Protection Act 1984.

During the third IT generation, financial services organizations invested heavily in client/server technology. Telecommunications costs were high, but server and workstation processing power was cheap so it made sense to move from the centralized approach of the second generation to the use of client/server – generally cooperative processing.

This resulted in networks as follows:

Figure 16.2

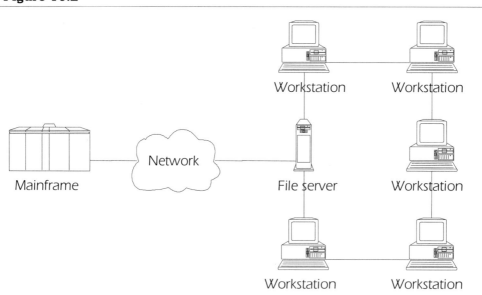

Application processing is split between the mainframe and the workstations. The applications themselves are stored on the file server and loaded onto the workstations when they are needed. Some data is stored on the server to save telecommunications costs, but this is a copy of data from the mainframe so this is not true distributed database.

The problem was that any changes made to data or programs on the branch servers had to be rolled out to every branch. Depending on the amount of information to be sent this could take days or even weeks – which presented a significant problem if the changes were being made to correct a fault.

Although financial services organizations developed various strategies to get round these problems they increased these organizations' costs. In addition, large roll-outs directly increased telecommunications costs, and there were further costs associated with their management.

Some of the problem avoidance strategies also increased costs. For example, one strategy is to keep processing on the mainframe computer as programs held on the mainframe do not need to be rolled out. This increases costs as it uses expensive mainframe processing power rather than relatively cheap workstation processing. Another example is the ability to 'switch' new versions of software on the server on and off. This avoided problems with errors on the software: if there was a problem the new version could be switched off and the branch could go back to using the old version. However, it also meant that the branch servers had to hold several versions of the software, increasing storage costs.

16.2   Move to Internet technology

Internet technology offered an alternative to client/server. Organizations can still benefit from the processing power of servers and workstations but they achieve additional benefits relating to:

● Cost of ownership;

● Robustness;

● Changing nature of information;

● Knowledge management tools.

Cost of ownership

When we discussed cost of ownership, we considered the cost of upgrading computers to the latest version of a particular type of software. This may not matter greatly to an individual – a two-year old version of a word processor will still work, even though it may not have the same features as a more up-to-date version – but it is a problem to organizations.

Large financial services organizations may have hundreds or thousands of branches with tens of thousands of workstations. If the organization needs to change an application program it faces the problem of making this available to all the workstations in the network. Before client/server, this was not a problem as all processing was carried out on the mainframe. A change made to the mainframe would be available to the branch network the following day.

This is more difficult in a client/server environment. Changing the software on thousands of servers is time consuming. The problem is greater if software on tens of thousands of individual workstations needs to be changed. There are also security issues – financial services organizations do not want it to be easy to change the software on their servers and workstations because of the threats to data security we discussed in Chapter 4. Therefore the changes are usually made overnight using the data communications network. Even using this approach it may take days or weeks to change the software on all workstations.

Internet technology avoids this problem. The branch will always receive the latest version of the software when it is required, without any requirement to manage this centrally.

Robustness

It may not always seem it, but the technology used for the Internet is very robust. This may be a legacy of the US Department of Defense involvement. The Internet has no single point of failure, and practically all messages arrive at their destination eventually even though up to 25% of the individual message packages are lost. Further, the Internet has managed to cope with an exponential rate of usage growth without coming to a complete stop – few financial services organizations could claim their networks would be capable of this.

That said, performance on the Internet would not be acceptable within a commercial organization. But the Internet's performance problems are a result of too many people trying to use too little telecommunications capacity (bandwidth), not of any weaknesses in the underlying technology.

Organizations using Internet technology for their internal communications can ensure that they have sufficient bandwidth for the number of users and can guarantee acceptable response times. Further, as we have already discussed, the network will be able to handle sudden increases in the number of messages without failure.

Changing nature of information

The change from data through information to knowledge that we have seen in the different generations of IT reflected not only the limitations of the available technology but also the needs of financial services organizations. We have discussed how this also involved a change from structured to less structured data.

Most application software is not designed for unstructured data. The exceptions – for example, word processors and desktop publishing software – are not designed for processing transactions over a network.

The Internet is different. It combines structured and unstructured data, using a web browser to bring these together. It is designed to operate as a network and, because of the potential importance of electronic commerce (e-commerce), Internet transaction processing software is available. The software available for the Internet is much more suited to the type of information now needed by financial services organizations than traditional types of application software.

Knowledge management

The wide range of tools developed for the Internet, including search engines, push technology and intelligent agents, can also be made available to users of the intranet.

16.3   Intranets

The use of Internet technology for internal WANs is called an intranet and is one of the fastest growing areas of the Internet market. As intranets use internal communications links they overcome the security problems associated with the Internet.

The intranet combines access to applications and data with email. Financial services organizations are able to use a single interface – the browser – for both. This reduces training and software costs.

Many organizations restrict the use of tools such as search engines and push technology. These can use resources quite heavily, and have cost implications when rolled out across an entire network.

16.4   Extranets

Some financial services organizations would like to communicate with their customers using Internet technology but are unwilling so to do because of concerns over security. An alternative is an extranet.

Extranets use exactly the same technology as the Internet but customers connect directly to the financial services organization's servers, without going through an ISP. This means that there is no possibility of messages being intercepted.

16.5   Affinity networks

Affinity networks are private networks using Internet technology to connect groups with a common interest. An example of this is the World Insurance Network (WIN). Affinity networks are also used as 'metropolitan area networks' linking organizations located in a geographical area.

16.6   Virtual private networks

In Chapter 15, we discussed how we can use a firewall to provide a virtual private network (VPN) by wrapping messages in a digital envelope. This allows us to overcome the security problems associated with the Internet.

Therefore we can provide the same level of security as an extranet or an affinity network over the public network. This is more convenient for our customers or affinity network partners.

There are some disadvantages. Operating a VPN imposes a heavy workload on the firewall, and we may need more powerful hardware to ensure that system performance is acceptable. The VPN uses public lines (which can be PSTN or the faster ISDN lines), and we would not have the option of installing a very high speed link to particular customers or partners. On balance the use of VPNs to provide extranet or affinity network services seems likely to increase.

17

INTERNET BANKING

Introduction

Most major UK financial services organizations now have web sites, and many allow direct banking either through the Internet or through a proprietary PC banking system.

From the customer's point of view, Internet banking and PC banking provide much the same services. These will generally include:

- Balance and statement enquiries;

- Ability to transfer funds between accounts;

- Ability to set up standing orders;

- Ability to make bill payments.

Bill payment is the only service developed specifically for direct banking – originally for telephone banking and now for PC and Internet banking. This allows the customer to set up a bill payment arrangement and to make payment (either on demand or on a specified date) through the BACS system. Unlike the electronic cheques (e-cheques) offered by US banks such as Bank Boston and NationsBank a bill payment arrangement must be set up before a payment can be made.

Financial services organizations have tended to use their web sites as an advertising medium. Therefore they have offered other services – both financial and non-financial – to attract visitors. These include:

- Branch and ATM locators;

- Mortgage repayment calculators;

- Links to personal financial management software;

- Links to virtual shopping malls;

- Sporting and other non-financial information.

These systems provide customers with access to the financial services organization's mainframe systems. Therefore we need to consider:

- Ease of use;

● Security.

The customer must find the system *easy to use*. It must look interesting, and the screens must be clearly laid out. The customer should be able to get help if needed.

If the system is delivered over the Internet, we need to consider how quickly it will load and how it will work with different browsers. If we want to use Java or ActiveX for special effects we need to consider how customers who have disabled these features (owing to concern about viruses, for example) will use the site.

Security is paramount. The system provides customers (or anyone with a PC) with access to the organization's main computer systems. Protection of data, systems and messages is essential. There must also be certainty – if the customer loses the connection to the organization's systems in the middle of a transaction, has it taken place or not?

The world's first Internet bank is the Security First Network Bank (SFNB), set up in 1995 in the US. SFNB carries the virtual banking concept to its limit – it does not have any branches and it does not itself provide financial services. SFNB acts as a delivery channel, and the financial services it sells are provided by other financial services organizations. SFNB's unique method of operation gives it a very low cost base.

17.1 PC banking for personal customers

The main financial services organizations to have adopted the PC banking route for personal customers are Barclays and Citibank, although both organizations also have a web site, and Barclays also plan to offer Internet banking.

PC banking works as follows:

● The financial services organization provides the customer with the software, which he or she installs on a PC, and security information such as a PIN.

● The customer can access banking services through the PC. The software stores the financial services organization's telephone number and dials it automatically as needed. The software also encrypts messages sent.

● If the financial services organization changes its PC banking software, the customer will only receive the new version if he or she requests it or if the organization sends it to all customers. Even if the organization does this, it cannot guarantee that all customers will install the new software on their PCs.

In principle the PC software could be Internet enabled, allowing changes to be loaded to the customer's PC from the financial services organization's web site. There do not appear to be any PC banking systems that do this.

Barclays have linked their PC banking system to the personal financial management product Microsoft Money. Money provides a range of tools allowing customers to balance their chequebooks, create budgets and produce long-term financial plans. Linked to the Barclays on-line system it can be used to get account information, download statements and make on-line payments.

Financial services organizations offering PC banking use their web sites for providing information and customer recruitment. Barclays have developed their site into a portal linking to other members of the Barclays group (such as Barclaycard and offshore banking) and to the virtual shopping mall Barclaysquare.

17.2   PC banking for business customers

Many financial services organizations use PCs to provide banking services for small business customers (office banking). The organization provides the customer with a smart card reader. A new smart card will be issued every month. The smart card is used to confirm that the system is being used by an authorized person (to prevent fraud) and also to encrypt the message sent to the organization's mainframe computer. Encryption is used to prevent the message being read or altered: this is discussed in Chapter 4.

Office banking allows customers to manage their accounts and make payments without needing to visit the bank. Systems usually allow more complicated transactions such as applying for a letter of credit or a loan.

We discussed Bank of Scotland's Home and Office Banking System in Chapter 9, and this can be used for both personal and business banking. HSBC's office banking product Hexagon has been extended to personal customers through Personal Hexagon, which can also link to the personal financial management product Microsoft Money.

17.3   Internet banking

Royal Bank of Scotland was the first UK bank to offer full service Internet banking. It was followed by the Nationwide Building Society and the TSB. More recently most major financial services organizations have followed this route or are announcing plans so to do, including Barclays Bank, which already offers PC banking.

Internet banking works as follows:

- Customers will need to prove their identity in order to register. This is sometimes possible through other direct banking services such as telephone banking. They will be sent security information allowing them to use the service.

- Customers can access the financial services organization's web sites through the Internet. A small amount of information may be stored on the PC but this will not include any computer programs.

- When the financial services organization changes its web site all customers will automatically see the latest version. There is no need for the customer to install any software.

The Nationwide Building Society's web site carries information about the Football League which it sponsors. This is an example of a financial services organization using sporting information to attract visitors to its web site. The Royal Bank of Scotland have linked their system to Microsoft Money.

The next development for Internet banking may be to allow access to the Internet over a mobile telephone. This is already possible using Internet-enabled mobile telephones such as the Nokia 9000, but Cellnet have worked with Barclaycard, First Direct and French bank BNP to offer some Internet banking services, with information such as statement entries sent to the mobile telephone as text messages.

17.4 Internet non-banking services

Most financial services organizations have web sites, whether or not they offer Internet banking services. They use their sites as a source of recruitment, and offer a range of services including:

- Calculators for foreign exchange or for loan or mortgage repayments;
- Financial planners;
- Locators for branches and ATMs.

Other services include property sales, travel insurance and links to Internet shopping malls. Some financial services organizations are becoming Internet service providers – the Nationwide Building Society pioneered this, and Barclays Bank is also adopting this approach – and it is possible to foresee organizations such as these positioning their sites as portals providing access to a range of financial services.

One of the most important non-banking financial services to be delivered over the Internet is share dealing. The success of Charles Schwab in the US and its entry into the UK has demonstrated the possibilities of this, and at least two UK financial services organizations have plans to offer share dealing services.

17.5 Risks and problems

The slow adoption of Internet banking in the UK can be explained by security concerns such as the risk of hackers, which have already been discussed in Chapter 15.

Security is not the only problem with the Internet. Response times can be very slow, and financial services organizations have been concerned that customers would blame them for problems beyond their control. There are also issues if the customer loses the Internet connection during a transaction – it may be difficult for the customer to determine whether or not the transaction has been processed.

The legal status of the Internet has also been a source of uncertainty, and a legal framework for e-commerce is only just starting to develop. Financial services organizations are under an obligation to establish the identity of those with whom they are doing business if they are not to be exposed to risk of fraud or under money laundering legislation. Prior to digital certificates and digital signatures this was impossible to guarantee.

Index